Pelé Can Wait... Some More

*To Julie
Thank you AGAIN for the support
Best Wishes*

P.S. HONEY

Pelé Can Wait ... Some More © P.S. Honey 2024
ISBN 978-1-915962-50-8

First published 2024 by Compass-Publishing UK

Edited by AJ Humpage
Typeset by The Book Refinery Ltd

The right of Phil Honey to be identified as the author of this work has been asserted in accordance with the Copyright, Designs and Patents Act, 1988.

All rights reserved. No part of this publication may be reproduced, stored in a retrieval system, or transmitted, in any form or by any means (electronic, mechanical, photocopying, recording or otherwise), without the prior written permission of the publisher.

This book is not a work of fiction. There are deep scars to prove it.

Names, characters, places and incidents are either a product of the author's experience or have been artistically modified so that the chances of being sued for defamation of character have been significantly reduced. Any resemblance to actual people living or dead, events or locales is entirely possible.

A CIP catalogue record for this book is available from the
British Library.

Contents

1 - Day Break	7
2 - Hammersmith Hospital	14
3 - Roy	20
4 - Going Down	27
5 - A Trip to the Theatre	39
6 - Alive	46
7 - The Aftermath	55
8 - Alarming	66
9 - The Other Two	72
10 - Fingers Crossed for Friday Morning	77
11 - Doctors' Rounds	84
12 - The Pain Team	92
13 - Friday Night (is Gonna be Alright)	102
14 - Saturday - The Calm Before The Storm	111
15 - The Storm	121
16 - An Oasis in a Desert of Despair	138
17 - The Bizarre and the Ridiculous	144
18 - Sunday, Please Save Me	164
19 - A Target to Aim For	173
20 - Away From the Bay	186
21 - A New Week for the Weak	194

22 - Find a Happy Place	203
23 - Monday, Get Behind Me	217
24 - Tuesday. Hopefully Not a Newsday	220
25 - Second Half, Downhill, Surely?	231
26 - Another Day in Paradise	235
27 - When Wishes and Prayers Come True	240
28 - The Race For Home	244
29 - Rejoining my Favourite Timeline	259
Epilogue	266
Acknowledgements	269
About the Author	271

For Patricia.

And our unbreakable bond. I love you.

1

Day Break

The alarm that Ali and I heard was more important than our usual one, and therefore it stirred us differently. It was exceptionally early for starters, but it was other factors that meant we reacted to it immediately.

The day had come. I'd had a restless night's sleep because of the worry and, just like setting the alarm for being *airport-early*, whenever I'd heard the blare of that alarm - my brain kicked into gear straight away. As predicted, within moments, Ali was very much awake. As was I.

Unfortunately, we weren't going to the airport. It felt many miles away from an enjoyable summer family holiday.

Ali rolled over.

I recognised that knowing look; it meant we didn't have to say much to each other, except a gentle, 'Morning.'

It was going to be a tough day for both of us. I needed to be at Hammersmith Hospital at 6:45am and that meant we had to leave home just before six. The numbers on the digital clock pushed on regardless, and the morning felt like any other normal routine - but on steroids - because there was no way we were going to be late.

Everything had to work like clockwork. It simply had to.

5:00am on the red LED display (one hour before departure) and we both sprang into our separate bathroom routines. I jumped into the shower first - it was a thorough yet efficiently quick affair. Ali just needed to be washed and dressed and to simply *be there* for me, so she started her day off by taking a seat in the ensuite and showing the toilet bowl exactly what the morning nerves had already done to her insides. At least the dinner she barely ate the previous evening came out the way it should. The state of anxiety Ali was in meant her frazzled nerves could have expelled any unwanted matter that was inside her in either direction. Or worse, both.

She planned to take a shower later, when she got back from my drop off, and then she could begin her typical routine to get ready for work at a more reasonable time. Ali had decided that a day at work might just help provide some sort of distraction from the craziness ahead. She knew that her own brain would be her worst enemy in the absence of any news about me. She didn't want to be at work on such an important day, but the alternative of pacing around at home, as she waited to hear some news, seemed even more torturous.

Ali also knew that a good stomp around at work wasn't much more attractive, but if she wasn't going to hear from the hospital (or me) until deep into the afternoon, any distraction would help.

Ali worked in the school office at the local village infant school. It was always a busy day, every day was completely different from the next, and whilst some days could get a bit chaotic, she always felt that most days whizzed by. If all went to plan, Ali would be far from bored and should get more interruptions than she could possibly want. She also predicted that if she wasn't massively distracted, each hour would feel like a day. Ali had been supported by her colleague and friend Sandra since I'd fallen ill, so I was reassured that her day-time rock would help her through the worst part of the day.

'I've just thought,' I said as I came out from the bathroom, 'they didn't say anything, but do you think I should have had a proper shave? You know, do my body to save them some time?'

Ali smiled. 'No. I'm sure they do everything there.'

She wasn't sure at all, but there was no way she was going to fuel any doubts or anxieties that I might have had. She knew my coping mechanism well. Each step in the situation had been handled as just that, a step. Whilst Ali had calculated every single permutation (and then absorbed herself within each of those outcomes), I had refused to go down any train of thought other than to deal with single, daily ordeals. Ali endured all the worrying and that was often the case for those living with people that were going through an illness. It was true in our partnership – I was going into battle and Ali was the one shitting herself with worry.

'Would you even know where to shave?' she asked.

'Errm, no. I thought about just clearing the whole area.' I pulled open my white bathrobe to reveal some middle-aged spread not particularly well hidden by the hair that I'd left unshaven. I had lost about a stone in weight since I had received a diagnosis of diabetes the year before and had done my bit to eat better and to do a bit more exercise, so my impressive belly wasn't quite as rotund as it had been in previous times.

'Take a final look at this gorgeous body, wifey. It might never look quite so sensational after today.' I intended to keep everything light-hearted between us. I was more than happy to joke about the mountainous elephant that took up every square inch of space in whatever room we ever found ourselves in. That elephant was not only enormous, but it was also hard to shake off, a bit like herpes.

Ali reached over from where she sat in front of her dressing table and gave my tummy a loving caress. 'You'll always be gorgeous.' She smiled and her blue eyes twinkled. 'Just make sure you get back to me safely.'

'Yeah, Baby. That is certainly Plan A.' I was so confident in my reply, I almost believed it myself. I claimed her arm at the wrist and bent down to kiss her left hand that had touched me. Then I bent down even further to kiss her full on the lips. 'I love you.' I straightened. 'I'll be back.'

'Alright, Arnie. Just make sure you stick to the plan,' Ali scoffed, and pushed me away, and I wasn't convinced that she didn't like my corny line.

I appreciated the light-hearted joke we shared. We both danced along a delicate emotional line that morning. The event was hugely important and scary, and if one of us cracked at any time, it could have resulted in a lot of hugs and tears. In reality, we needed stiff upper lips and total focus to get the first step, to arrive at the hospital on time, done and dusted, with minimal fuss. There was no way on Earth that either of us would show the other any sign of weakness whatsoever.

We had approached the day in totally different ways. My coping mechanism had been to attack the whole illness-diagnosis-treatment-recovery as if it were a series of tests or mini-ordeals that could only be overcome in order, one step at a time. Simple, methodical, logical. I had been disciplined and not asked Google to confirm anything, not listening to anyone's stories, and not wasting time or energy thinking beyond each event. The whole fight was like a boxing match that could be split into manageable rounds. Round one, the starting point back in June at Wexham Park Hospital, had been brutal. I had scored it 10-9 in favour of myself because of the outstanding defence and resilience I showed but, on reflection, maybe I hadn't landed that many punches in reply - so that score could be challenged as biased. In between then and *operation day*, I had endured several other rounds. Whether it was a visit to a new hospital for a further scan; to be injected with radio-active ingredients, to have a camera shoved down my throat and into my stomach or have a biopsy bitten out of me - I, like Rocky Balboa, took the pasting and, exhausted, always found my way to the corner to recover.

Whilst I continued to get prodded by the experts, Ali and her supportive sister, Wendy, had to remain strong. Their mum and dad both fell ill, and their brother Robbie was also going through a tough time with his health. Rather than let the sense of doom consume us, Ali and I still managed to host a huge summer party to celebrate our joint 50th. So many of our wonderful friends and family came to celebrate the milestone with us and it was a spectacular success. Then, to further prove I wasn't prepared to curl up and die, I let GaryMan, Panda, and Sean take me up for a weekend of fun at Richard's up in Lytham-St-Annes. It was a crazy period of big highs and desperate lows.

To me, it had always been about a show of defiance and finding a way to get back to my corner. Catch my breath, get patched up, listen to my team that had waited for me, then *Bam!* - before I knew it, the bell sounded for a whole new round of punishment, and I was back out there – to bat back whatever was thrown my way.

The experience for me had one of uncertainty and frightening medical terminology. I hated that I had been forced to drop the tough guy persona and instead take on the role of a terrified rabbit - frozen, petrified, on a tarmac road waiting to be obliterated by an unstoppable force. The only positive was that Ali was with me at every turn. Yes, I had been the one that had been poked, injected, prodded, and pulled about all over the place, but Ali had suffered more than me in every other way, especially emotionally. As scared as I had been between the doctors finding the tumour and the day of the Big Op, I had relied upon my shield of denial and my rapier-like sense of humour. The feeling of shock had subsided over the previous two months, and I had accepted what had happened to me – and what was about to happen to me. I kept my imaginary blinkers on and just kept plodding along and took each (shit) day as it came.

Ali, on the other hand, had always been one of those people who needed to compute every possible outcome. That way, she felt in better control and a lot more prepared for whatever shit was to come her way. From the moment I called her with the first set of scan results, she had pretty much played out every single permutation possible, including what would happen in the event of losing me, either to the illness or maybe, later that day, on the operating table in my crucial attempt to fight it. I always said that she would be much better prepared for a true family crisis as she had already experienced everything at least once. Ali had never been able to stop her mind and thoughts from drifting off into dark places, especially late at night when she was tired and tried to fall asleep. Her incredibly active mind was both a virtue and a curse.

'Have you stirred them?' Ali asked, which meant had I begun shovelling two of our three children out of bed.

Harrison was going to work on that Thursday but would tag along to give his mother some support on the journey back, more than anything else. Lydia, our thirteen-year-old, was going to school but only after joining her mum and brother to give me a full and proper send-off. Plan A was that everyone (except Jayden, as he could never get up in a hurry) would make the trip into West London, but it was so early that everyone (except me) would be back in time to start their *normal* day.

'Yep,' I confirmed. 'Do you want some toast or a coffee? Or both?' Like a six-foot Gremlin, I hadn't been allowed to eat anything since midnight, so someone might as well eat. Hospital rules, they don't want to operate on someone that had just gorged themselves on a full English.

'If you've got time, I'd love a coffee. Thanks.' She did her best to emulate my single-step method. She tried hard not to overthink but there was little point in accepting an offer of toast as she felt as if she could vomit at any given moment.

I hadn't been up long, but I was alert and the gravity of my situation stood right in front of me. It was undeniable. A big part of my worry was the niggling doubt that I could be in the 1% club of patients that died on the operating table. It sometimes happened. I wasn't worried for myself – I was worried about Ali and the kids and how that awful event would affect their lives from that point onward. It was too painful and too stressful for me to consider for any length of time, so I parked that grim possibility to one side.

What about brain damage though? That might be worse than death.

Or some form of paralysis? Shit.

What if I woke up in the middle of the operation? That happens right?

The anaesthetic part is the complicated bit – what if they fuck it up?

What if they discover even more tumours?

What if I start to bleed like an Icelandic geyser and they can't stop it?

They constantly send me reminders to donate blood because they're so low on stock.

Yeah, Phil – and what if you died in a car wreck just driving there? I gave myself a bollocking so that I didn't let panic ruin all the fun. Up until that point, I had done a fantastic job to remain positive. The operation I was to have had been carried out hundreds of times before and, like flying on a plane, it was out of my control and in the hands of experts.

No point in worrying about something I couldn't change. Or so I kept telling myself.

The multiple layers of fear gripped my insides and made me feel nauseous. If I had been allowed to eat – I think I would've only managed a cup of tea at most. The physical sensation of feeling lightheaded, and therefore a bit sick, was brought on by my ever-increasing anxiety rather than the big, fat tumour that had been booked for extraction later that day.

We got dressed. All of us were kitted in our most comfortable gear. My holdall had been packed the day before. It had felt strangely different, to pack for such a traumatic experience – I could only ever remember good times whenever I'd previously packed that navy holdall. Optimistically, I packed underwear for 7 days and enough T-shirts to see me through the week. Seven to ten days I had been told. Fuck that. Seven days or earlier was my plan. I packed all my toiletries into my black washbag, but I kept my glasses on – it seemed daft to wear my usual contact lenses considering what I had planned. The conscious act of choosing glasses over contacts made me feel uneasy. I pictured my eyes being shut for several hours whilst Mr Chai hacked into me. Errgh. Thoughts of those horrific and graphic images did nothing to ease my queasiness.

As it approached the time to leave the sanctuary of home, I felt the distress build up proportionally. Every time I checked my watch or my phone to see if it was nearly time to go, my stomach gave a little wave of nausea. Time did not wait – it pushed me and the family towards the departure time. My nerves were jaded, and I could not sit still.

It would soon be over.

Soon.

In a matter of hours – everything would be all over.

I sent God a little prayer, even though I knew He had other things to bother with, and I politely asked, if it wasn't too much trouble, to return me back home, as soon as He could, in one piece. I had major doubts on the success of my prayer as I was sure God wasn't big on helping out agnostics ahead of His faithful.

Hammersmith Hospital

The journey to the hospital went to plan. The traffic had been light at that early time in the morning and we experienced that incredible phenomenon when the sunrise welcomed everyone into the brand new day. To keep me occupied, I drove us all into London. The conversation remained casual, as I refused to contemplate what was due to happen that day – whilst Ali couldn't help but contemplate everything dreadful that could possibly happen that day. We had made the trip once before to meet Mr Chai, my specialist surgeon, to discuss the operation, so we had overcome the initial anxiety of finding a new place or working out the deal when it came to parking. As I turned off the A40, and despite acting calm and doing my best to appear stoic in front of my family, I secretly wished that the car journey could last forever.

We pulled into a space in front of the main entrance. That was a lucky find, surely a good omen. The digital clock within the car dashboard told us we were bang on time. It was 6:40am. Clockwork. So far, everything had gone like clockwork. It helped to ease my nerves because it felt that everything was under control.

We all got out of the car and there were a lot of kisses and even more hugs. I exchanged 'I love yous' with the three of them and they all hugged back harder than they usually would. I heard 'Good luck' and 'See you later.' I told both my son and daughter to look after their mum until I was back. Ali didn't want to make a fuss, she knew it would unnerve me, so she dug deep and kept herself together. She asked me if I wanted her to come inside to help me settle in but I declined. She took my holdall from the boot and hoisted it onto my shoulder. With a free hand, I held my A4 folder that contained every piece of paper that I had accumulated from various doctors and hospitals over the previous ten weeks – all sorts of reports, appointments, and correspondence, and on top was confirmation of the day's arrangements and what department I had to head to for my 6:45am start.

Rather than walk towards the entrance, I put down the bag and laid the folder on top so I could exchange the proper, final, passionate hug I needed with Ali.

'Make sure you give them my number so they can call me straight away, OK?' she said, and kissed me.

'I will, wifey.' I returned the kiss.

She kissed me again. 'I love you.'

'And I love you, too.' I gave her a final kiss. Our embrace ended and I gathered up the folder and my bag and turned.

Ali joined the other two that were back in the car; she'd moved to the driving seat, and she watched as I walked towards the automatic entrance doors. I knew she must have felt sick to the pit of her stomach, but she hid it well from me and our children. There didn't seem to be anyone else walking in or out of the hospital. It *was* early. Ali didn't drive off immediately, and she waited for me to stop and give her a final wave. Except, I didn't stop. I strode directly into the building; I was on my most serious mission. By the time I realised that they would have waited for that last look, the moment had gone. Ali had pulled away and they were on their way back. Back to start a day that would centre around an unbearable wait, not knowing if I had made it through major surgery or not. In many ways my part was the easy one – I fully intended to sleep my way through the entire day.

There was nobody behind the Perspex screen of the main desk. The usually hectic atmosphere seemed calm and eerily quiet. I was sure I needed to head through the entrance and take a right once through the double doors, so that's where I headed. I didn't see a single soul as I made my way to the lifts and, after double-checking the letter I'd been sent, I went up to Ward 21 on the second floor in 'B' Wing. If I got lost, then I wasn't far away.

I passed many signs on the way. I recognised the names of some of the departments and wards (radiotherapy, oncology, neurology), and they were all scary enough to give me a chill - the unfamiliar ones even more so. Some people had some serious shit to go through.

Hammersmith specialised in the digestive system, pretty much the whole tube from the mouth to the anus. I stopped and studied a poster that showed the anatomy of the human digestive tract. The important parts were labelled, and various complaints and diseases were also annotated to every organ. That is what we animals were, to be blunt – a tube. Food went in at one end and once nutrients were consumed, the body forced out waste at the other. Arms, legs, head, and everything else were just extra bits to help the tube get what it needed to survive, and they also helped distinguish humans from the worms. I focussed on the pancreas and its defined tail.

'*Bye, bye*,' I said to my own tail. '*Oh, and you too, Mr Spleen.*'

As I entered Ward 21, I could tell that nobody had turned up the lighting to announce the day to all the patients, and I noticed an elderly lady in a wheelchair at the curved reception desk. It was reassuring to finally see another person – the day was surreal enough as it was without crazy thoughts that I'd entered a post-apocalyptic world with only a handful of survivors. The lady was being checked in by a nurse and I made an assumption that the lady's daughter was in attendance to help because she stood next to the wheelchair and was the one who did all the talking and form filling. I stayed back, socially distanced, and waited my turn. Everyone had conformed to Covid rules and wore light blue medical facemasks, including me.

Another nurse came out from behind the desk and said in a gentle, girlie French accent, 'Good morning.' She looked much bigger than her tiny voice suggested, and it seemed fair to think that I wouldn't be the only one that would have felt immediately calm and safe in her presence. I figured that she was from a French-speaking African country, and I could tell that she was one of those magic nurses and was exactly the person I needed to see. Although, I had always been a sucker for a cute French accent.

'Good morning,' I whispered in response, to make sure I didn't wake anyone up from their last minutes of precious sleep. 'How are you?'

'I'm very well zank you. Ma name is Ami,' she said behind her mask. 'Would you like to zit down over zhere?' She gestured towards a chair that would take me out of the main trafficked area. That little French voice was not an act and I thought, how wonderful.

'Yes, OK. I'm Philip. I hope you are expecting me.' I moved towards the chair.

'Yes, we are,' Ami said, and giggled. 'Please can you fill out zis form for me?' She waited until I'd set down my bag and folder and settled down into the chair and then she handed over a clipboard and a black biro. 'Let me know when you are ready.'

'Of course.' I took the clipboard and pen and got stuck into the questionnaire. It was all standard information and a lot of ticking boxes to help give the medical team as much information as possible.

Had I ever had an anaesthetic before? I ticked that as a *yes*. I remembered a successful operation when I was seventeen to remove all four wisdom teeth. No adverse reactions back then, and no reason to think anything would be any different.

False teeth? – No.

No, I wasn't wearing contact lenses – gold star for my anticipation of that one.

No, I did not have any jewellery - I'd given my neck chain back to Lydia and Ali was wearing my wedding ring on her own necklace. I was acing the questionnaire.

I skipped the section dedicated to women – no I was not pregnant. Imagine having to operate on someone that was pregnant, I thought.

Form completed, I stood up, gathered my belongings, and made my way over to the desk. Ami spotted me and asked me to go with her to the weighing scales at the end of the corridor. With my shoes off, I stood on the sturdy, old-fashioned scales. The big dial in front of us declared my weight and I saw her write down 87.5kgs. She asked me to stand up against the wall and brought down a small bar that rested on the top of my head. I hadn't had my height measured like that since my school days. They measured my height at 185cm. Ami then asked me to sit down again so she could take my blood pressure, whilst clipping the peg on my forefinger so that they could see my oxygen saturation levels at the same time. After so many weeks of medical attention, I had become a pro at all the required tests. Finally, Ami gently probed her digital thermometer into my right ear to check my temperature. All vitals looked good.

'OK. Zat is all fine. Follow me please.' Ami led me down the corridor towards my new home. On the right, I saw a long reception desk, and behind it, I made out an office and two other doors that I guessed might be cupboards for storage. To my left were all the bays that contained the beds for the patients. I couldn't help but glance in, but it was still too early to gauge any action, and nobody stirred. Ami took a left turn at the fourth bay.

My thoughts were - *Here we go*.

The four beds had been arranged two on one side and two on the other, which faced each other. The first two beds were curtained off and quiet. The next pair of beds were not curtained off and Ami happily showed me the unoccupied bed on the left. She opened up the bedside cabinet and suggested that I could put my things (my sings as she called them) inside it. I had been lucky enough to have been allocated a bed next to a window. The roller blinds were half down but I could make out a splendid view including an athletics stadium and, in the distance, the arch of Wembley.

On the bed I saw the dreaded gown, neatly folded and ready to be worn.

I didn't like the gown. I hated it. It represented illness and hospitalisation. I had been doing well; I had been positive and let Ami do her checks without a problem. But that fucking gown. It killed the mood for me. The fear rose up. Denial left the building – there was to be some serious shit going down that morning and that gown symbolised it perfectly.

'I zink ze anaesthetist or someone from ze surgery team will come up to talk to you soon. Zen we will get you ready.' Ami was so sweet, she made it sound like we were possibly going wine tasting.

'OK,' I replied, 'but I may need some help tying up the gown.'

'Yes, of course. Zere is a front and back part but when you are ready, I can help.'

It seemed like double trouble with the gown situation, but I was glad I would be helped into it. The gowns were still new to me, and I wasn't sure if I was supposed to present myself *as front opening* or *back opening*. They would need to get to my belly eventually and I guessed that getting dressed properly was probably the least of my or anyone else's worries.

'Thank you.' I confirmed my gratitude and Ami left me to settle in.

Ami said, 'Good morning, Roy,' to the man in the bed directly opposite me as she left.

I also heard the man, Roy, I assumed, happily repeat the greeting.

3

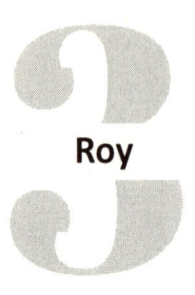

Roy

Dead opposite me there was a senior gent, fully dressed and lying down on top of his made bed. He seemed calm and serene as he read a paperback, but I couldn't make out what it was, other than guess that the cover font looked like it was a Grisham or something of that ilk. He looked quite smart, with a sky blue sweater over a collared shirt, trousers with a proper crease down the legs and tan shoes that looked more on the comfortable side than formal. I couldn't make out if the guy had just got there like me or had done his time and was all ready to leave. I saw the chap's whiteboard on the wall, and it told me that the man's name was Roy. There were some initials or abbreviations that only meant something to the medical team – and also, written in red, "*D.O.D 23/09/21*". I hoped it didn't mean Date of Death as I didn't want to look at a ghost that early in the morning. I checked out my own whiteboard above my bed and found that Ami had written on it whilst I had been checking out the room and my surroundings. Neatly, she'd put 'Philip - NBM', which I assumed meant Nil-By-Mouth, and also, 'D.O.D - 01.10.21'. Based on the information I had been given, that I might be in the hospital for a week, I figured that it must mean the Date of Departure. Based on that, Roy, who relaxed with his book, had indeed completed his sentence and was on his way out of Dodge. Good for him.

Roy peered up from his novel; he must have seen me looking over.

'Morning.' His voice sounded quiet, yet friendly.

I replied with a standard, 'Morning.' I've never been sure about the best way to strike up a conversation with a stranger.

Roy didn't look back down to continue reading, but instead paused before he spoke next, after all, it was now his turn. 'Did you have far to get here?'

'Not too bad,' I replied, 'pretty much straight down the A40. Not many cars on the road at this early hour. Not like it used to be, before all that *working from home* thing. Took us about 40 minutes door to door.'

Roy had lowered his book to his chest and sat up a bit. 'Oh, that's not too bad. I'm heading out on the A40 this morning once they sort all the paperwork out.'

'Well done to you.' I smiled as I congratulated the free man. 'You look well. How long have you been here?'

'Six weeks. I've had a few setbacks. I was at Harefield in June having an operation on my heart, so I am really looking forward to going home today.'

'I bet. Well, I hope that is you all done for hospitals now.'

'Yes. Me too,' said Roy and raised his eyebrows to accentuate his feelings as our brief conversation came to an end. He returned to his book and read on for a few minutes so that he could reach the end of the chapter. I saw him put in a bookmark, close the book, and put it on top of his bag that he had previously finished packing. Then I noticed he had swung his legs around to the side of the bed, then he stood upright and took a couple of steps as if he was too agitated and impatient to wait around, and it looked like he'd decided to stretch his legs to kill some time.

That plan did not happen.

As Roy began to take a few steps, he stopped. I could tell he looked a bit unsteady, but maybe that was how he always looked. I thought I saw him sway a bit. Maybe he had just got up too quickly after lying down for so long. I was relieved to see him take a couple more tentative steps towards the foot of his bed – maybe it was an attempt to walk-off the light-headed sensation people get as the body adjusts to the effect gravity has on the vascular system. That sensation must have got worse for Roy because he stopped again. His movements weren't normal but, I considered, maybe they were normal for Roy. I hoped he wasn't going to keel over – I was the only one around.

He locked eyes on me, and I saw something in Roy's eyes and his general aura. He looked worried, lost, scared even. It only took a second to get a feeling from someone and although I'd been minding my own business, I got up from my bed and approached Roy.

'Are you OK, Roy?'

'Err...' Roy responded but it was not convincing.

I felt concerned. I stood in front of him and noticed that Roy had turned light grey. 'Maybe, you should just sit on the bed for a bit?'

'OK...' Even his voice had changed to sound frail and unsteady, but he hadn't moved despite the suggestion. Instead, he seemed to stare right through me, his mouth slightly open.

There was a pause as I waited for Roy to sit down.

'Here, Roy.' I gestured towards the bed. 'There's no rush. Just sit down for a bit. You don't look too good. Are you sure you're OK?'

There wasn't anyone around and I wasn't sure if it was all normal for Roy or if he needed me to go and find some proper, professional help. I was sure that Roy should not continue his walkabout mission. That was clear as day.

'Um...I feel cold.'

'Come on Roy, sit down for a minute.' I really wanted him to sit down. His words and the way he talked seemed strange to me. I thought maybe he had dementia, if anything it was warm in the ward.

Roy appeared to have come around from his wide stare. I felt some relief as he touched the bed with his left hand and lowered himself enough so he could half-turn and sit down as instructed. I stood in front of him, not sure what to do but I felt that I couldn't leave my new cellmate just yet.

'That's better,' I said to encourage Roy. 'Just get your breath back, until you start to feel better.'

That was something I suggested to anyone that looked as though they were having some sort of episode or panic attack – get them to concentrate on their breathing and nothing else. If it worked for women in the throes of labour, it should work for everything. Luckily for us both, Roy was breathing, but it was shallow and a bit erratic.

I was about to start to coax him through a series of focused breaths, but he looked vacant, and his face had turned from grey to a deathly white. He seemed so distant and unresponsive I wondered if he was going to be sick, and I hoped to God he wasn't planning a heart attack, a stroke, or something else equally serious.

Just as I wondered what he was going to do next, I witnessed Roy's eyes roll back and then it seemed as though the rest of his body rolled back with them. It bordered on the comical – the way he fell backwards, but somehow, he'd twisted slightly and managed to get his head to land back onto his pillow. Anyone that had seen us from a different angle might have thought that I had given dear old Roy an uppercut, but the truth was that there was nobody else around to see any of it.

'Roy! Are you OK? Can you hear me?' As the words left my lips, I knew that there wasn't going to be a response and I kicked into some sort of auto-pilot mode. I knew I was going to need help. Fortunately, for everyone concerned, I had already experienced what pushing the alarm button meant in a hospital ward. It meant waiting around until an overworked nurse eventually came by – since hospitals worked to different timescales. I had only just arrived at Hammersmith and therefore had no idea where the alarm button was. I looked at the bed head, saw the button, jumped at it, and hit it with the side of my fist.

On the ceiling, at the foot of Roy's bed a little light came on. A gentle 'ping' sounded in the corridor to gently alert anyone nearby.

My previous hospital experience hadn't been that extensive, but I knew, because it was so early in the day and quiet, that it was not going to get the desired result of immediate, qualified help. It was going to be exactly like sitting on a plane to Majorca and waiting for the cabin crew to see if the little bulkhead cabin light meant passengers wanted another gin & tonic. Or wanted to be conned by the airline's duty-free scam. No time for jokes – things had got serious.

Holy Shit. I was going to need much more of an alarm.

'HELP! NURSE! HELP!' I started off loud, but then I guessed that I needed people from the front desk, all the way back down the corridor, so I began to get even more shouty.

'HELLO, SOMEBODY! CAN WE GET SOME HELP, PLEASE!'

Nothing came back. Shit – *fucking* shit.

'NURSE!' Panic started to set in. 'HELLO?' Anger teamed up with panic in my voice.

I didn't want to leave Roy, but realised I might have to. I considered I might have to put him into the recovery position or something. I couldn't tell if Roy was still breathing or not as everything happened incredibly quickly. I desperately wanted someone to make an appearance right that fucking second. The idea of performing CPR flashed into my thoughts. Christ, Roy was out cold.

Someone else called out for help. 'IN HERE! IN HERE!' The voice came from behind the curtained-off bed next to my bed. It wasn't a powerful voice, but the urgency was there.

I heard movement and action, and I sensed that help, finally, was on its way. The staff had heard my battle-cry, and thank God, they responded. There must have been three, maybe four, nurses that had marched into the bay and I stood back so they could get to the unconscious Roy.

'ROY?' One of the nurses tried to get a response out of him. 'Roy? Can you hear me, Roy?'

'He was just sitting there,' I told the huddle of nurses. 'He seemed to pass out and then fall back...'

Although they had listened to me, all their attention was focused on Roy. The nurses on either side of him put their arms under his shoulders and moved him into an upright position. I looked on intently.

Roy responded. His eyes had opened and although he looked a little frightened and disorientated, he tried to focus on the nurse that talked to him. I felt a huge surge of relief.

Phew, I reflected, that was bloody hairy. For a moment I thought it was all going to kick off.

The wannabe doctor inside me wondered if Roy had suffered some type of seizure or maybe a stroke. Hadn't Roy just been talking about heart problems?

Roy still looked groggy. He seemed to drift out of the darkness, but he still couldn't function properly, and his communication skills were not firing on any cylinders at all. I wondered what his brain might be up to. It was misbehaving and I hoped Roy would click back into the real world as quickly as he'd left it.

The nurses had set him upright and a young, male doctor had joined the team and stood in front of him. Exactly where I had been a minute before. He spoke calmly to Roy, as one of the nurses expertly looped a cuff around his bicep, Velcro-ed it in place, and then took his blood pressure. They were all trying to keep Roy, and themselves, calm.

I hoped everything would settle down enough and we could all just carry out some simple tests to determine what the hell that was all about. The blood pressure monitor would have told the medical team that Roy's blood pressure was critically low – but events were just about to take a turn for the horrific, before the numbers on the machine were even recorded.

The sounds that Roy generated were equally as terrifying as the sight of him projectile vomiting what seemed to be the entire contents of a bottle of quality Malbec from his sitting position. There was no real warning as Roy appeared to have gone into himself and wasn't able to speak. Everyone looked mesmerised for those few seconds as the splattering sound, mixed with Roy's groans, filled the air.

It was always astonishing how much mess just a small amount of blood (or wine) could make. But it was not a small amount. Roy's torso bucked again, and more blood gushed up from his stomach and onto the floor and that second wave was bigger and noisier.

The blood in that second tsunami appeared thicker and darker.

That bucket-load looked like it meant business.

Everything within six feet appeared to attract some of it. Everyone's shoes, socks and the bottoms of their trousers, the walls, and the wheels of the bed; nothing escaped. I had been trans-fixed from a safe distance by my bed and although unsplashed by Roy's blood, I was connected by the sight before me. A fast-acting nurse cut the scene off by quickly swooshing the privacy curtain around Roy and the team.

Now that I was outside of the scene, I struggled to connect all the voices with the people that were behind the curtain. I tried to listen to what was going on as much as I tried to *not* listen. There was clearly something urgent happening and no sooner had the curtains been drawn than they were pulled open again. I watched a gang of about six people wheel Roy's bed out from its previously snug setting at a distinctly swift speed and they charged out into the corridor. Some team members had their hands on the bed, some were holding Roy in place – he'd been rolled on to his side - and some jogged along and held various bits of equipment. They weren't talking as they all seemed to know exactly where they were headed.

I was left behind in silence as the commotion of staff, patient, and equipment took a left turn once they'd stormed the corridor and then suddenly, that was that, and they were gone.

I was left with a deafening silence after such a fast and fraught storm.

After a brief spell of reflection and with hopes that Roy was in safe hands, I checked back into the real, current world and back to my own private mission. Sombre, I silently sat back on my bed and looked at the empty area opposite that used to be Roy's space. My plan had been to prepare for my surgery in a peaceful and certainly unspectacular way. It was incredible how things could escalate in the blink of an eye.

I was left with my thoughts of Roy, and I slowly unpacked for a good five minutes and then, as expected, the anaesthetist made his appearance – just to really get my party started.

Going Down

The anaesthetist introduced himself as Adam. He came across as young and enthusiastic. I liked him. Adam was my sort of anaesthetist. He told me that he was pleased that I was a bit younger and in better shape than most of his typical customers. I lapped up the flattery as it wasn't every day I was called young and fit. I tried to focus on the job at hand and my situation, but I was still reeling from the drama with Roy's blood explosion – I tried to park my worries for him to one side, after all, Roy was in the best possible place. Adam went on to explain that me, being a healthy specimen of a man (or words to that effect), made his job just a little bit less stressful, as he didn't like to work with those that were already tapping on Death's door, or roughly 90 years old, or at either end of the BMI league table. I hoped that he was experienced enough to know that looks could be deceiving, and so I made the point that he wasn't to be complacent just because I was so incredibly fit and healthy. He gave a friendly chuckle and said he and his team would certainly not be complacent. Dr Adam carefully read through the notes and paid particular attention to all my observations – height and weight – and I had no inclination to interrupt him.

'Have you had a general anaesthetic before?' Adam asked whilst poised with pen in hand.

'Yes, I have,' was my positive response. 'When I was seventeen, I had all my wisdom teeth removed.'

'And I take it that there weren't any complications?' Adam wrote as he spoke.

I didn't have to think back too hard. I remembered that previous experience to be a complete success. Lovely private hospital, the operation went well and the recovery (apart from odd bits of food that got stuck in the caverns left behind) had been remarkably quick. Some suffer from swollen cheeks to ridiculous hamster-like sizes, but I managed to be lucky on all fronts. I'd always been such a lucky guy.

'No. No complications. I survived,' I joked. I felt a bit guilty that I was able to make a joke about survival whilst Roy was probably in some theatre fighting to stay alive. Shit, I felt a bit fragile; maybe my luck would run out one day.

'That's good,' Adam continued. 'And you're not allergic to anything?'

'Nope. Not that I know of.'

Adam carried on down his checklist. 'Have you ever had an epidural before?'

'Er...no.'

I had been told what was wrong with me several weeks prior, and I had also been told exactly what they were going to do to me. Various scans and dozens of tests had shown that I had managed to grow a fist-sized tumour on the back end of my pancreas. I would never know for sure what caused this to happen, and I doubted that they would ever be able to calculate for how long it had been steadily increasing its mass inside me. I would have said that I had experienced no symptoms whatsoever, but in its defence, my dear old pancreas hadn't performed brilliantly over the previous eighteen months – which made sense, due to the unwelcome guest stuck on its back. My insulin production had been hampered and, following a routine MOT offered out by the local GP surgery in the previous year, it had led to a diagnosis of diabetes and a daily dose of Metformin. The medication did well to keep my blood sugar levels in check. A diagnosis of diabetes was a weird one for me. I didn't feel like I had a health problem at all – I felt no different than I had 20 years before (apart from the aches and pains that came with middle age). Yet, I was a bit scared to think that the food that I loved (and especially chocolate and ice cream) might have the power to kill me. The dedicated diabetes team had me in for an eye screening test and a foot sensitivity test – to make sure I didn't have advanced diabetes that could make me go blind or caused my feet to rot and result in amputation. The more I researched what diabetes was all about, the more frightened I got. So I ditched my research and, suffice to say, had not become an expert.

I did respect the illness and tried to *do my bit*. I had begun to eat better and literally got on the treadmill to shift a few pounds. I made a conscious effort to walk to the shops rather than drive and generally tried to become more active. I became a little obsessed with the need to get blood flow to my toes.

However, although my overall health appeared to be perfectly acceptable, the truth was that there was a significant mass of unwanted cells that were on a mission to grow and multiply stealthily within my body. If I were to have had any negative symptoms because of the monster within, they had been cloaked by the medication and my own effort to improve my well-being. Luckily, that unrelated illness three months ago had led to a CT scan that finally detected the truth, before it had become large enough to engulf or cause irreparable damage to organs that were neighbours to the pancreas. I knew my spleen had come under attack, but plenty of other important vessels (gall bladder, bile duct, hepatic artery) were also in the vicinity and under threat. I imagined that my insides may have looked like a biological version of that classic horror film, The Blob.

As I headed toward the day of my operation, I had undergone numerous appointments, tests, and scans in every hospital in and around London – Chelsea, Charing Cross, and The Royal Marsden – it felt like I'd been caught up in a real-life version of Monopoly (hospital edition). Each appointment was an ordeal. I was in the loop with many others to wait to find out how bad the cancer was. That process was designed to find out everything about my enemy, and to calculate what my odds were of beating it. I felt a bit like a mule being carted from one place to another, something of a medical experiment or possibly a research project. Those sessions left me emotionally drained. I remained positive for my own mental well-being and that of Ali's and the kids, but I was exhausted after every trial.

I thought back to a few weeks before surgery day to when I'd attended a different department at Hammersmith Hospital. Ali came with me that day, and I had been sedated with drugs so I wouldn't mind so much about the endoscope that they eventually shoved down my throat and into my stomach. The sedation (or was it sheer exhaustion?) had worked like a dream. Literally, a dream, because I found myself drift off and fall asleep for a short while. That ordeal (for me) was nowhere near as uncomfortable and traumatic as it had sounded. The main purpose was to enable the team to use some modern bit of equipment to probe through the stomach wall and with a state-of-art camera they could locate the pancreas and spleen, and anything else affected by the tumour. Once in the right place, they extended a nifty tool to bite out several chunks of matter from the slow-growing blob. Those cells had then gone on their own journey back to a lab and been used for the purpose of a biopsy. Once the team had checked over the images of what the cells were playing at, they delivered their verdict to the specialists and me.

The results from all the many examinations had been favourable and positive as far as the attempts to determine spread and how aggressive the whole situation had become. Other organs and lymph nodes gave back optimistic results when it came to the indicators and tracers that the oncology team searched for. The spread seemed to be *not far* and *under control*. Back then, when Ali and I waited to hear my fate, each hour of waiting felt like a day. Those days where I heard nothing back lasted forever, they were like void days, wasted days of nothingness except worry and stress. The NHS had been on the case though, and I could not fault them, and after four days of waiting the verdict came back from the lab and the people in white coats. Their results set the path for me, and with MDT recommendations, I heard what treatment I had to endure.

Prepare for the Worst – Hope for the Best.

'We can class the cells as well-differentiated,' is what I heard Mr Chai tell me. He went on and explained that this news, when considered with all the other factors, was about as good an outcome as we could all expect. I will confess that I was frightened to ask, but because Ali pushed for maximum information, I had to ask if we were dealing with a cancer that could be described with that terrifying M-Word or (please God) the almost-safe B-Word. We were on a knife-edge with that one. We hoped with all our hearts that the tumour was a lazy benign bastard.

'We cannot be 100% sure until pathology carry out all their tests on the tumour - obviously after we have removed it. They will slice it up and give it a proper investigation. In my opinion, and with all the information we have to date, I would say this is a Grade 1 tumour and is about as friendly as these things can be. It is just the sheer size of it and the location of it that is our problem.'

Friendly? I pushed a little bit more to establish that Grade 1 was at the nice end of their rankings because, for all I knew, number 1 could have been the most aggressive. Mr Chai confirmed we were on the right side of their Grades. Halle-fucking-lujah!

At that point, Ali and I had accepted the verdict and, because it was generally good news, it was full steam ahead. No more uncertainty – we knew precisely what had to be done. I wasn't exactly *out of the woods,* but I don't think I could have received anything much better from Mr Chai. The hope and positivity from the specialist inspired a drive in me to attack the next round which was to be 'The Treatment.' I had been fearful of the prospect of hormone or radiation therapy and obviously chemotherapy, but it seemed I had been able to dodge multiple bullets, like Neo from The Matrix. Unfortunately, the one bullet I knew I couldn't dodge was surgery. Major surgery, as they kept calling it.

'If you were in your 80's we probably would not do this procedure at all,' Mr Chai had said in his consultation. 'We would just regularly scan you and deal with any symptoms as they would occur. Luckily enough, you are very young and have many years ahead of you. You can appreciate that we cannot just let it keep growing because it has already projected into your spleen and the vessels around it, and I have to tell you that we will have to completely remove your spleen as well as the tumour.'

Mr Chai had crossed his right hand under his ribcage on his left and drew an imaginary line from his side to the front of his belly to demonstrate where the incision would be. It looked like the cut would be a foot long. I don't think Ali or Mr Chai noticed or heard my gulp.

'So, to get to where we need to be we shall make an incision here and this should be enough to see what we are doing.'

I suggested Keyhole surgery. Scars can be interesting, but I would have much rather just have a few puncture wounds to back up my story, should anyone get cornered and have to listen to my dramatic tale of woe. My colleague from work, Tony, had undergone the delightful process after receiving a diagnosis of prostate cancer, which ultimately led to the removal of the offending gland. He had continued to be a great support to me throughout the whole cancer journey and although we had different illnesses, we spoke a lot, joked a lot, and generally dragged each other through our respective conditions. Tony had his surgery privately and everything had been carried out keyhole-style. I assumed if they could extract a prostate – they could extract a tumour and maybe a spleen?

'Unfortunately, not,' Mr Chai confirmed. 'I will try my best to remove as little of the pancreas as I can. But I have to make sure I get everything I need to, everything that is attached. Because I will have to remove your spleen *and* the tumour, I can only do this safely by opening you up. It is quite a major procedure; you will be in surgery for at least five hours.'

He let the stark facts sink in with me before he ladled on more information.

'It is probably at this point that we should talk about the risks. There is a very small chance that we have some sort of complication and, although we're *almost* certain, we have to all be aware that sometimes, even if they're incredibly rare, things don't always go to plan. So, I have to tell you that any operation carries the small risk of death.'

I knew that and I had expected his declaration. I had already guessed at a 1% chance of everything going belly up. I didn't want to clarify my estimation with the expert – just in case the reality was any worse.

'Yes, I know. It's fine,' I confirmed, even though it wasn't exactly fine. I didn't intend on being the 1 in 100 that died on the operating table.

'The other risks that we need to be aware of are...' Mr Chai had grabbed his left thumb when he began his list, starting with death, and then he moved on to grab each finger in turn to announce the other delightful members of his danger club. 'Infection. Which is something we can't 100% predict and we shall deal with it if this were to happen. Pancreatic leakage is also something we need to look out for. We will physically staple the pancreas and we will use drains to keep this leakage down to a minimum. A lot of the time we operate on people that are much older than you and their pancreas is a little bit more used up. Yours is a bit more juicy and so it is important to keep any unwanted secretions away as this could make you ill.'

I noticed that Mr Chai had released his fingers and was now sat back in his chair, a bit more relaxed. Maybe he was relieved that he'd delivered some scares, and his patient hadn't keeled over with a heart attack.

'You'll be recovering in the hospital for somewhere between seven to ten days. All dependant on how everything goes'

Seven to ten days – that's what I mulled over as Dr Adam asked me if I'd ever had an epidural before. He might have been asking a question, but I was side-tracked, and my thoughts were already beyond Adam's work - I had to endure a week, as a bare minimum, in that sodding place. I had no intention of staying a minute longer than was necessary. A week – maximum.

Sorry? An epidural?

Lovely.

It was one of those bitter-sweet things. Sure, it would help take away the pain, but the thought of having a ridiculously long needle shoved into the spinal cord would give most people a shiver down their spine. Ironically, a spine that needed to be perfectly still. I had previously seen the length of an epidural needle. I was there when Ali gave birth to all three of our children, but only the first needed the help of pain-numbing injections, forced directly into her nervous system. Ali had coped admirably and also suffered back problems for many years after, so I took great inspiration from my wife, the mother of those beautiful children – I was glad to embrace the whole epidural procedure. If I had been born a woman, there was no way would I have ever chosen to give birth *naturally*. Just like I would never choose to have a broken leg reset *naturally*. I didn't care if it made me sound a bit cowardly, but I was fully on board to make the entire episode as pain-free as it could possibly be.

'Am I OK to assume that you haven't eaten anything over the last 8 hours?' The anaesthetist enquired. He certainly didn't want the unwanted complication of food lurking in my body.

'That's right. I haven't eaten anything since about 7 o'clock last night. I'm lucky that this is an early morning gig,' I confirmed. I'd always been a morning person, one of those people that liked to get important stuff done before lunchtime.

'And can you confirm what procedure you are having today?'

I considered a witty response but instead bumbled through my not-very-technical version of; general anaesthetic, incision, remove endocrine tumour from pancreas, remove spleen, and sew me back up.

'That's great, thank you, Philip. Everything seems to be fine, so what I now need to do is to ask you to sign here, so we have your formal permission and consent.'

He handed me the clipboard and indicated the space near the bottom of his form that waited for my scribble. There was a fair bit of writing for me to read through and I did make a start to carry out some due diligence, but after 30 seconds of legal jargon, I came to the quick conclusion that if I didn't sign on the dotted line I'd have to call Ali to come and get me (and my tumour) and bring us both home. I just wanted to get on with everything – so I signed.

I handed the clipboard back to Dr Adam.

He thanked me and said, 'OK. If you can change into the gowns, we should be coming to get you in about 15 to 20 minutes.' Dr Adam had got all the confirmation he needed so it was all systems go.

'Sounds wonderful,' I replied a little too sarcastically. 'I probably shouldn't be asking you this, but is it true that you guys don't actually know *how* an anaesthetic works – you just know that it does?'

Adam probably hadn't expected my line of interrogation, but I'd like to think that he could tell that I was just being provocative in a friendly tone rather than being overly anxious or downright obnoxious. However, he couldn't just laugh it off, and he couldn't admit that they have never had a clue, so instead, he attempted some credible explanation.

'Yeah well, there are plenty of theories that would help explain how the chemicals work. Something to do with how they attach to cells in the brain. But you don't need to worry, everything will be working just fine and that is what is most important, right?'

There was no need for me to press that one any further. It was true, they didn't know how it worked. What I did know was that, although Doctors still had a lot to learn, they were bloody good with the things they did know.

I concluded the matter. 'As long as I'm totally out of it and you are looking after me, then I'm more than happy.'

'Superb,' said Adam brightly, slightly relieved that he wasn't about to endure the Spanish Inquisition on a topic he probably wished he knew more about, after all, it was his job. 'We'll see you in a bit, OK?'

'Perfect, see you soon,' I replied. I still liked him.

Once Dr Adam had left the ward, I considered the two gowns on my bed that Nurse Ami had neatly folded. Not only did they fill me with dread, but I knew I would need help to get them on. They never showed me how to put on a gown properly when I had first been admitted to hospital three months before. I had struggled like hell to tie it up behind my neck. Everyone else seemed to cope majestically with that most simple of tasks. I picked up the garments in turn. I could see that they were different designs - one of them had short arms and the other didn't. What the hell? Ami was out doing her rounds and I made sure I caught her eye.

'Are you alright?' she gently asked with her sweet French accent.

'Can you help me with these please?' I showed her the gowns, one in each hand.

'Ah, oui, yes of course I can,' Ami said. She had helped many patients get dressed. 'If you first take off your top - you can put zis one on first.'

We worked together and Ami helped me put on the back-half first. She held it up behind me so I could feed my arms through one at a time. She expertly knotted the tie-ups, and we repeated the process with the front-half. All done. I had a grim vision of the surgical team whipping off the front of my ensemble as soon as I was out cold, on my back, so they could begin hacking into me with their knives and saws and whatever tools where needed to fillet a human.

Ami seemed thrilled with how my outfit looked. She told me that I would need to wear the bright red socks provided, as these helped to prevent blood clots. Ami asked if there was anything else she could help me with. I only had one thing on my mind. I asked Ami to double-check that she, or someone from the team, would definitely call my wife as soon as I was safely out and to let her know exactly how everything went.

'Mais oui, yes, of course, we will call her,' Ami confirmed and, after an exchange of *see you laters*, she closed the curtains behind her so I could complete my strip, in private.

I felt lonely.

Thoughts of a disastrous operation attempted to infiltrate my otherwise positive attitude. The gown was on, but it wasn't a dress rehearsal, it was the real thing. I craved some distraction; being alone was not good.

I sat on the bed and removed my blue Adidas trainers. I took off my socks and stuffed them into each shoe like I used to do when I went swimming as a kid. I'd only worn those socks for an hour and a half, so I figured they'd be fresh enough for another go in the not-too-distant future. I replaced my rather conservative black socks with the new racy red ones. They had white, tacky (as in sticky) stripes on the soles, and they looked exactly like the Totes that my mum might have bought me at any given Christmas. It didn't feel much like Christmas. I let the small joy of pulling on new socks wash over me – still one of the best feelings in the world. The red socks felt good, nice, and snug, and I slid off the bed to stand in them so I could remove my tracksuit bottoms and then my pants. I couldn't help but compare my new socks with the ones I'd been asked to wear when I stayed at Wexham Park in Slough – these were a massive upgrade from the silky green stockings I'd been given back then. At least these ones were warm – and with no holes.

I laid my trackie bottoms on the bed, but I had a slight doubt about whether I should keep my pants on. They weren't going that low down on me. It was a dilemma normally saved for the rare occasion

I've had the pleasure of a massage – pants on or off? After two seconds of deliberation, I considered there might be a reasonable amount of blood flying around (thoughts of Roy still preyed on my sanity) so did I want my blood on my pants? Fucking hell, was I really having to worry about blood on my pants?

Anyway, I thought, *no*. I was sure they'd told me to take them off. Commando. Whether they had said off or not – I made the executive decision to go into battle double-gowned, Commando-style. I was never sure why Commandos didn't wear under-crackers – I've always felt far more safe and secure with a nice pair of comfy pants on. I'm not buying into the *ready for action at any moment* rubbish because they could just as easily keep a clean pair of knickers next to their fatigues.

With the gown arrangement protecting my modesty, I stuffed the trackie bottoms and my pants into the holdall. I was pretty much ready.

I looked down at the gowns I wore, which had become a symbol of my anxiety. I hated them; they made me feel the illness. They were the Kryptonite to my positivity. If I were to die on the operating table, I vowed to myself, I would make sure my spirit found a way to attach itself to that bloody shroud. Then I could return as a proper old-fashioned sheet-wearing ghost and frighten the shit out of everyone there. The tubes from the IV drips wouldn't be quite as effectively noisy as chunky metal chains, but I couldn't have it all when it came to revenge.

Countless fears raced through me. My life was in the hands of others. I did my best to sit calmly on the armchair next to my bed. I tried to focus on my breathing. Easier said than done. I wanted to find a happy place, but I failed miserably. I quietly read my book for a few minutes and then I sent a final text message to Ali:-

> Phil: Going down now - see you on the other side - I love you.

I signed off with a kiss-blowing emoji.

Ali came back within seconds:-

> Ali: I love you soooooo much. Dream Happy thoughts. Speak to you later. I love you xxxxxxxx

Then the porter arrived, with a wheelchair in tow. He was there to take me down. We exchanged pleasantries. I put my phone and my book in my holdall and then hid that within my bedside unit and closed the little door. They were ready for me. There had not been a mistake. I said I could walk there. He insisted that I was in his care, and it would help him if I just let him wheel me there. I complied. I gulped.

Showtime.

A Trip to the Theatre

It wasn't a long journey from the ward. The lift arrived soon after the porter had pushed the button and the two of us sailed down the two floors in silence. If I had been left with any food in my digestive system, I would have shit myself.

It was still relatively early in the morning for the hospital (and for the outside world, too) and, other than the porter, I hadn't seen another soul on my trip to the theatre. Strange then, that when the lift settled on the ground floor and the doors opened, the only person that I knew in the entire hospital was stood right in front of me. It was Mr Chai.

I didn't wear a facemask and I beamed a smile his way. I was genuinely delighted to know that Mr Chai was there with me. Everything could simply coast along – it was all going to plan.

'Hello there,' said Mr Chai, who hadn't planned the welcome party. He extended his hand.

I assumed that there would be a lot of scrubbing up to happen after physical contact, so I accepted the surgeon's hand, and we exchanged a brief pump. I made sure not to crush my saviour's hand in my excitement, but also, I didn't want to freak him out with a horribly limp handshake. I only had a split second to gauge it, but I think I got the pressure spot on.

'Hello!' I was grateful to share a handshake that had become a rare thing during the pandemic era.

'How are you doing?' Mr Chai had his face mask under his chin, so as he asked his question, I could see a kind face that reciprocated a smile with sincere warmth.

'I'm fine,' I responded keenly. 'The question is - how are *YOU* doing? Because, if you're all right and feeling good – then so am I!'

Mr Chai chuckled a little. 'Yes, I'm all good.' He seemed glad to see that I was up for it – up for the challenge ahead. 'Don't you worry; we have a fantastic team to look after you.'

'OK. Thanks. That is good to know,' I replied. I liked Mr Chai. In the previous eight weeks, we had met a few times and he had gently explained to me (and Ali) what had happened and what he was going to do to help. He hadn't sold his soul to the private healthcare organisations, and I liked him more because of that. He had said that I could have gone private, but I wouldn't get any better care and when it came to recovery, his team were experts at helping patients with my type of recovery. Whilst a private room might sound nice, the private team did not have the same pool of talent that were available at Hammersmith. It had been an easy decision to ditch all the benefits of my private healthcare scheme and put all my trust, and my life, in the hands of the NHS and their Mr Chai.

'Well, I need to get ready for you,' Mr Chai said, and made a move towards his room. He was not dressed and ready for action at all. Obviously, he was dressed. Dressed as a civilian in a work shirt and trousers, but not as a Superhero in blue overalls, latex gloves, and a surgeon's hat. All of that costume was ready to be donned, just in time for some life-saving action. 'See you on the other side.'

'I certainly plan to,' I said whilst I maintained my smile. As we parted company I called out, 'Good luck!'

Mr Chai gave me a 'You too!' and waved goodbye as he walked away.

My porter wheeled me in a different direction. We headed towards the preparation room.

They had been expecting me.

There was a welcome party of four. Between them they had an arsenal of needles and masks that they used for their effective knock-

5 – A TRIP TO THE THEATRE | 41

out gases and injections designed to paralyse, numb my nerves, and keep me asleep throughout. The room was pokey. It was no more than eight feet by eight feet, with a whacking great bed on one side and me stuck in a wheelchair, the four of them looked squeezed in and on top of each other. Dr Adam was there, two other men and a female nurse. The vibe in the room was upbeat – but with a detectable, sinister undercurrent. Like they were preparing to take me up for a solo sky-dive.

Everything moved quickly along. I barely had time to crap myself with the fear of what was about to happen. Dr Adam asked me to confirm my name and my date of birth – which I did. The nurse had asked me to get on to bed. It was a beast of a bed – perfect for operations. Under her guidance, I shuffled up and down but eventually ended up sitting at the foot of the bed, where my legs dangled off the end. She then proceeded to get out the old blood pressure cuff and, as expected, the machine squeezed out a reading from my arm. She then put the oxygen-reading clothes peg on my finger and jammed the thermometer into my ear – I got the full works. I noticed that the cuff wasn't removed – an indication that the cuff would be employed to send out readings throughout my time in theatre. Whilst all the action with me was going on, the others talked between themselves and flipped over pages on their clipboards. One of them had an iPad or some tablet thing. I didn't ask the three I'd never met before, if they had a better idea than Adam about how an anaesthetic worked.

The nurse took hold of my left arm and got to work with the insertion of a cannula. I looked away as she warned me about a sharp scratch moments before the needle penetrated my flesh. The process happened with efficient speed. I didn't have time to think about whether that cannula set up was a good one or not. She taped it into place. Before I had time to admire her handiwork, she plumbed an IV drip into the cannula and hoisted a bag of liquid on a metal stand.

Here we go.

I barely had a moment to think of all the many people I knew, that were either at work or on their way to work, that would experience a perfectly normal boring day – whilst I was committed to an operation that should, fingers crossed, save my life. I thought of Ali and the children – but I wasn't allowed any time to dwell on them as I found myself being quizzed by the nurse.

I was asked similar questions to those that Dr Adam had thrown at me earlier. Had I had an anaesthetic before? An epidural? Any false teeth? Was I allergic to anything? I wondered if the doubling up on everything was necessary, or maybe she was being nosey. She told me that they were going to put the epidural into my back. Fucking hell. I had been scared about that part. A bloody great long needle was about to be forced into my spinal column. Ali's back had been screwed up for a few years after her first epidural. I knew it was all necessary, but it was the fallout from the procedure that bothered me. I grasped at the inspiration I got from my wife - if Ali got through all that shit, then so must I.

Before the big needle went in, they needed to give me a local anaesthetic, which I was distinctly in favour of. I was asked to lift up my gown to expose my back. Then I had to lean forward and curve my spine for them. The nurse cleaned my back with some surgical wipes. Then one of the other doctors gave me a first injection that I barely felt. I could tell it was half-way down my back from where he touched me. I guessed, just where my ribs ended, the bottom end of my chest. Maybe the wipes contained a special ingredient with the power to numb the skin. Either that or my body had already started to go into shock. The team carried on with their conversation whilst we all waited for the local to take effect.

The nurse was lovely. She spoke words of encouragement and reassurance. I didn't listen properly because I was in the middle of an overwhelming precursor to a panic attack. Whilst everything had sped along, I had been fine and happy to get caught up in their confident done-this-hundreds-of-times procedure, but when there was a pause, especially a two-minute pause, my mind started to race.

Fuck – these thoughts might actually be my last thoughts.

I might be in that 1% club. Someone had to be.

When I get put to sleep that might be it. No more me.

Goodnight Vienna.

What idiotic, crap thoughts to have as your last ones, Phil.

The big needle that was to carry the plastic sleeve into the cavity of my spinal cord had been coiled up in a bag. I had seen it. I was impressed with its flexibility. Quite an incredible invention, really. I wondered what sort of crazy psychopath first tried this out on someone. No doubt it had been tested on our animal friends before humans got the pleasure, but still.

There was a sense of calm as Dr Adam went for it.

I was asked to stay curled forwards and remain perfectly still.

The nurse was in front of me. My left hand held my gown behind my neck, but then the nurse reached out and held my free hand. I think it was more for my benefit, but it might have been for hers.

Adam and his two colleagues were fully focussed on the middle of my back.

Due to the intensity of the situation, my thoughts continued to race – *If these jokers screw this up, I could be paralysed from the chest down.*

Despite feeling some prods, I could sense that their first attempt hadn't worked.

They'd all pulled away from my back and although I didn't hear groans of failure, there were no whoops or high-fives either.

'Just stay still for me please, Philip,' said Dr Adam calmly.

I didn't say a word as he went in for another go.

I barely took a breath.

I guessed a millimetre of movement might be disastrous.

The second attempt hadn't worked either. The team pulled away and had a little chat and the nurse and I looked at each. She told me that everything was fine and that they were going to use a different needle, that was all; perfectly normal, nothing for me to worry about.

I began to feel warm.

My lack of breathing didn't help quash a sensation of nausea that had begun to brew.

I didn't have to wait too long; Dr Adam was back.

'Sorry about that. Are you OK?' he asked.

I had no intention of responding. Instead, I thought: *Can you please get this over with?*

The three wise monkeys were in attendance at my back for the third time. It seemed like they had got somewhere. I could tell from the difference in the pressure of Adam's hand on my back – a sensation of something (not painful) had entered me, maybe something like that of an acupuncturist's needle. The work continued behind me. I pictured them slipping in the plastic sleeve that was to be the conduit for all my future pain relief. Then I could sense them all pull back again, the difference was that I felt something had been left behind, and I guessed they were behind me admiring the epidural that stuck out from my spine. Third time lucky, boys, third time lucky.

'OK, we are in now,' confirmed Adam. 'That's the tricky bit all done.'

'Great! Well done guys,' I responded jovially. I could still feel my feet, so I guessed that they had taken their time and not permanently crippled me. Which was nice.

I stayed hunched forward whilst they connected a tube to that needle in my back and then taped down the tube along my back in several places up to my neck using strips of medical tape to ensure the whole set up stayed securely in place. The end of the tube was looped up onto the metal stand next to the IV drip. The nurse checked out a different bag of clear solution, and then clipped it up high before she plumbed the tube into the bag. A valve was in place high up the tube – the flood gates were held back until needed. That solution was to be my new best friend for the next few days.

They asked me to release my grip on the gown to let it fall and cover my back again. I hadn't realised how tightly I'd held it whilst I allowed them to force a bit of metal into my central nervous system. Then Adam asked me to lie back down on to the bed.

Lie back? Lie back and risk dislodging the epidural we've just spent five minutes getting exactly perfect? Worse than that, what if I lay back and my movements forced that needle even further into my spine? I'd be in a wheelchair for the rest of my days for sure.

I couldn't help but check. 'Are you sure you want me to lie back on all of that?'

'Yes. Don't worry. It's all secure now,' was Adam's clear response.

Firstly, I shuffled all the way back until my feet were well and truly on the bed, then I tentatively lay back. I could feel the tube's cool presence against the top of my back, but it wasn't uncomfortable. I must have got my location spot on because I wasn't asked to shuffle up or down, which would have stressed me out even further.

I lay motionless; I only allowed my eyeballs to move, so I looked straight up at the square lights in the ceiling. The team did not hang about – my vision of the ceiling was interrupted by a big mask that came down and over to cover my nose and mouth.

Christ, no warning, it was knock-out time.

Or so I thought.

There was air in the mask; I guessed they would soon pump in the nitrous oxide to take me far away from the shores of reality.

I wasn't sure if I had imagined the sound of gas being released somewhere in the room. I remembered the drill from back when I had my only other operation and every other instance I'd seen in the movies or on TV. One of them, probably Adam, would now ask me to count back from ten to zero. I reckon I had only reached up to seven on that first go. I wanted to see if I could beat my personal best.

Oh. Everyone had gone quiet. The mood in the room had changed from busy to frozen.

In my final moments I thought: *It might be happening now.*

Hold on. Where was my sodding countdown?

Then, blackness.

Alive

A thought. A brief, conscious thought.
Barely a flicker.

Then back to the darkness and the nothingness.

Another thought made itself known. It didn't have much power behind it, but it didn't need to. The thought was something like, *I've had a thought. And. This thought is another one.*

It was a strange experience; it was as if I had been a bystander that watched the scene whilst my brain attempted to regain consciousness. The darkness was everywhere, but it wasn't scary. It was neutral. My first cognitive thought that felt like my own, that felt like me was - *I'm alive.*

Time was a complete unknown. There had been a gap between my two states of consciousness, and I had no idea of how long it had been. It might have been seconds, or it might have been decades. The gap was totally different from being asleep, which was joined by some activity - dreams and nightmares. It wasn't a dramatic sensation of rebirth. It wasn't like a switch that had flicked from off to on. It was more of an initial inkling of a spark that might turn a cog. A cog that might start to turn up a dimmer switch.

Let there be light.

Please.

No light yet, but one of my senses broke free. I was grateful for it. It gave me a location. I heard a sound.

I could hear.

The sounds evolved into something I recognised - a voice.

I could tell it was a woman's voice.

My sense of touch deceived me. I could feel something. My brain tried to work out the messages from all over my body and it told me that I was lying flat on my back. That made sense because I could think back in time. I thought about memories. Latest memories. My situation came back to me.

I was in hospital, and I had been about to have operation. I had been given an injection and, I could only assume, I had woken on the other side of it. Maybe, the operation was all over? I'd experienced a general anaesthetic once before and had been knocked-out from a clash of heads twice playing sport. I guessed my brain had entered that same recovery process. I was rebooting - in safe mode. Groggy, I felt weak, and my thoughts were limited. I could only muster basic thoughts and even they were unclear.

I might be OK.

As the stages of regaining consciousness creaked along, I sensed I was not in pain or discomfort.

I concentrated on the voice. The female was having a conversation with someone near to her. Oh! Maybe she is speaking to me? I must try to concentrate more.

The voice came from the foot of my bed. Quite near to me. Maybe just off to the left. I don't know why but as she continued to speak, and I gauged her to be mid-twenties with a British Asian accent. Had I seen her before?

Another voice was present. It wasn't mine, but it was a male voice.

The two voices talked about someone. The male voice sounded young as well, but he was further away and muffled so I couldn't comprehend what he said. The female voice, possibly because it was clearer, seemed to be in charge. They continued to chat about one of the patients.

"...did you hear about that? It was a shame because there was a *big* tear in the skin..." The female spoke, but I could only make out snippets of the conversation, which was frustrating.

Were they talking about me?

I wasn't quite aware enough to feel scared or angry with the words my ears had picked up. I just lay there and listened. I thought, *I hope they're not talking about me*. A BIG tear of the skin didn't sound like good news. The tone of the voice had made it sound even more horrific.

Maybe I should be scared? My emotions seemed as scrambled as my thoughts.

I counselled myself – be positive. It might not be me that they were talking about. The woman stood just off to my left and I could sense the chap was a little further beyond on that same side. There was every chance that there was another body/patient/corpse that lay on another bed, over to my left in that black, godforsaken place.

Anyway, if it was me that they were talking about – fuck it – I was alive, and I was sure that they'd managed to stitch me back up. Surely there would be a flurry of a trauma team if my broken body hadn't been fixed? They were professionals and had overcome similar situations hundreds of times. There was no sense of panic in the darkness – all was calm.

I wanted my eyes to work. Seeing was believing.

No. That seemed to be too much to ask.

I felt that my eyes were OK. Or, at least, they were not *not* working. I could sense my eyeballs there, in my head.

Everything remained black. My eyelids were definitely shut and closed for business, but at least it was something new that I could physically feel and sense. No need to panic, all part of the process. My eyes felt like they normally would have if they were shut at any other point in my life. I didn't bother to force them open and instead, I let tiredness win. I was exhausted from all the brain activity – thoughts, memories, senses, and the whole rebooting process had taken it out of me.

Or maybe it was the drugs? Is that why I was groggy, disorientated and not in pain?

Whatever it was, I let myself get taken away. I drifted off into a different state that was somewhere between unconsciousness and normal sleep.

The voices seemed to get quieter as they floated away from me.

Those words I'd heard about skin being torn (my skin?) hung in front of my thoughts, like a horror movie banner. My mind (my brain) wasn't prepared to process anything; it needed to recharge and to do that, it needed a full-on shutdown. At that point, I wasn't scared of a sleep that could be my last. There wasn't a euphoric feeling of being alive either. I was perfectly content to bank a neutral position – I was too tired to experience anything significant. My brain had a self-preservation thing going on.

I fell asleep.

I was not blessed with sweet dreams.

More importantly, I don't remember being plagued with frightening nightmares.

'Hello, Philip?'

A different voice. I detected an older voice. It had a faster pace.

'Hello. Can you hear me, Philip?'

I wasn't sure who was talking to me, but I automatically replied with my own, 'Hello,' as I could tell that the voice tried to resurrect me from the depths of deep sleep.

'Hello, Philip.'

I repeated my hello again. But the conversation didn't seem to move on much.

Faster and louder. 'Hello. Hello, Philip. Can you hear me? Are you OK, Philip?'

I tried to say *yes. I can hear you*. But I couldn't get the words out. Shit. I can't even speak. I realised that I hadn't said *hello* at all. That is why the voice kept on saying the same thing. They weren't deaf – it was because I was mute.

My throat felt strange. There was something actually *in* my throat. Bollocks. Speak? I can't even fucking breathe properly. Hang on. Yes, I can breathe. I concentrated on breathing. I could physically feel a tube in my throat. I could still breathe – there was no blockage. No need to panic. I'd get to speak in the future. One step at a time.

I felt a need to swallow. It was because I had been thinking of my throat. The power of suggestion had stirred my subconsciousness and demanded that I check out the simple process of a swallow. It seemed totally unnatural and uncomfortable. The muscles I usually relied upon were obviously hampered by the plastic tube. *So, Phil – you can't swallow, and you can't speak.* I guessed that those two things would have to wait. I was happy to lay there and breathe. Those doctors would sort me out, I was sure of it.

A negative thought attacked me. Are you 100% sure the doctors can sort you out?

Fuck off. I was too tired and confused to believe that I had become a blind cabbage that couldn't see or communicate. But it was a possibility.

'Hello, Philip. It's all over, Philip. Everything went well,' the woman said, and her words sounded clearer, calmer.

Did she just say *it's all over* and *everything went well*? Because if she did, that would be fantastic news. Quickly, someone must tell Ali.

I mumbled something. God knows what it was or what the lady thought it was as she tried to eke out a response from me. I reckoned that she recognised my sounds as standard mumbles that all of us post-op patients give out to announce to the world that we're alive.

'Can you feel my fingers in your hand, Philip? Can you give them a squeeze?' She said a little faster, and I detected a degree of urgency in her voice. Not in a panicky sense, more of an efficient way like *come on, you – I've got another 50 cases to wake up before my shift ends.*

I tried to do my bit, but I felt too slow, and my body didn't want to co-operate. I concentrated my thoughts to my left hand and there was definitely something foreign in my palm. I felt the warmth of whatever was there on my skin. I felt that they were the size of fingers, just as the lady had suggested. I felt confident they were human fingers with bones, rather than room temperature chipolatas, so I attempted a squeeze.

My hand worked!

It felt good. I held the fingers and wanted to show the voice that I was responsive, and her efforts had worked. I had no idea if there was any power in my squeeze, but it got the desired response.

'That's good, Philip. Are you alright?'

I didn't know if I was alright or not. My natural reply would have always been, '*Yes, I'm alright, thanks*', but that probably wouldn't have been helpful in that situation. Honesty was the best policy. If I could just prise open my sodding eyes, I'd have a much better idea on how I felt. Apart from the uncomfortable throat tube, I wasn't in any pain, and with some senses back, and my brain giving me signs of encouragement, yes, I guessed I was doing alright.

If I could squeeze my fingers, maybe I could creak open my eyes.

For a fraction of a second, I thought that maybe my eyelids were still taped down from the operation. Maybe they were just sticky. Hang about, I could do this. Come on! I focussed – both eyelids complied with my brain's instructions and like a pair of rusty metal security shutters, they began to yield to the motors that controlled the opening-up mechanisms. That effort, that event, was a biggie.

Blurred light.

Murky, unfocussed, and dull light probed its way through the slits of my eyelids as they slowly opened.

Fantastic.

An unspectacular shard of light to everyone else, and yet to me, in my desperate situation, as I waited for any improvement, it felt fantastic. Murky, dull light was good enough at that time. I was confident that I could work with that as a starting point. I remembered that my eyesight was poor anyway. I'd been myopic for the last 30 years and it had conditioned me to accept blurred images whenever I woke up. I blinked and tried to re-focus.

I could see.

Well, I could see the ceiling. Not the most exciting sight, but I was encouraged as I considered all my circumstances. I looked down at my left hand. Yep, definitely my hand. There was a cannula and a tube that joined into it. I didn't bother to lift my hand up, it had done alright in the squeeze task, but I wasn't sure if my mind had played tricks with me or not. Could I move the muscles in my arm? The strangeness of the wake-up process could not be trusted.

Within the first few minutes after I'd creaked open my eyes; I felt my faculties fight their way back. I began to feel a bit more like me. My thoughts were familiar. I moved my head and I saw the nurse that was in charge of resus. I couldn't see her well, but just being able to make out a shape and identify colours was incredible. She looked back at me, at my eyes. I was calm and satisfied that my sight would be decent enough for when I put my glasses back on. Before I could strike up a conversation with the nurse, exhaustion came over me again. I fell asleep. All that lying around being operated on was so tiring.

I must have been semi-conscious when they wheeled my bed out of the recovery room and down maze-like corridors. I wanted to wake up and find out what was happening and, equally, I wanted to sleep. I was aware that we went in and out of over-sized lifts. There was no conversation at all. I couldn't seem to stay awake for more than a few seconds. Unless, maybe, being wheeled around the hospital had been an exceptionally naff dream.

No, it wasn't a dream. Eventually, they rolled me back to the safety of my bay, and my corner space and then they engaged the foot brakes. I had made it back. I wasn't able to verbalise my thanks to the porter, but the thought was there. I looked down at my torso. A crisp white sheet covered me. I couldn't work out if I was thinner or more bloated than I had been the last time I'd looked down at my body. I hated the confusion. Christ, even that journey had been too much – I felt myself drift off back to sleep. I attempted to fight back the feeling. I thought that maybe the operation had changed my life so that I wasn't able to stay awake for longer than a minute. Had I caught narcolepsy? You can't *catch* narcolepsy. *Get a grip*. I was too tired to stress about it. Once again, I slept.

Something or someone disturbed me from my sleep. A nurse fussed around me as I stirred. After I took a minute to gather my thoughts, I took a few gulps, assessed the tube in my throat and made an attempt to speak.

'Hello,' I croaked. My voice sounded awful to me. It sounded weak and bordered on pathetic.

'Hello,' the nurse replied brightly. 'Are you OK?'

I paused a moment to consider if I was OK or not. 'Yes.' I had to swallow against the tube between my words. 'Please...can you...pass me...my phone?'

'Of course. Where is it? Is it in here?' She moved towards my bedside unit as if she had answered her own question. She found my navy holdall that I'd stuffed in there earlier that morning, before the carving had happened.

'Yes...in the...side pocket.' The tube scratched inside my oesophagus. It had become uncomfortable and wasn't far off painful. My throat had always been a weak point for me, if I ever got a cold, I knew that it would result in a sore throat.

The nurse found it straight away. 'Here you are.' She handed it over. 'Do you need anything else?'

I didn't know the answer to her question. I should have known, but I was only firing on one cylinder at best. I had no idea if I needed anything or not.

'No, thanks,' I squeaked. As I spoke, I felt all the tube. It started at the back of my mouth, went down my throat, and most of the way down to the indent where my collar bones met. I touched that indent – it was so sore there. I had been sliced right across my belly and yet the only pain that troubled me was that point at the base of my throat. The tube caused me a stress I didn't want – I wanted it out.

I assumed that someone from the hospital team had already let my wife know that I had survived the surgery, but I wanted her to hear from me. Straight from the horse's mouth. I held the phone and pressed the button at its side to bring the device back to life. My eyes were a bit squinty, but I achieved my aim, which was to send some messages to Ali:-

> Phil: In recovery xxx
> Sore throat - Obviously. Can't speak yet.

I noticed the time was 15:59. Call it 4pm. Ali hadn't heard from me for eight hours, since my 8am message to say I was going down. I knew she would have been worried sick all day. I hoped that someone from the hospital had found two minutes to at least let her know I was through the worst of it. I must have sent my messages whilst half-asleep, as I had told Ali I was in recovery when I actually meant that I was recovering. It didn't matter in the big scheme of things – I didn't have the energy to correct any miscommunication. I just wanted to let her know that I wasn't dead.

> Ali: OMG!!!! So lovely to hear from you xxx

> Phil: I'm okay.

> Ali: That's all I need to hear. I love you xx

> Phil: I'll call later. I love you x

> Ali: I haven't stopped thinking of you all day...My heart jumped when I read your message. Take it easy and we will speak later xxxxxx

I took Ali's advice to take it easy. I crashed out and went back to sleep.

The Aftermath

As it approached the end of the working day, I had become aware of all the additional love and attention I received from the nurses. No doubt they'd been there constantly, even when I'd been unaware. Ami had seen me numerous times with her happy demeanour and her testing machinery. She seemed to be satisfied with the regular readings she had taken from my compliant existence. Blood pressure, temperature, and pulse all continued to behave themselves. Otherwise, I was certain, I'd have been whizzed off back into surgery.

Ami had put some of my things within reach on my adjustable wheelie-tray. My book, my phone, my glasses, and a cup of water that I was ordered to only sip – no big gulps. The time had come to assess the damage. I pulled my sheets down. My horrible gown had gone – I could see my bare chest and I could see a lot of white. There were huge white dressings that covered a massive proportion of my torso. A five or six-inch wide padded strip started at my solar plexus and covered a wound, all the way down to my naval. Then, I could make out another wider dressing that began on my left side and ran horizontally, all the way past my naval to halfway across my right side. It was a truly professional job, there was a clear, waterproof film (something a bit more substantial than cling-film) that held everything in place and offered a further barrier against unwanted moisture. I felt secure but it did look like their incisions had been three times longer than the visual impression Mr Chai had given me weeks ago in his office. Fuck. They had cut me up good. I was grateful that I couldn't see the actual wound – out of sight, out of mind. I knew it would look horrific, but I hoped that my inevitable first sight of it would be later – when it had healed somewhat and looked at least a little bit prettier.

I put my glasses on and was able to have a good look around. Roy was back! Thank God. I could see he was covered up as he lay in bed, and he looked to be asleep. Poor sod should have been at home with his feet up. I was so pleased that I hadn't seen an empty bed in front of me – that would have upset me. Yes – Roy was breathing.

I took a moment to consider my state. I felt OK. I wasn't sure if the pain I felt was all in my head. I'd been sliced open. I felt tightness across my belly. The pain wasn't acute and was more of a grumble. They'd cut through layers of skin, muscle, tissue, sinews, and whatever else was in their way, like a jungle guide, violently hacking through vegetation with his machete, to make a path that wasn't supposed to be revealed to human eyes. Whilst I remained still, my pains were like the manageable sensations of feeling bloated and that of trapped wind. To combat anything worse, I made a conscious plan to not move at all. I was scared. Scared that any movement below my chest would gift me the most intense pain I'd ever experienced. I didn't quite have the energy for that degree of agony, so I'd vowed to my body that I wouldn't move it.

I prayed that I would not cough, sneeze, laugh, or top of the list – be sick. Any uncontrollable spasms would feel like I'd been ripped open. I was worried that maybe internal stitches would rupture, and I would feel everything because I was not under the protection of Dr Adam's anaesthetic.

As long as I stayed still, my throat continued to be my biggest source of discomfort. It was fine when I was asleep but as soon as I was awake the internal scratching had become painful. There didn't seem to be much I could do about it. I scouted around the rest of me to see what else had happened whilst I'd been out for the count. I deduced that they had really gone to town on me. I had on an oxygen mask that covered my nose and mouth and, although it was no doubt doing plenty of good, I found it suffocating in a claustrophobic sense. In the handful of times I'd worn them, I'd never liked those oxygen masks, I felt like they prevented me from taking a big deep breath and that sense of restriction was something I found unsettling. As I lay there, it wasn't the mask as such that bothered me, but the way the mask put pressure on a tube that sprang from my nose. I worked out that the pull from the oxygen mask tugged at the obstruction that was glued into my right nostril. That nose-tube continued down into my throat and, I assumed, into my stomach. I sensed the thick and incredibly sticky plasters caked around my nose that held everything in place. There was nothing wrong with my medium-term memory as I thought of Michael, my gypsy friend from my stay at Wexham Park. I remembered how ill and beaten up he'd looked with his nose distorted with the mass of grotesque plasters that held drains in place. I guessed I must have looked just like he had back then. Those plasters were heavy-duty and the thought of having to rip them off in the future and then knowing that I'd have to scrub like fury to remove any left-behind adhesive – yeah, that didn't fill me with much pleasure.

I followed the tube out from my nose and figured there were three or four feet of it before it ended with a bag. The bag was clear, and I could see a small amount of liquid inside. It looked like watery blood. Not much in there, maybe a tablespoon's worth.

Next to my stomach drain bag, there were two other identical bags. Three bags in total lay on my left, like obedient lap dogs. Christ – three bags. I followed the tubes that connected the other bags to me and discovered that they both entered my left-hand side half-way between my ribs and my pelvis, about two inches apart from each other. The wounds where the tubes entered my body were nicely dressed. I imagined these two plastic tapeworms were coiled up inside me and oversaw any discharge or leakage that could come from my chopped-up pancreas or possibly from the void left from my spleen. It was bearable, but the points where the tubes entered me were bothersome and I guessed that after a while those points of entry would become sensitive and, ultimately, very sore. Any pain in that location would be made worse if the tubes got knocked, or pulled, or pushed in – if that was possible. The thought of the tubes becoming kinked or bent or the threat of pain if they got angled badly started to play on my mind. I knew I would have to protect that area of my body. I'd resigned to the reality that I would have to sleep on my back (on my epidural) for several days.

Three bags, and yet I discovered another tube.

A thicker tube snaked across my left thigh. It had a weight to it, but I couldn't see its head or its tail end. One end went off to my left and, out of sight, down from my bed. I used my left hand to track where the head was sited. Because I could see a yellow liquid in the tube I knew where to go. I followed it toward my groin and, I don't know why, but I gave the tube a little tug. As predicted, my penis felt that gentle pull. I felt revulsion; I didn't want to see that tube go into the end of my dick. Similarly, I didn't want to blindly feel around it either. I felt totally compromised. It was great that the catheter did its job so well (I hadn't even thought about needing a wee) but I was worried that my pride and joy had been damaged. What if I was now incontinent? What if I could no longer get an erection? Or an orgasm? Genuine fears of non-performance filled me. Yes, my child-making days were well and truly behind me, but I still had some adventures planned for my little friend. I knew Ali would be compassionate and sympathetic, but Mrs H would not be impressed if my manhood had become a useless flop for the rest of our time together. I tried to stop thoughts of problematic sex and made myself grateful for the fact I was still alive.

It was then that I decided to not only make the pact to not move my body below my chest, but I also to vow that I would do everything in my power to not get an erection – that event would surely mess everything up. Fortunately, I didn't feel particularly horny, and the nurses' uniforms weren't quite as sexy as I'd previously fantasised about.

After thirty seconds I realised that it was impossible to avoid thoughts of my breached cock. At least it wasn't sore. Quite incredible really when I considered what the poor fucker had been through. Or was it beyond pain? Had the epidural blocked out everything below the waist? I wondered how painful the procedure would have been, had I been conscious. I imagined a tube, a suitably thin tube, shoved into the slit at the end of my dick, expertly diverted down my urethra (I'll avoid the opportunity to exaggerate the length of my urethra) to snake its way to eventually nestle at the base of my bladder. Once there, it could happily siphon up my piss. I wondered if my enlarged prostate gland had given the tube-pusher much resistance. If there was to be a silver lining – maybe my previous poor urine flow would be improved after my sensitive pipework had been re-bored.

I looked down at my freshly mutilated body and my catheterised penis. I felt genuinely sorry for myself, but also for my poor, violated willy that had become an innocent casualty of a brutal war.

During my self-inspection, I heard something jangle next to my right ear. As soon as I'd brought my hand up to feel what it was – I put that hand back down. I'd stumbled across the King of Cannulas. Fuck Me! Stuck in my bloody neck was a monster cannula. What the hell? I thought the needle jammed into my lower arm was more than enough, but that thing was a beast. It must have had about four entry points to it.

Did they need that thing in me? I guessed it might have been necessary for an operation, but now?

I made a mental list of the things I needed the doctors to help me out with:-

- Throat tube (Please take this out)
- Face Mask (Please take this off)
- Monster neck cannula (Please take it out)

All the other scary things like drips, tubes, bags, and dressings all seemed to be necessary, so I decided I'd not make a fuss of any of those things until I had to.

The final thing I noticed was the computerised contraption to my right, which seemed to be in control of my pain relief. Ami had explained it before, when I was half-asleep, but now I was alert and was interested to see what it was all about. It was the morphine machine. There was a cable that came from the computer that ended in a small hand-held controller. I reached over and held it in my hand. It was a similar size to a highlighter marker pen. It only had one button. As it lay in my palm, I looked at that solitary button. It glowed an LED lit green around the circular shape, and it invited my thumb to press it.

I hesitated.

I didn't press the button.

Despite the safe green light.

I put the controller back on the side of the machine where it had been.

I knew it was there to help, but at that point, it scared me a little.

Morphine = opiates = Heroin.

I lay back and considered the opiate-based pain-relief that was a simple button-press away. Bolus – I think Ami had called it a bolus. Yes, my throat hurt. Yes, I had trapped wind and could do with releasing a big fart. The bloating was uncomfortable and there was a tightness and strange tenderness across my belly – but I wasn't in a state of out-an-out pain. I reckoned that the epidural in my spine was doing a grand job because I was sure that my body should have screamed out in agony. Except it wasn't. I was already being fed morphine; the bolus was a turbo boost. There was a distant hum of some latent pain – but I didn't want to test how bad things were, which is why I kept as still as I possibly could. With all of that considered, I didn't think it was time for the bolus. As fascinated as I was to see what it could do to me, I decided to save it for when I truly needed it. With a bit of luck, I mused, maybe I would never need its services.

I must have been totally out of it, because I finally registered something that had repeatedly happened every thirty or forty minutes. I realised that I had been blessed with a magic bed. They didn't have magic beds in Slough, or if they did, I'd never seen them. My magic bed had some sort of inflatable air mattress within it. Every so often, just when I started to feel uncomfortable, there would be the sound of a small motor and the entire mattress would deflate in some areas and move the air around to another part of the bed. I could hear the air move, but most importantly, I could feel it. It shifted the pressure I felt on some parts of my body to another, different part – and I felt the joyous relief. I meant I didn't have to shift my body at all – and therefore didn't have to risk sending shockwaves of pain through my injured body. It had obviously been designed for patients that could not move or were bedridden for a long time. It must help prevent bed sores. I certainly welcomed the shift – it felt like I'd stretched out my legs and back, without actually stretching at all.

Unfortunately, as magic as it was, it did feel as though I had a beach lilo beneath me – it wasn't completely comfortable and the plastic that coated it might be the main factor that contributed to the sweats that seemed to have plagued me. The design wasn't 100% perfect, but I was grateful that I didn't have to shuffle about like I would have done on a regular bed.

Mr Chai came to see me.

It was great to see him; it uplifted my mood and woke me up. It must have been his last task of the day. He was dressed in his blue hospital scrubs, topped off with a funky, colourful bandana. If he had been splattered with my blood (and God knows what else) earlier that morning, he'd changed, as he looked clean considering the battlefield he'd been in all day. He was on his own.

'Hello, Philip. How are you doing?'

'Hello.' I beamed at my hero and responded with a croaky voice. 'I'm pretty good thanks.'

'You did very well. Everything went to plan,' Mr Chai began. He seemed in a buoyant, positive mood. 'We got everything out that we wanted. That tumour was quite something. I explained to you before that we would have to take some of your pancreas with it– but I'm happy that what we have left you will be good enough for many years. We have a great aftercare team that will help you look after it. Also, there was no way we could save your spleen – so, I'm sorry to say that has come out as well. But, again, we can manage that situation, so you don't need to worry about that either. So, how are you? Are you in any pain?'

'No,' I replied honestly. 'Well, a bit, but nothing too bad. The epidural must be doing something.'

'Yes – yes,' Mr Chai said.

'The worst is this tube in my throat. Is there anything you can do about it? And also, do I need this oxygen mask on now?

'Unfortunately, we have to keep that drain into your stomach for a little while longer.' Mr Chai had become a little more serious. 'But we can give you something to help soothe your mouth and throat.'

He moved over to me and fiddled about with something to my left.

'And yes, I can take the mask off you now,' he said. 'Maybe we can see how you get on with the oxygen feed from here?'

I soon found out what he had fiddled with. Mr Chai gently removed the mask from my face. I felt instant freedom. Then he expertly took some thin air-tubes and looped them behind my ears and kind of locked them in place with a clasp under my chin – like it was necktie. Finally, he positioned two little nozzles that sprouted from the tube, directly into my nostrils. My nasal hairs were agitated by the fresh flow of oxygenated air.

'Any better?' he asked.

'Much better, thank you.' I felt I could breathe more freely, but I wasn't sure the jets of air achieved a great deal.

'We need to keep your oxygen levels up. You won't be quite ready yet, but the physio team will call on you soon because if we can get you up and about it will really help speed up your recovery. What do you do for work?'

The thought of physio wasn't attractive. I couldn't lift my legs up and I felt a million years away from the thought of a sit-up.

'I'm a Quantity Surveyor,' I answered and wondered if I would then have to explain what the hell a Quantity Surveyor did. I was used to that scenario.

'And is that a physical job?'

'No. Not particularly,' I confirmed. 'There used to be a lot more walking about on-site before the introduction of computers, but now most of my working day is me sat down tapping away at a laptop.'

'OK,' he said. 'You won't be able to drive for about six weeks. You may feel OK, but it comes down to the ability to make an emergency stop. Your body won't quite be there for several weeks. So, you'll need to give the physio a chance to speed everything along.'

'That's alright with me,' I replied. 'I can work from home. I'm actually in the process of being made redundant and they know about my situation, so work isn't a problem.'

Mr Chai' eyes showed some surprise. 'You're being made redundant?'

'Yeah. It's alright though. They've given me until the end of the year, so I have enough time to get myself sorted. I just need to get myself fit first of all.'

'Yes, that is our priority,' Mr Chai said whilst he began to check over my body. He changed the subject away from my work situation. 'Apart from all the stitches, you have 48 metal staples holding you together. When we let you go home, we'll give a special tool that the GP will need to remove them.'

I had never been squeamish. I hadn't seen my wound and at that moment, I didn't want to talk or even think about it. Although, I was a little curious. Maybe, once the dust had settled, and the scars had healed, I would be able to handle it.

'Did you take any photos? Or is there a video?' I chanced, as we had become great friends (in my head).

My question must have tickled him as he chuckled. 'Ha-ha. Yes! I did take some photos – you'll have to remind me to show you next time.'

Even though I struggled to talk, I kept up with more questions. 'And did someone call my wife do you know?'

'Ahh. I'm not sure. I'll go and check.' Mr Chai did just that. He turned away and marched off.

Within two minutes, Mr Chai was back with another doctor in tow. He closed the curtains and introduced Dr Christakis. She seemed like an intense character. I wondered if her senior had given her a hard time because I got the impression that nobody had made the promised call to Ali. I guessed she was in her mid-thirties. She had dark, curly hair that had been pulled back and tied behind her head. Her unbuttoned white coat was also pulled back and her hands were in her trouser pockets to keep it open. She appeared defensive.

After we exchanged greetings, Dr Christakis apologised as she admitted that they had not made the call. She went on to say that she could make the call right then if I still wanted her to. It seemed somewhat obsolete – Ali knew I was alive, so her agonising wait to find out if her husband had died was over. Maybe the doctor wanted to apologise directly, or possibly they had some news for Ali that I wasn't supposed to hear. Maybe she just thought it was the right thing to do.

Although I had silently sent messages, we hadn't spoken to each other and suddenly the urge for direct contact with Ali was irresistible.

The other patients in my bay had been exceptionally quiet (except for Roy's violent blood-puke episode and the guy next to me shamelessly farting every half an hour like a flatulent Big Ben) so it did make me feel self-conscious about a phone call – but I had just been given a free pass.

'Yes, OK. Let's call her,' I said.

'Hello!' Ali had answered my call on the first ring. 'How are you?'

'Hi wifey,' I croaked back. 'I'm alive!'

'Oh, Phil. It's so lovely to hear from you. It's been the longest day of my life.'

'It's been the shortest of mine. I've been unconscious or asleep for most of it.'

'Shut up! You sound husky. Are you alright? Why are you calling me? Is everything OK?' Ali had quickly jumped from being delighted to hear from me, to thinking the worst.

'Yes. Apart from the obvious, I'm OK. What about you? Is everyone there alright?'

'Er...yes, we are all fine.' Ali's tone was - why are you asking about us? 'Apart from worrying ourselves sick about you.'

'Yeah, sorry about that.' I was conscious that I had two busy doctors in front of me that weren't enthused about spending a chunk of their day listening in to my call to Ali. 'This was supposed to be a quick call. The doctors are here with me, and they wanted to talk to you to let you know how today went.' A few sentences and I felt out of breath.

'Oh, okaaay.' Ali sounded suspicious.

'I'll pass you over to them now. I'll speak to you later. I love you.'

'I love you, too.'

I handed my phone over to Dr Christakis and I heard her say, 'Hello, Mrs Honey...' but that was about all I could hear as she walked away from my bed and out through the curtains, to have a more private conversation away from me, I assumed. I didn't have the energy to be concerned that there was something wrong. I looked at Mr Chai whilst the ladies had their chat – surely, he would've told me if there was a critical problem.

Mr Chai sounded positive. 'Keep sipping that water this evening and we should be able to give you something more substantial tomorrow. Like yoghurt or something to start building you up gradually.'

A question popped into my head. 'Do I need my Metformin this evening?' Up until that point I had taken medication to regulate my sugar levels twice a day.

'No.' Mr Chai was a mixture of confidence and mischievous pride. 'You can throw that medication in the bin. You don't need it anymore.'

'Really?' I could hardly believe it. It sounded like my surgeon had completely cured me.

'Yes.' Mr Chai settled the matter.

I didn't challenge him further in case he changed his mind. To be free from any medication seemed incredible.

Dr Christakis came back to join us after her call with Ali and handed my phone back to me. I checked it in case the call with Ali was still live – it wasn't, one of them had ended it.

'Everything OK?' Dr Christakis asked us both. She looked from Mr Chai, to me, and then back to him again so I could tell her question was aimed at us both.

'Yes,' I said, and added a nod in case my growl hadn't been understood. I was happy that I'd been given the all-clear.

'Yes,' Mr Chai said straight after me.

We made a great little team, Mr Chai and me.

'Great,' said Dr Christakis. She then turned to me. 'I've let your wife know that everything went as expected, you're recovering well, and that we are looking after you.'

'Thank you,' I said with relief and a little happier that Ali would have felt similar emotions now that she had heard confirmation from a qualified doctor, rather than three-word texts from her half-conscious husband.

We all seemed satisfied that Plan A had gone well. The doctors said their goodbyes and told me that they would be back in the morning to see me.

Alarming

The fire alarm rang. It was an old-fashioned one with a metal clanger hitting a metal dome at speed. Not a modern one with an artificial sound. No, that fire alarm penetrated the ears and speared the brain. After only a short while my brain started to vibrate. I couldn't see it, but that alarm must have been near because it was so bloody loud.

My immediate thought was that it was a test. It couldn't possibly be the real thing. Could it?

Alarm tests usually last, what, three or four rings? We had gone way beyond that. I'd lost count. The sound was a shrill *brrrinnng* for a constant two seconds followed by a one-second break, and it repeated on and on at the same loud volume. It blared out for well over a minute, as I lay there crippled, and wondered why nobody had shut it off. If it was a fire drill, then we weren't doing a good job at clearing the ward. If it *was* the real thing then we were all in deep shit as nobody was around to wheel us to safety.

As much as it annoyed me, I knew that I could handle the racket, but what did worry me was that were so many ill people that would struggle with the noise. As we entered minute two, I sensed that the stress levels from others would reach a point that would be unbearable. What was equally strange was that there didn't seem to be anyone reacting to the persistent din. The other three patients in my bay hadn't moved or said a word and I sensed nurses and staff move about in the corridors, but there was no urgency or even a desire to get the alarm shut down.

Three minutes of loud noise was a long time.

Four minutes was even longer.

Was there something wrong with me? Was I the only one that could hear that alarm?

Roy was propped up by the angled bed and some pillows, but he'd been stirred. I could see him awake, directly in front of me. No, I hadn't gone mad because I could tell that he, too, had heard the alarm.

Finally, after at least five minutes, the noise stopped. The vibrations within my inner ears carried on for a good while after, but the relief was wonderful.

Roy caught me looking at him. 'It's broken.'

'The alarm?' I clarified, even though I knew exactly what he meant.

'Yes. There is some electrical fault. It goes off at least two or three times a day. It's been like it for three or four weeks.'

Roy had given me enough information for me to understand why I had been the only person in the hospital that had reacted to the alarm – everyone else was used to it.

'It's not particularly helpful if there is a real fire,' I said. 'We'll all be burnt alive.'

'They keep saying they've fixed it, but it doesn't sound like they have to me.' Roy seemed coherent and articulate but his previous confident *I'm going home* mood had been stolen from him.

We were chatting away, and it struck me that the previous time we had spoken we both seemed completely fine, but all that had changed within a matter of hours. We both found ourselves bed-bound and in a bad way.

'It's great to see you talking, Roy,' I said. 'Are you OK now? What happened?'

'Yes. I'm much better now. I should say, with thanks to you.'

'I'm not sure I did much,' I replied modestly.

'Well, you were there for me, and you did raise the alarm.'

'What happened? They've cleaned up the mess well.'

Something even more alarming than the broken fire alarm was

Roy's story. He spoke in short sentences because he was exhausted and to re-live the event so soon after was probably extremely traumatic. I didn't interrupt.

'What happened? I nearly died this morning. Sorry, you had to see all that. What I remember was feeling cold more than anything else. And you, helping me to sit on the bed. I remember being sick. Sick a few times. Sorry. Then I must have passed out. Apparently, they took me into theatre and repaired a tear I had around my stomach. They haven't said how or why it happened but rather than pumping blood around my body, my heart was pumping blood into my stomach. I don't know how much blood ended up on the floor and on everyone around me, but they say I lost four pints. They told me that I was worth two blood transfusions. It was a close one, but I was lucky I was here, in hospital. Had it happened an hour later, I would have been at home. And I would have died. So, thank you again for saving my life.'

'Anytime,' I said, dumb founded. I knew that Roy had been bad, but I hadn't expected to hear a story of such significant blood loss and drama. Four pints was half his total volume and if he hadn't sounded so confident, I might have thought it was bullshit and not even possible to survive. What could have caused it? Selfishly I thought that maybe that same thing could possibly happen to me. Had I just had the same operation as Roy? Was I at risk of the same danger? Out of the frigging frying pan.

'And what about you?' Roy asked. 'How are you?'

'Not too bad. Can't shake the tiredness and this tube in my throat is painful.'

Roy patted the soft spot where his collarbones met and said, 'Hurts right here doesn't it?'

'Yeah,' I said, and nodded back. Roy understood the discomfort I experienced.

'Did you have a Whipple as well?' he asked.

I didn't understand what a Whipple was. I thought he may have said Whip-all – as in, having a load of important stuff whipped out. I didn't want to appear ignorant so rather than say yes or no I opted to just confirm what had been cut out.

'Apart from the tumour, they took out my spleen and the back end of my pancreas.'

'Oh right,' said Roy with some interest. 'Are you on Creon as well?'

My ignorance continued to simmer; I had no idea what Creon was but assumed it was some medication that related to pancreatic activity. Maybe it was a form of insulin or possibly, it was taken to help produce insulin or pancreatic enzymes. I guessed I was in the minority of humans that didn't ask Google to diagnose or explain illnesses. I should have been an expert in every pancreas-related thing, but ignorance was bliss – and I'd always loved a bit of bliss. Bliss had always been so much better than the alternative of scaring yourself to death.

'No. I've only been taking Metformin, but the doctor told me to chuck it away.'

'That sounds positive,' Roy said before he changed the subject. 'Did I hear you say that you are a QS?'

I didn't mind that Roy had listened in on my conversation with Mr Chai earlier. I thought he'd been asleep recovering, but he'd been aware the whole time. 'Yes. Although, the company I'm working for has decided to have a change of direction, so I'm currently in the process of being made redundant.'

'That's a shame,' said Roy sympathetically. 'I used to work in construction; would I know who you work for?'

'Probably not. They're a property developer called EcoWorld. They're big in Malaysia and bought out the residential arm of Willmott Dixon – of whom you may well have heard of. We've built the new stadium for Brentford Football Club and all the residential buildings around it. If you follow football at all we've had EcoWorld emblazoned on Brentford's shirts. As a QPR fan, it hurts to see how well they're doing.'

'I don't know EcoWorld,' said Roy. 'But I do know Willmott Dixon. Very good company. I used to work for a contractor in Maidenhead called JM Jones.'

'Really?' I gasped. I'd hardly heard that company name since it went bust at the end of the 1980s. 'Me too!'

Roy smiled. 'Oh wow. I was there for many years as the personnel director.'

That was the point when our extraordinary coincidence struck me.

'Roy, your surname isn't Sanderson is it?'

'Ha-ha. Yes, my surname is Sanderson.'

'Roy! I have a letter at my mum's house that was written by you. You gave me my first ever job at JM Jones as a trainee surveyor, when I'd just turned eighteen.'

'How incredible!' Roy seemed as pleased as me with our newly discovered connection. 'And now, here you are, decades later, to come and save my life. That is amazing.'

'It's been over thirty years,' I said. 'It was a big shame when the company was shut down; there were some good people there. I was so young back then; I didn't know what was going on. I hadn't been made redundant since then – well, until now. Are you still working, Roy?'

'Still working? No, no, no – I retired when I was 57.'

'Fifty seven!' I was shocked that anyone could retire so early. I had resigned to the upsetting fact that I'd need to work until I reached 70 – with the assumption that someone would still employ me. 'That is really young.'

'Yes, it is, but I've enjoyed my retirement. Grace and I have done so much. Lots of travelling. I'm 73 now and we've done alright.'

'That is so good to hear. Good for you.'

We continued our chat for a long time. We spoke about colleagues that we remembered but had failed to keep in touch with. Roy lived ten minutes away from me, I even knew his next door neighbour. Roy proudly told me about his daughters and grandchildren, and I (equally as proudly) replied with stories of my wife and three children. We spoke a lot about work and how things had changed since the advent of computers and the internet.

Roy told me about his exceptionally tough year. He'd spent two months in Harefield Hospital and had undergone open heart surgery. They'd found cancer in and around his stomach and his specialist team were hopeful that a mixture of radiotherapy and surgery would get Roy back home and to some normality. The dramatic events of the morning were simply a setback. I thought I was a patient man, but Roy took it to another level.

Whilst I seemed to be on the crest of a wave and felt like I could talk forever, Roy was exhausted, and the day had taken its toll on him, so he politely ended our friendly chat.

'I'm sorry, I don't mean to be rude but I'm very tired, I really should get some sleep.'

'Of course, Roy.' I agreed. 'You go for it. We can speak later; I'll still be here.'

Overall, it had been a welcome and uplifting conversation. We had so much in common, not just the fact we had both been through the mill, but Roy was such a calm, friendly, and grounded person. His outlook on life was akin to mine; he was a true gentleman, polite to all the staff and I could tell that he was well-liked by them during the brief interactions I witnessed. It felt good to have someone to connect with; it would help with the loneliness I expected during my recovery upon that inflatable bed.

The Other Two

Roy drifted off. I, on the other hand, still had a buzz about me. Maybe I was still on a high from the anaesthetic, but I had become ridiculously alert, and as the epidural kept my pains dulled down, I was able to observe my immediate environment. I didn't want the job, but I had become Roy's watchman. He slept on his side, and I was sure I could see his chest move, so assumed he was breathing. He looked perfectly serene; it was bizarre to think that he'd had such a near-death experience only hours before. I felt it was my responsibility to keep an eye out for him. He had mentioned that he had felt cold again as we had chatted. That scared me as it seemed to be the main sensation he had felt when it had all kicked off before. That feeling must have passed for him, because he had managed to carry on our conversation without any further incident.

Relief!

Relief had come in spray form. Ami had brought me a small tube that had a nozzle attached to the top. I pointed the nozzle to the back of my throat and squeezed the top down (similar to a Ventolin inhaler). Three blasts of the medicine seemed to take the sting away from my throat within a few seconds. It was good stuff. I kept it nearby, as I figured that the pain would soon return, but I had a weapon to fight back with. I could swallow without the sensation that broken glass had been rammed down my gullet.

The other two residents of our bay were awake. To my right was someone whom I hadn't seen, but I'd heard plenty from him. I knew his name was Stefano because Ami and the rest of the nurses said his name. He'd obviously been there several weeks because he referred to them all on first-name terms. Just as his name suggested, he was European – he sounded Italian to me, but his English was faultless. Like me, Stefano suffered from terrible flatulence. Unlike me, he was able to release his wind at regular intervals – my wind was trapped, and the build-up bothered me and had become painful. I was scared to force out even the smallest of farts, but mostly I was worried about the resultant pain in my abdomen. Added to that fear was my Britishness and, for some ridiculous reason, my body wanted me to hold in all my pent-up gas rather than (God forbid) let out a huge fart that complete strangers could hear or (God forbid) smell. I was also terrified that, because I didn't have 100% control of my nerves below my waist, the slightest push might have caused me to shit myself.

In the back of my mind, I imagined that during my operation they pumped air or gas into my abdominal cavity to help them to see better. I'd heard that it was quite common to suffer from trapped wind after an operation. Or was it sterilised water they used? Whatever it was, I was one of the common people that needed to fart.

Stefano was cheeky and was the sort of character that I could tell enjoyed life. From what I picked up from the overheard conversations and also *how* he spoke to the nurses, he was a terrible flirt and sometimes bordered on the inappropriate rather than outrageous or offensive. I could tell he was older than me; his voice was gravelly, like someone that had damaged their vocal cords through many years of smoking. Most of the nurses addressed him using his first name, but Ami referred to him as Pappy. The relationship between them was a comical one. When Ami was by his bed, which was quite often, Stefano acted like a little boy talking to his mum, and yet when Ami replied (probably because of her small and sweet French accent) she also sounded like a young schoolgirl talking to her father.

The latest drama with Stefano was the state of his cheeks. No, not the cheeks on his face but the ones that were gatekeepers to his overactive, noisy bum hole.

'Ami. Please-a can you check my bottom? Itza so sore.'

'Of course, Pappy,' was Ami's response. 'Turn on to your side.'

There were several seconds of silence, apart from the sounds of them shuffling about, but with a curtain between us, I could not see what went on to my right. All I had was my imagination and their conversation, which filled in a lot of blanks for me. I guessed that Stefano had indeed rolled over and Ami had opened his gown to inspect the old man's bum.

'Oh. Yes, I can see. Eet looks all red, Pappy.'

'It-a hurts to lie down-a. It-a hurts more than the operation did-a,' said an anguished Stefano. He upped his little boy act to harbour some extra sympathy. 'Please-a, Ami. Please-a can you put some cream-a on my poor red bottom?'

Ami giggled. 'Ahhh. Of course, Pappy. I'll go and zee what I can find for you.'

I wondered how long their 'Allo 'Allo double act had gone on for. Based on the movements I heard, I sensed that Ami had walked off to hunt down some medication that would help the Italian's bum. I guessed that whilst Ami had gone, Stefano remained on his side with his arse stuck out for all and sundry to admire. I would have been mortified, but I got the impression that he didn't care if anyone caught a glimpse of his backside, and I wondered if he was an exhibitionist.

Ami returned, armed with some appropriate medication. 'Ere you go, Pappy. Zis cream should 'elp you feel better.'

'Grazie, grazie,' Stefano whimpered. 'Please-a Ami, please-a can you rub it in for me?'

If the words weren't suggestive enough, Stefano had made it sound as sexual as he possibly could.

Ami seemed to be used to his ways because she happily played along. 'Of course, Pappy.'

The brief pause in their verbal intercourse must have been filled with Ami opening the tube of cream whilst her patient eagerly waited, with his arse hanging out.

'Oooh,' Stefano moaned out in mock ecstasy. 'That-a feels so good. I feel-a better already.'

Ami let out her cute giggle again. 'Iz zhat nice, Pappy?'

'Oooh, yes. Itza wonderful!'

'Stop eet,' laughed Ami. 'You are not zupposed to enjoy zis.'

'Keep going, keep going,' urged Stefano.

Ami kept on with the treatment.

The silence whilst she continued to rub the ointment into Stefano's raw bum cheeks became more uncomfortable for me than having to listen to their flirty banter.

After what I thought was way too long, Ami ended their session.

'Zhere! OK. All done.'

'Grazie, thank you, Baby. That-a was incredible,' rejoiced Stefano. He had clearly loved every second of Ami's treatment. 'You have-a made my little bottom all better.'

'He-he,' Ami laughed. I think she may have enjoyed their liaison as well. 'I will check on you later, Pappy.'

'Ciao, Ami. I love you. See you later,' he said, managing to keep up his little boy act right to the end.

Whilst Stefano had returned to silence, the guy in the other bed picked up the slack.

Dean was what I called him. I couldn't think of a more appropriate name. Dean was either asleep or talking on his phone. Dean seemed like a normal guy. When the side curtains weren't fully extended, although I couldn't see Stefano on my right, I could see Dean in the opposing right corner to me. He looked younger than me – maybe early to mid-forties. Dark hair, medium build. I would say that the most notable feature that Dean had was that he possessed the most incredibly boring drone of a voice. No accent as such, other than a middle-England, Home Counties one with no added flavour to it. I might have forgiven Dean and the drone that came from his mouth had he said anything of any interest, but no, not only did he sound boring but the content that came out was equally as mind-numbingly bland.

Dean was so boring, so dull, that I was rapt with fascination. I tried to distract myself – I sent the scene from Jaws when Quint gets bitten in half by the shark to my friends in answer to how I felt. That helped for 30 seconds. I tried to play chess on the app on my phone but, despite my intense concentration, thoughts of any moves were cast to one side by that inane drone that came from about twenty feet away.

'Yeah...oh...right...did you? Yeah...are you walking now? Really? What? No petrol anywhere? Oh...so, where are you going? Really? Oh...did you? What, with the dog? Oh...and then what? Oh...right... in the shop? Yeah...not at the moment, no...what flavour are you going to get? Really? Are you? Oh right...salt and vinegar...nice...or maybe cheese and onion. What? On the way home? No, it's alright...on the path? Is the grass still damp? Oh...right..yeah...'

Fucking ship me off to Dignitas, right-fucking-now.

Fingers Crossed for Friday Morning

There was no dinner for me. I had no appetite anyway, so I sipped at some water, and I seemed to be able to handle that. Dean the Droner kept on and on and it was an effort to not go insane or shout out to get him to shut up. Stefano continued to fart, whilst my pain grew. Roy slept quietly. The calmness was only ever broken by nurses that came in to check on us or to take some observations or dish up some medication.

I summoned up some bravery and tentatively touched my wounds. The padded dressings (loads of them) offered such good protection that I couldn't feel where I'd been cut. I touched some bare skin below the bandages that had escaped unharmed, and it felt different. The sensation was all one way – I could feel skin with the tips of my fingers, but my belly felt numb, and it was almost like I'd touched somebody else's body. I considered that the surgeons may well have cut through many nerves in and around my belly to get to my insides. I wondered how much feeling, if any, I would get back in my skin once the epidural was out and my scars had healed. Would I ever feel Ali's touch the same way?

The care team had their changeover around 8pm. What a ridiculously long shift to be expected to perform at such a responsible job. Twelve hours minimum, plus the additional time at each end to make sure the handovers are carried out correctly. Throw night shifts into the mix and the fact that they dealt with some of the most stressful, life-threatening situations on a daily basis...they truly were the most remarkable people.

Ami's replacement was a big man called Lukas. He was a no-nonsense sort of character. His accent was from central Europe. I asked if he was German, but he said that he was from Austria. He must have been six foot four as a minimum and probably 24 stone (or 150 kilograms or 330 pounds). He had a big belly and kind of countered that by forcing his shoulders backward when he walked or stood still. In a strange way it made it look like he was proudly showing off his obese shape as if he was an expectant mother. He wore a white T-shirt under his scrubs, but his guts prevented him from tucking that, or his top, into the front of his trousers, so I got glimpses of belly flesh far too many times. Lukas had a pasty face, like a peeled jacket potato, a large nose, and big lips and although his face was clean-shaven, he had a grade one clipped haircut that helped distract his otherwise receding hairline and bald patch that I noticed when he bent down to attend to me. He had big, meaty forearms but I could tell his chunky fingers were deceptively dexterous as he flushed cool saline through the cannula in my neck and changed over my drip with minimum fuss. I don't mean to make him sound ugly, but his manner was efficient and direct rather than kind. He never smiled, even when I thought we shared a joke. As I said, no-nonsense.

When I admitted to Lukas that I was uncomfortable, he was sympathetic and held out one of his meaty forearms. I held on with both my hands and he hauled me upright without me having to crunch up my abdominal muscles at all. Lukas was as strong as his size suggested, and I was grateful for it. His breathing was laboured as he plumped up my pillows and after completing all the usual tests he left me there, a comfortable and satisfied customer.

I was a little apprehensive (alright, I was scared) to go to sleep. I'd dozed off so many times since coming out of the operation that I doubted I'd get the refreshing, deep sleep that I craved. I feared a night of tossing and turning – without being able to move an inch. I had tubes attached to me, drains coming out of me, and that huge epidural needle was stuck beneath me – hardly the best recipe for a good night's kip. I wanted to curl up into a comfortable foetal, sleeping position, but that basic pleasure had been taken from me.

Everyone around me seemed to be asleep. There was a noticeable change in the atmosphere outside of my bay and out into the rest of

10 – FINGERS CROSSED FOR FRIDAY MORNING | 79

the ward. Lights had been turned off. There was barely any sense of hustle or staff moving about. Things had quietened down. The night shift was on.

Lukas had made sure that everything I needed was within easy reach. The remote that altered my bed position, my book, my iPhone, a cup of water, the help alarm, and the bolus from the morphine machine – whatever I wanted was all there for me. He'd been able to dig out my wash bag from my holdall, so I managed to brush my teeth and spray some deodorant under my arms. Not exactly my usual bedtime routine, but considering the circumstances, it was good enough. I didn't need to go for a long, final piss as the catheter had slowly emptied my bladder throughout the day. Lukas had recorded how much urine had collected in the bag attached to the left side of my bed. It looked orangey to me – Ali would have words about how I wasn't drinking enough water, and that dehydration was bad for me. With Ali's warning rattling around my thoughts, I sipped some more water – a big gulp was not possible.

Before I attempted my first sleep I killed some time, to make sure I was at maximum tiredness. Although the euphoric feeling I'd experienced in the late afternoon had subsided, I still felt active and alert, so I needed to occupy my mind because nodding off was not an option. I played some chess on my phone. I was in the middle of four matches and the tournament I was in allowed players to make a move within 24 hours. There was a chance that I would have to forfeit the games because of my situation, but no, I was well enough to concentrate and made doubly sure that I hadn't made any mistakes before sending over my moves. I was playing well, and it was a great distraction from the perilous situation I was in. After chess came poker. Poker for me was either a quick five-to-ten-minute game or several hours slugging it out. I chose the quick five-minute game and ended it £2 up. No early retirement for me. As an attempt to calm down my adrenalin, I read my book. I was almost ready to attempt a sleep.

I assessed myself. There was an ache in my middle, but it wasn't an acute, unbearable pain. I figured the epidural was responsible for keeping it dulled. I hadn't sneezed, laughed, hic-cupped or suffered any other involuntary convulsions – but my breathing wasn't great. I slowly tried to inhale fully as my breaths had been shallow. Rather than feeling a pull around my tummy, my chest and back felt something. Again, nothing acute as such, but there was definitely a noticeable pain that made me stop at about 90% lung capacity rather than trying to force myself. *No point over-doing it on day one, Phil.* I returned to standard breaths, nothing too deep, which was nicely comfortable. I was doing OK.

It was time to say goodnight to Ali – so I sent a message.

> Phil: Gonna say goodnight now…Nighty night
> I love you wifey.

> Ali: You've made my night saying good night.
> You OK still? I'll dream of you all night… x
> I love you xx

> Phil: Yeah I'm ok - not in pain xxx
> Bit uncomfortable but what do you expect eh.

> Ali: Your poor body x

> Phil: Vitals all good btw

> Ali: Well that's good xx
> I hope they are looking after my most precious gift well x
> Let me know when you're awake.
> Hoping you have a restful night gorgeous x

> Phil: Will do wifey x

We signed off for the night with a few dozen emojis, love hearts, and kisses. Then, despite being miles apart, we attacked the mission of going to sleep together. My chances of a decent night's sleep were minimal, but they were still massively better than Ali's as she continued to worry about whether her husband would make it through that first night.

Thursday night melted into Friday morning. As expected, it was an unsettled sleep, so the changeover from night to day was something I witnessed. Lukas came by at regular two-hour intervals and changed my drips, which always involved the initial cool flush injection into my neck via the cannula. He meticulously recorded the standard observations each time. There was no way I would ever sleep through those visits. Each time we would have a quiet chat and bit by bit we started to get to know more about each other. He seemed to be noticeably interested in finding out as much information about me. Yes, I was married – yes, to a woman – yes, I had children – yes, I lived with them all. All the usual questions a potential stalker would ask.

My pain was kept in check and the spray for my throat helped, but I never managed to get comfortable. The magic bed continued to move and shift, yet I found myself in a crooked position. Although my back was straight, both my legs were together, but they kinked at my waist to the right. Ordinarily, I would have lifted my legs up and straightened up – that relief had been denied to me. There was no way I could lift either leg up – I didn't even attempt it. I was uncomfortable, but I managed to put up with it.

At 5am I'd given up on the idea that I could grab any more sleep. Nobody else seemed to be up that early and I held back from pinging a message to Ali for fear of waking her. I rested and quietly played with my phone. My chest hurt more than it did the night before, which was a concern. I didn't quite understand why my lower, floating ribs ached so much. The operation hadn't been that high up on me. I was grateful that my breastbone had not received the attention of the surgeon's circular saw – poor old Roy must have gone through that precise experience (and painful recovery) over the previous couple of months. Thank Christ I was just dealing with soft tissue repair.

At one minute to seven, I finally broke from my loneliness and sent a message to Ali. If she hadn't been awake, her alarm would soon go off. My message was nothing profound, I just said good morning and declared that I was pleased to let her know that I had survived the night. Ali, as I suspected, came back to me within the same minute. She seemed pleased that I wasn't dead and asked me if I slept well. I told the truth and said that I'd stolen a few broken hours. Ali, on the other hand, had slept like a log. She put it down to sleeping on my side of the bed and letting Lydia cuddle up with her. I put it down to her being emotionally exhausted.

I was delighted to see that my roomies had all survived the night with me. Roy sat upright and we exchanged a greeting of, 'Morning.' Dean was already mumbling into his phone about something or other and Stefano let us all know he was fine with a morning trump.

'How are you doing, Roy?' I asked. 'You know you said last night that you felt cold again. Are you OK?'

'Yes, I'm alright, thanks,' he answered gently. 'How about you?'

'Well, I'm alive, so that's a good start.'

'Hopefully today will be a nice calm one,' said Roy with real intent.

'Amen to that,' I said.

Big Lukas must have finished his night shift and handed over duties back to Ami because she came into our bay to check up on me and the guys. She'd wheeled in her testing kit, so we knew what the visit was all about.

'Ah, 'allo, Roy. Good morning. Ow are you feeling?' Ami asked.

'I'm OK,' was his reply.

You'd better be, I thought, because there was no way I could leap out of bed and help out due to my recent immobilisation.

Ami stayed with Roy for a while. I couldn't hear their conversation, but it seemed like the usual chit-chat as Ami recorded her tests. She sounded calm and I assumed that Roy must be back in the normal range because she calmly said her goodbye to Roy and moved over to my bed.

'Allo, Philip. Ow are you diz morning?' Ami asked.

'I'm alright, thanks.'

'Are you een enny pain?'

'My throat, my tummy, and my chest. So keep the drugs coming,' I said as jovially as I muster.

10 – FINGERS CROSSED FOR FRIDAY MORNING

'OK. Iz eet all right if I take your blood pressure?'

'Of course,' I answered and at the same time I offered up my right arm for the cuff to be Velcro-ed.

Ami busied around and the clip on my finger seemed to give off an unfavourable oxygen reading because she asked me to take some deep breaths to boost up my levels. It hurt my lower ribs to comply with her request, but after three or four bigger breaths I must have done enough to reach Ami's 94% threshold because she eventually moved on to concentrate on my temperature. That too was stable enough, so Ami left happy and said that she would be back with some painkillers. Opiate-based morphine – the breakfast choice of champions.

I was just about comfortable. The drugs held back the true agony I should have suffered. I had totally underestimated what major surgery was all about. I remembered back to when I told my boss that I needed time off.

'I'll check in on the Thursday. They're cutting me open in the morning, taking out what they need to, and then they'll stitch me back up again. Should be back home within a week. Piece of piss,' is what I told Mike (my boss).

'Yeah,' he'd scoffed. Piece of piss. And when I thought back to that exchange, it was quite sarcastic. I had come to the realisation that, when it came to how difficult my surgery could be, I had been in denial to myself as well as to everyone else around me. I felt like an idiot. The stark reality was that it had been a massive deal. Physically, it had become the biggest hurdle I'd ever encountered in all my 50 years.

Breakfast came and went. They weren't prepared to dish out anything to me until Mr Chai said so. To be fair, my appetite still wasn't back with me. I didn't see what Roy got, possibly a yoghurt and a cup of tea, but he definitely got something despite his ruptured stomach. Fair play to him. My other two inmates, Dean and Stefano, were able to tuck into something more substantial because I could hear the clang and clank of spoons and knives as they hit bowls or plates as they enjoyed whatever they'd ordered. That will be me soon. With a bit of luck.

Doctors' Rounds

By mid-morning, I was visited by three doctors. They stood at the foot of my bed and stared down at me. The bed had shifted me, but I was still crooked at the waist. I must have looked grotesque but the three of them seemed quite pleased with their creation in front of them. The scene must have looked like a mash-up between Dr Frankenstein's monster and Scrooge's three ghosts.

Dr Haji introduced himself as he was a new face to me. The other two, Mr Chai and Dr Christakis, were now well known to me. Mr Chai did most of the talking. I still liked him. He was friendly, caring, and more importantly, intelligent, and brilliant. Most of what he said was an action replay of what had happened the day before. All four of us were still content that the day before had all gone to plan. They were now dedicated to the next phase, which was to monitor my recovery, manage my pain, and help me achieve a successful discharge within the week. I had conflicted feelings. It was wonderful that they were all so super-positive and driven to get me up on my feet again (they told me that the physio team would be making a visit later), but I also felt it was all a little bit rushed. Christ, I'd only just been stapled together.

Dr Haji was taller and slimmer than the more rounded Mr Chai. Maybe of similar age to my hero. He had more hair, but it looked greyer. Dr Haji showed interest in the drains that came out from my damaged body. He muttered out the volumes of the fluid collected in each bag and Dr Christakis made notes. The two tubes that came from my left flank led to two different bags and therefore two different stories. One bag had about 30ml of bright scarlet blood and the other had twice as much, but it was a horrible brown colour. It was a mixture of blood and pancreatic juice. I reminded myself about one of the risks associated with my surgery – pancreatic leakage.

Once the volumes had been recorded, Dr Haji turned the little tap at the bottom of the bags and extracted a small sample of each into different vials. I assumed for them to check out what the liquids were made up of. I didn't ask, I just let him do his job.

My nose and throat tube led to a third bag and there was hardly anything in that one at all. The bag was flat and, at best, had enough in it to constitute two decent spits: a mixture of phlegm, snot, and saliva, which was not everyone's cup of tea. We discussed it and Mr Chai hinted that if all went OK, they might remove the tube later that day. The other two doctors nodded in agreement. I also nodded, for what it was worth.

The fourth bag was the one I couldn't see, until Dr Haji lifted it up. It had a nice collection of strong-coloured urine in it. They checked the volume against the previous and told me that my kidneys seemed to be behaving themselves and I was to continue to drink water throughout the day even though I was connected to a drip. Mr Chai said that he wanted to see if I could handle a bowl of soup for lunch and I replied that I would love to.

Mr Chai asked me how the pain was. I tried to be as honest as possible rather than act like I normally would do – which would be to say that I was OK. I told him that my tummy did hurt (as expected) and so did my throat still. I didn't want to admit that the sprayed medication had helped in case they considered keeping the tube in my throat for a second longer than necessary. I also said that I had a bit of a pain high up in my lungs when I took in some deep breaths and that my lower ribs, my floating ribs, felt bruised.

'I'm not surprised,' said Dr Christakis and as we looked at her, she did a movement that some might say was inappropriate. With her clipboard under her arm, she made two fists and made a motion as if she was slowly breaking an imaginary twig in front of her. To further emphasise the image of my ribs getting extended out in surgery, she let out a sound to imitate a rusted-up door creaking open. 'Kerrrgh'

I could picture my ribs being cranked outwards on stiff hinges to allow easier access to the soft treasures inside my torso.

Mr Chai was far from impressed, and he shot her a sideways glance. Her joke would have probably been funny if there hadn't been a pathetic victim laid out before them. Too soon, Doctor, too soon.

'We'll keep up with the morphine for now, but if your pain gets worse, we can give you some ketamine,' said Mr Chai after he had turned his eyes and attention back to me.

Ketamine? I'd always thought that it was something given to horses to tranquilise them. I secretly wondered what it would do to me. Strange that I had resisted the morphine bolus and yet seemed to be all over having a drop of K. If I was to start on the slippery slope of drug use, at least I'd get some comedy mileage out of it on my WhatsApp groups.

Mr Chai then came right over to me and with latex clad hands, he checked out my dressings. There was a small, dark patch of dried blood that had seeped out from where the incisions had crossed. Otherwise, everything looked to be in order. He checked out my left side and although it was uncomfortable where the tubes entered me, I wasn't in any real pain. I was a touch fearful that those exposed areas could well be susceptible to infection. If I had been at home, I would have rubbed in a bit of Germolene or some Savlon to help stave off any nasty germs. All I could do was monitor the situation and raise the alarm if I thought the puncture wounds were getting red or noticeably sore. In the back of my mind, I had my good friend Sean's words lurking there – *will you have a colostomy bag?* I prayed that everything was perfectly normal.

'That all looks pretty good,' Mr Chai declared, once he'd finished his visual inspection. 'We won't need to change the dressings today.'

'OK. Thank you,' I replied, but only because I didn't fancy having all those sticky bandages ripped off me – everything still seemed way too soon for any more action in that sensitive area. 'Oh. I nearly forgot; did you take any photos?'

'Er. Yes, I did,' answered Mr Chai, but he was noticeably sheepish. He looked back at his two team members, but nobody said anything. He pulled out his iPhone from his back pocket and turned back to me.

After a few moments he had pulled off a glove, turned on the phone and began to scroll through his photos. Whilst he did that I wondered if it was against protocol – had I just got the guy into trouble? Was showing graphic images to patients completely frowned upon? I truly hoped I hadn't put him in an uncompromising position.

'Here, this is the tumour,' Mr Chai said as he held out the phone for me to see the photo he'd taken the day before.

I was a bit stunned. I didn't know what to expect. In the weeks I'd had knowledge of the uninvited growth inside me, I hadn't formed a picture in my mind of what it might look like. I'd only considered it to be a colourless, round ball of soft tissue. Why would I have thought it could possibly have any distinguishable characteristics?

My first thought, bizarre as it sounded, was that my tumour looked like a wet Fozzie Bear from The Muppets. Without his brown hat, it wasn't *that* bizarre.

The photo was a close up so I couldn't tell exactly where it had been taken, but I guessed it had been staged in the operating room. The tumour bathed in a stainless-steel dish. It was glossy yellow with a tinge of orange. It looked fleshy, soft, and irregular, possibly further distorted by the surgeon's knife as he'd cut it free from my organs. It was ugly or, as the kids call it, fugly.

It made me feel sick and the most unsettled I'd ever felt, to think that the blob on the screen had lived in me undetected for so long. It looked chunky and meaty and must have weighed a pound or two. How could I have not felt it? How could my body shape have hidden such a sizeable intruder from me or Ali? I've been a chunky fella for many years, a bit of a belly on my dad-bod – well, I have had three children – that was my usual excuse. Despite that, I don't think that I'd walked about with the look of someone well into their second trimester.

'Mmm. Lovely,' I said, unsure about how I should react, like being confronted with a piece of modern art that actually looked crap.

'And this is the spleen,' Mr Chai said, and scrolled on to the next shot.

First impressions are important. I knew I was wrong, but the purple-brown organ in the picture looked like liver. Or, I should say, it looked like *my* liver. I'd been confronted with a proper organ, and, like the tumour, it was lifeless and filled its stainless-steel dish. It looked bigger than what I'd thought it would be and I had a sick image of Hannibal Lecter drooling over the photo, whilst firing up a pan of fava beans on the hob.

When Mr Chai had said, '*is* the spleen,' he may as well have said *was*. It looked like a dead lump of meat. No longer able to function (unless that function was to do an impression of half the filling of a steak and kidney pie). No longer able to keep the balance of my white and red blood cells and no help in the battle against future infections. Redundant. As glad as I was to say goodbye to the tumour, I felt pangs of sadness to say goodbye to the other chunk of meat. Plenty of people survive without a spleen, I told myself. Maybe I had wished that once inside me, they would have had a better look and say, 'Oh, the spleen looks OK, let's try and save it.' But, sadly, there was no stay of execution for the innocent bystander in that situation. Collateral damage. The poor fucker had done nothing wrong, other than be in the wrong place at the wrong time, as the silent intruder moved on to engulf its next victim.

'Oh, right. Nice,' I said to the picture and Mr Chai. What more could I say?

I had wanted to see it. It was an image I'd never be able to unsee. Always be careful what you wish for.

My three visitors of surgeries past, present, and surgeries yet to come, concluded their visit with some small talk with me. Finally, Mr Chai said that he would send someone from the pain team to come and check on me. They left me and my mixed-up emotions.

Stefano had got out of bed and came over to the window. It was the first time I'd seen him despite spending a day and night right next to the man. He was short and chubby. He made a great doppelganger of Silvio Berlusconi. He looked well into his 70's, yet he was a lively one. He had a nice enough tanned face and, like Danny De Vito in some of his films, he tried to give an impression of long healthy hair by pulling back as many strands of grey hair as he could into a ponytail, when really, he was 98% bald. He confirmed his Italian roots and kept his accent, although he'd lived in London for over 40 years. He had asked me how I was doing before telling me his life story, so he wasn't totally full of himself. I was happy to let him ramble on; he was interesting and clearly loved life. He was still working six days a week and was itching to get back to his antique shop on the King's Road in West London. He stopped his story to go and get me a business card from his stash by his bed. Not that I'd asked for it.

I got the impression that Roy wasn't too enamoured with our Italian Stallion. Like Roy, he'd been in the bay for several weeks. These older guys were taking a little longer to heal than my targeted 7 days. Stefano was certainly an acquired taste and, maybe, Roy had experienced too much of him and his stories, his relationship with Ami (and all the women that worked there), and no doubt, his farting. I was certain Roy rolled his eyes as he overheard our chat.

I took the card and was given a personal invite to visit his premises when all the hospital shit was over. The card was simple – white with a plain font, but it had all the basics like his name, the shop name, address, and phone number. It looked like it might have come from a print run he'd done twenty years ago that was still handing out. He went on to tell me about all the exotic pieces he had from India, Iraq, Iran, Israel, and Indonesia – clearly, he had a thing for countries starting with the letter 'I'. I played my part as the listener and asked appropriate questions such as what sort of things he sold and how expensive some of his pieces were. I only had his word to go on, but apparently, he didn't sell utter tat. His bread and butter was carpets and rugs. Some of his Persian collection had already sold for several thousand pounds. He couldn't be more passionate about his dealings and could not wait to get back to the hustle and bustle of it. Not only was his shop calling for him, he had an Alfa Romeo that was his pride and joy, and he also had a daughter that, by the sound of it, didn't seem to mind putting up with his shit. Stefano's daughter had been roped in to run the business for the seven weeks he'd been in hospital, although most of her working day seemed to consist of moving her father's car from one parking space to the next to avoid paying a penny for parking and dodging traffic wardens. Stefano took great joy in updating me about all the women he was having sex with. I did my best to shut down my ears, but I was trapped, so I was forced to hear his impression of some poor woman called Maggie having an orgasm whilst he 'Gave it to her Doggy-a'. Not only was he full of wind – he was also full of shit.

They were of similar ages, Stefano and Roy, yet they craved totally different lifestyles. I'd only had half an hour of Stefano and wasn't sure I could take much more. To some (and certainly Roy), he would be considered a boorish misogynist, but I found Stefano to be harmless and such a ridiculous caricature that offered me some mild amusement.

My chat with Stefano was interrupted by the arrival of lunch. Stefano, and his slightly less raw bottom, gave me a 'Caio,' and he toddled off back to his bed. I don't know what he had been served, but he seemed to get stuck into it without too much bother.

The catering lady wheeled the trolley around to me. She confirmed, by reading from a little card, that I had chargrilled, grass-fed 10oz fillet steak, with a flambéed brandy and truffle sauce, French beans, and thick-cut chips.

In my dreams.

In reality, I was told that I had vegetable soup.

It was hot and watery. There were some bits in it that I presumed qualified as vegetables, with small flecks of some kind of plant that floated on top, which looked more like a warmed-up puddle.

Although it would be near the top of my list for most pathetic, disappointing lunches – it was probably ideal for what I needed and could handle. The taste of the watery soup wasn't too bad. At least I felt happier that I had taken on some sort of nutrition to help my recovery. Each spoonful was slow. The tube down my throat was a constant sodding nuisance throughout, but I supped it all up. I kept it down as well, which was a relief. I was genuinely frightened that my body might react to a disturbance in my stomach and attempt to turn itself inside out – that pain would not be denied by my epidural. After ten minutes, I felt I'd passed through the danger zone and my anxiety of an unwanted reaction faded. Mission accomplished; I'd eaten my first meal. Albeit only hot, tasty water.

The Pain Team

Soon after lunch had been cleared away, and after being aurally tortured for ten minutes by the broken fire alarm, I received a visit from Mandy.

'Hi, Philip. I'm Mandy and I'm from the Pain Team here at Hammersmith.'

Australian. That was my first thought. Although, she could have been from New Zealand as I've always struggled to detect the subtle differences between their accents. She was possibly my age, but if I'd been asked to guess I would have said 37, as knocking off ten to fifteen years was always the correct way to go when it came to having a stab at a woman's age.

She was friendly and professional and held such strong eye contact with me that I suspected an intensity that I wasn't sure would be good or bad for me.

'Hi, Mandy,' I replied. 'How are you?'

'I'm fine thanks. How are you today?'

We discussed my levels of pain. Again, I moaned about my throat first, but kept consistent with what I'd told Mr Chai and his gang of surgeons and told her about the tightness across my middle, the pains in my lower ribs, and also high in my chest at the back.

'OK. What I want to do is check your epidural. If that's alright with you?'

'Sure.'

With my six-pack (I wish) slashed to pieces, I had no chance of sitting up without help. I'd developed an excellent technique of grabbing the side rails of the bed and by using the strength of my arms, I could bring myself upright, but it was a real effort. Mandy grabbed my left arm and gradually hauled me up, and we both groaned out with the exertion.

'You're stronger than you look,' I said to her.

'Comes with the job, I guess,' retorted my Antipodean professional.

She then asked me to hold my gown to one side whilst she inspected the needle that was still embedded in my spine.

Everything was in order, or so she told me. She gently tapped at where I assumed the point of entry was half-way up my back. She reassured me that the epidural was in place and the tube was clear of kinks and twists, so we were looking good back there. Just to make doubly sure, Mandy applied some extra strips of tape at various locations so that nothing would move. The plan was for me to stick with the epidural for another two or three days.

She helped ease me back down, as gently as possible. I returned to my slightly inclined position and she then pulled out a leaflet for me to read. It was all about the dangers and risks of the epidural. I had thought that I was through all the risks, but apparently not. It made me feel unsettled to think that my spinal column was still so vulnerable. In fact, Mandy told me, the dangers would carry on for a few more weeks, even after leaving (please God) hospital. She told me there was no bleeding and it didn't look like infection was an issue, but those were things to look out for. She said I had to raise the alarm if I was to suddenly experience severe back pain where the insertion was, or if there was numbness or weakness in my legs. Similarly, I was to get to A&E if I lost function of my bladder or my bowels. None of it sounded much like a party.

She then asked me about my legs. They were all right. I could move them, and I could feel and wiggle my toes. I wasn't prepared to lift them up off the bed because that would mean tensing up my tummy muscles, but I could shuffle them left and right. In fact, my movements and the ever-changing air-mattress had caused the bedsheets to get crumpled underneath me. I'd put up with the uncomfortable feeling of being slightly crooked and lying on bunched-up sheets for too long. Mandy announced that she would get some help to sort all of that out. Great.

She returned with the smallest nurse she could have found. OK, I'd barely eaten for a couple of days, and I was down one and a half organs, but most of my 85kg bulk was still there. Those two women amazed me with their optimism that they would be able to shift me.

'OK, just hold still, we'll straighten out the bedsheet and you and the same time,' she declared positively.

I let them carry on. After all, they were the experts. I guessed they'd done this many times as I saw them take a position on either side of my bed. Then they both took a firm grip of their edge of my bedsheet. I couldn't lift my bum clear of the bed to make it easier for them. That meant they would need to use all their strength for the explosive tug of the sheet. I anticipated a version of the trick of pulling a tablecloth away from a fully set table, but with an assistant holding one edge.

They made a count of three. The tiny nurse held on whilst Mandy gave a powerful heave to shift the sheet below me. My body was snapped back into the a straight position.

The two of them might as well have drawn a lumberjack cross-saw across my tender belly. White heat tore me in half.

'Arrrrggghhh! FUUUCK!' I screamed.

'Oh no! Sorry! Sorry!' Mandy panicked and could not be more apologetic.

The pain that exploded through me was off the scale. Without any doubt, the worst sensation I'd ever experienced. I felt like a magician's assistant that had been cut in half and had the two halves of their body moved apart to show the audience. I hadn't been prepared for anything as violent. Apart from the sheer physical agony, I was equally struck by the thought that all my wounds had been ripped open. FUCK! The pain was red hot. Burning hot. The heat from my middle spread instantly up and down my body; it was a mind-blowing sensation, but luckily the rush did not last. Swearing as loudly as possible helps – the scientists, and I, can back that up.

At least I found out quickly why they were known as the Pain Team!

'I'm so sorry,' Mandy was still apologising. 'Are you OK?'

I couldn't answer because I didn't know. The blast of pain and the scary burning sensation had made me feel faint, weak, and on the verge of throwing up my watery soup. Fortunately, the sheer intensity of the agony had subsided. It had to; otherwise, I would have passed out. My heart rate had already increased, and I was breathing heavily. Sweat broke out all over me. I needed a minute to see where I was and to see where the hell I was headed.

The two of them waited for me to regain some composure.

'Yeah,' I said, as my breaths had become more normal. There remained a dull ache across my middle, and I thought that I would be able to handle that. 'Sorry. I wasn't expecting that.'

'Just take a minute,' Mandy suggested.

'Yeah, I'm OK,' I confirmed. I was, at last, laid straight out on the bed with my upper body slightly inclined up. The bedsheets were flat and more comfortable. Once the jolt of pain and the shock of the ordeal had both faded, I was able to report that I was all right.

Mandy and her diminutive assistant apologised some more, and she asked me if I needed any pain relief. She pointed at the morphine bolus and hinted that it was all rigged up and ready to go. She told me not to worry as it wouldn't let me OD. It would give me a blast, which I'd feel shortly after I'd pressed the all-important green button. It wouldn't release anything more until a timer (5 minutes or so) made the bolus light up green again which, obviously, meant I could go again with some more self-administered relief. I said that if it got bad, I'd give it a go. After more apologies, the Pain Team left me.

I reached over and held the bolus in my right palm. The bright LEDs glowed bright green for 'Go'.

There was still a fair amount of pain that buzzed away across my damaged body.

I weighed things up and reached the conclusion that I had every right to start upping my opiate intake.

Fuck it.

I pushed the Go button.

It took a minute, but it hit the spot. A warm, calm feeling started in my heart, and I felt the rush spread quickly. If I had felt romantic in any way, I would've said it was like falling in love. It smoothed me out all over my body. Yep, it was good shit.

It was delicious. The drugs had returned me to a comfortable state of being. My pains had been diluted down to a manageable hum. Even the sharp stabs of pains in my lungs had been dulled down. I felt almost normal. My body wasn't bent anymore, and I no longer felt I was laid out on crumpled newspapers. I bathed in the joy from the relief and knew that if things got heavy again, I was just a little bolus press away from saving myself.

Things were looking up for me.

Ami had been given the all-clear to remove the annoying drain that started with one end in my stomach, rose through my oesophagus and exited my body through my throat and finally, out of my nose. The bag at the end of that long tube hardly had anything to show. I was sure that the absence of repulsive liquids was a good sign.

Ami carefully removed the heavy-duty band-aids from my right nostril. Fortunately, they weren't too hairy, so the waxing process wasn't too unbearable. No nostril hairs were damaged either, so no tears from me, even though a layer of skin had been torn off. With more care, Ami withdrew the tube. It must have been three feet long. It was so deep; I half expected a lobster pot to be attached to the end of it. There was a final scrape of the inner lining of my sensitive throat but the relief more than made up for it.

'Thank you, Ami. Thank you.' I expressed my sincere gratitude as much as I could, without sounding like the fawning Stefano.

'You are most welcome,' Ami said sweetly.

She then adjusted the little oxygen enriched air-tubes that fed directly up into my nostrils, looped it back around my head and tightened it up under my chin.

I celebrated this small win with a blast from the throat medicine and a squeeze of the bolus. The recovery business was a piece of piss, I thought, as I drifted off beautifully into a luscious snooze.

My forty winks were disturbed by the routine tests and checks. Once done, I reached for my phone to send an update to Ali to let her know how well I was doing. But I couldn't. Well, I could reach for my phone – it was just that it wasn't there. Unbelievable. I searched everywhere I could. It was gone.

I hated that I'd become a slave to that bloody phone, but it was my only link to my loved ones. Obviously, I could *and would* cope without it, but it would be maddeningly frustrating to do so with the knowledge it was somewhere. To have no contact – or at least no immediate contact – would be hard for me. I felt isolated and alone anyway, not having a phone made me feel even more so. Cast away, deserted. Like being shut away into solitary confinement.

I hated to admit the truth. I needed that phone as much as I now needed the bolus. Maybe even more so.

To cut the phone-based mini-adventure short, I managed to call over Divya, the nurse that was busy with my other hospital buddies. Once she had finished with Roy, Divya came over and I explained that my phone had gone AWOL. Nowhere to be seen. She understood how important it was so after scooting around all the places nearby that I couldn't get to – she soon realised that my phone had truly been phonenapped.

Divya went off to see if it had been handed in to the front desk. Nothing.

She returned empty-handed and suggested I give it a call. I said that was a good idea but my phone had been switched to silent since I'd arrived so it might not work. She rang my number...but we couldn't hear or see it and nobody answered. The mystery continued.

Divya spoke to both the catering and clean up teams. Still nothing.

She came back to me and said she'd ask some others that may have come into our bay. I'd been asleep but I doubted that many other people had been anywhere near my tray. I was getting a little anxious.

I thought about the loss of my lifeline to Ali a bit more. I tried to keep my anxiety caged, but a frantic sense of desperation had taken a foothold. Where the fuck was my phone? Who had taken it? Ali would only have thought the worst if she had not been able to contact me, or not heard from me for a prolonged period. I didn't know what I could do. That sodding phone had become a necessity, and I'd been stripped of it. I felt cut off and powerless to do anything about it. The situation in my head multiplied; I couldn't control it any more than I could control the whereabouts of my phone. Because I was physically tired, I became upset that the irrational panic had gained momentum. I was on the brink of losing my shit.

All the obvious places had been crossed off the search list. The other guys hadn't any clues and I was sure they weren't kleptomaniacs.

Just when I thought I'd become a raving maniac, I saw Divya stride over. She'd found it!

Praise the Lord.

'I'm sorry,' Divya said. 'Your phone looks just like mine. It was in my pocket the whole time. I must have taken it earlier – when I'd finished taking your blood pressure.'

'Oh. Great,' I was stuck between feeling grateful, surprised, and more than a touch annoyed.

'Yes,' she giggled. 'It even buzzed in my pocket when we rang it. I just didn't put two and two together...sorry.'

I couldn't stay annoyed; I was just relieved that my phone had turned up. 'No worries. Thanks for finding it.'

Panic over.

I rewarded myself with a bolus blast. Then, because I couldn't remember what I was going to say, I sent a message to Ali to let her know that a nurse had tried to steal my phone.

Ami didn't give me much of an explanation, but she asked me if I wanted to have a go on the nebuliser. I didn't know what she meant. She stood to my left and untangled the tubes and mask that had innocently waited nearby for that exact moment. I hadn't answered one way or the other, because Ami had already begun to get everything rigged up. I wasn't going to stop her, and I thought, let's give the nebuliser thingy a go.

Ami used the elasticated straps to fix the plastic mask to my face.

12 – THE PAIN TEAM

I still hated having a mask over my nose and mouth, but I went along with it. There was some sort of chemical that was in a little reservoir at the bottom of the mask, and it had a smell to it – it was menthol-like, and it reminded me of Vicks VapoRub, but nowhere near as powerful. She turned on the tap to send some air hissing through into the mask. It was loud and the menthol flavoured liquid bubbled and spat in and around the mask. I guessed it was all supposed to help clear my airways. Not that I thought they needed clearing.

Ami left me with the nebuliser and suggested I should relax and keep taking nice, slow, and deep breaths.

I gave it about two minutes.

It didn't do much for me. It was nice enough for the first minute, but I soon got bored, and I couldn't see the benefit of it. It was hard work to sit there and only think about taking in deep breaths and nothing else. My thoughts went elsewhere, and my breaths stopped being all deep and meaningful. It didn't seem like the treat that Ami had intimated. If anything, the restriction around my mouth and nose hindered inhalation. So, I took the mask off and left it to percolate noisily next to me.

Ami returned about twenty minutes later. 'Ave you finished?'

'Err...yeah,' I answered, a little sheepishly as I felt a tad guilty that I hadn't fully gone with her suggestion.

'Ah, fantastic!' Ami squealed. Her excitement at such an innocuous event seemed displaced to me. Then again, I can be a grumpy bastard. I didn't have the heart to tell her that I didn't get much out of it and I'd cast it aside before giving it a real effort.

I'd asked Ali via text if she had planned a trip to visit me. Friday wasn't ideal, mostly because I was just laid up in healing mode, so we agreed that Saturday would be a better day for us both. Had I been more local, Ali would have seen me every day.

The timing of my operation had messed up our plans.

I'd booked for Ali and me to have a weekend trip away at the Runnymede Hotel to celebrate her 50th birthday. Then, after some cancellations, the Macmillan support team called and asked if I was

OK to bring my operation date forward by a week. I accepted the date (I Have a Tumour, Get It Out of Me!) because I didn't want Ali to miss out on her big birthday treat, so I suggested she take Lydia and they could escape and have a rare girlie break together. The hotel booking was for Sunday, so it made perfect sense to arrange Saturday as visit-Phil-day. With the assumption that everything at my end went to plan.

Roy was the only one of us to receive a visitor on that first Friday.

It must have been near to 5pm. Roy's wife, Grace, walked in and she must have visited before because she knew exactly where to find Roy. She seemed fit and well and was clad in a thin plastic apron and wore latex gloves as it was all the rage when it came to fashion for those visiting the sick. She had a slim build, like Roy, with a calm and classy air about her and, like her husband, looked like she would be very much at home browsing around John Lewis, Waitrose, or a garden centre on any given Sunday. She came across as the sort of person that was kind enough to traipse around her neighbourhood collecting money for the Poppy Appeal every year. Their auras were so alike and to me, they seemed like a textbook match. In our chats, Roy had told me about all the travels that the two of them had enjoyed since his retirement and when I saw them together, I could tell that they loved each other's company, so their trips were probably as harmonious as Roy had suggested. Grace's hair was shoulder length and I thought, bless her, she had spent some time before setting off so that she could look her best. The grey streaks in her hair were probably not helped by the worries caused by her husband. She removed her facemask once she'd sat next to Roy.

Whilst they chatted, I used my phone to ping out some messages to Ali, my brother Richard, my mum, and some friends. They all came back instantly with their messages of support. GaryMan seemed impressed that I might start a Ketamine habit. I played a bit of on-line poker and some chess. My eyes grew tired, so after a short while I had to put the phone down and went into a bit of a doze. My fatigue was a strange thing. I wasn't convinced the epidural was still behaving itself as well as it had because during the previous hour or so my left-hand side seemed to have a nagging throb. That constant pain, the effort of taking deep breaths and the effects of the painkillers had all become exhausting.

When Grace's hour was nearly up, I could tell that they had discussed me. They were both looking in my direction. I was not the chipper self I wanted to be, but I couldn't fall asleep as I twigged that maybe Grace wanted to come over and say hello. I was right. She did.

'Hello,' Grace said gently, as she came over to my side of the bay. 'I just wanted to thank you for helping to save Roy's life.'

What can anyone say when someone you don't know says words like that?

'That's alright,' was my not-particularly-profound response. 'All I did was a bit of shouting.'

'I think we all know it was a little bit more than that.'

'At least I was still able to move at the time. I wouldn't be much help now.'

Grace ignored my modesty with her sincerity. 'Well, we are both extremely grateful.'

'Any time,' I said, with the hope that it would conclude matters. I was never much good at receiving compliments or even talking much about good things I'd done.

Grace and Roy exchanged their goodbyes, and she left us both with a lovely little wave and mouthed me another *Thank You* before she covered up her mouth with a facemask so she could move out into the corridor and head towards the exit.

Friday Night (is Gonna be Alright)

My appetite had abandoned me. The feeling was a rare one. I briefly wondered where the disconnection was in my body. Usually, my stomach had a hot line straight to my brain, and would call up and demand a meal, or a snack at the very least, every few hours. But on that Friday evening, the line was dead. It made sense that my guts just weren't interested. The conflict was that I needed some nutrition and was prepared to do whatever it took to speed up my recovery.

I was on a special diet. For dinner, they served up exactly the same vegetable soup I'd had earlier that day. The exception was that they'd upgraded me to have a slice of soft, white bread on the side. What a luxury!

It was a struggle. The expression a lot of people use is *gutted*. In a way I was gutted, it was my guts that were to blame. The soup was OK, and with that sodding tube gone, it was a lot easier to get down my gullet, but the bread – It was a proper challenge. I didn't feel sick, but there was an unfamiliar tightening up of my stomach after just two or three bites. They weren't big bites either. I did my best to keep to the easy-does-it instructions, but after half a slice it was almost like my body told me I was full. I'd never had the sensation before. If a doctor came along and told me that I'd had a gastric band attached during my operation I would have believed them. OK, I'd never had that procedure before, but I experienced a sensation that I guessed would be similar. In the real world, that slice of bread would have been gone in 60 seconds – in pain world, it took me 10 minutes. I got the job done though. I felt a bit like the guy on the TV show Man versus Food where there was normally some challenge to eat the biggest (coronary-inducing) burger that Pennsylvania (or whatever state they were in) had to offer. Adam (the guy in the show) had a 50/50 record and normally had about a hundred people cheering him on to beat the restaurant's challenge. I sweated myself through one slice of bread, with no fan club behind me. Even though it would've been the show's worst ever episode, I gave myself a pat on the back. As I completed my self-congratulations, I also tried to convince myself that it was early days, and my poor knackered digestive system would soon get itself back in the game.

Part of a speedier recovery involved oxygen. It would have been a stretch to ask the NHS to whisk me off to an oxygen chamber to speed everything up a gear, but at least I had some little tubes.

As I lay there, I became conscious of the plastic tubes Ami had poked into both my nostrils. I hadn't paid much attention to them, but I felt jets of air agitate the hairs up my nose. The clear tube had been looped behind my ears and across my face just under my nose. Unfortunately, the nozzles from the tube didn't quite hit the spot. Two factors prevented their true efficiency. Firstly, the tube seemed to be twisted and this made them point outwards rather than upwards and into my nostrils. Secondly, even if the tubes pointed in the right direction, my nose might not have been compatible as my nostrils naturally flared backward. I probably should have been set up with longer nozzles as the ½-inch-long ones I had been given were simply not penetrating the desired orifices. I didn't make a fuss about it; I just let the oxygenated air blow vaguely around under my nose. I hoped that I might breathe in some of the oxygen and, as a result, it would still help my recovery - even if it was by only a fraction. Every now and then I attempted to jab the nozzles back into my nose. The trouble was that because of my shaped nostrils and the twisted tube, after only a minute, they would give up the ghost and they'd let themselves ping loose. Every other patient in the world seemed to handle the oxygen feed. If I'd had any energy, I would have been annoyed about my failure.

In truth, my energy levels were flagging. I'd had a day of small sleeps, but the fatigue had got the better of me. As the evening session approached, I knew I was not going to have a late one. At 8pm, Lukas had begun his Friday shift. The big guy, with the big attitude, came by to have a chat as he changed my drip bags. I stayed silent but the way he flushed my canula wasn't as gentle as I would've liked. It seemed a little rushed. I didn't think I would ever get used to the cool, wet sensation every time the cannula was flushed. I found the cannula in my arm bad enough – but the fucking neck monstrosity was something else. I kept my neck still but looked away, as Lukas was close to me, and I let him get on with it. My theory was that the sooner he got it done, the sooner he'd be gone.

It was a good theory, except that Lukas hung around even after completing blood pressure tests and everything else. He quizzed me about personal things. He wanted to know more about my children. He asked how old they were and where I worked. It made me feel a little vulnerable and uneasy. I had it in my head that Lukas was gay. I can honestly say that I wasn't homophobic at all. I didn't give a shit if Lukas was gay or not. I just thought he'd become over familiar too quickly and there was some sort of sinister undertone that I couldn't put my finger on. If I'd been asked to pick someone that might spend their weekends trussed up in PVC (complete with gimp mask) – I'd have picked out Lukas. Sexuality had nothing to do with my train of thought. I would have been more than happy to pick out a straight guy that loved expressing himself in a kinky sex-dungeon with an orange in his mouth. Maybe I was going a little bit crazy; I actually wondered if Lukas had some sort of liking towards me. I felt uneasy in his presence. I had a sick thought that he might want to take advantage of me. I did my best to shut down such weird thoughts because I also knew that in the darkest hours of the hospital night, Lukas would be my only saviour.

I'd scared myself, and even though I'd calmed down a little once Lukas had left to continue his rounds, I sickened myself with thoughts that there was almost certainly an abusive someone out there who had taken advantage of a vulnerable person at some point today. I felt helpless, vulnerable, and lonely, and it was a dreadful feeling. I was desperate to get better, get well, and get the hell out of Hammersmith

Hospital before fate realised that I was next in line for a dose of malpractice.

I hated being a victim, even if it was just thoughts of being one. In an attempt to raise myself up from the doldrums, I grabbed my phone and called up Ali for a video call. A video call? I'd always been a tech dinosaur. It was the best thing I could have done. I kept the volume down at my end (conscientious to the end) but Ali and Lydia (who had bounced up to her mum) were joyous and raised my spirits exponentially. All my negative emotions were quashed by the love they gushed my way. I switched the camera and discretely panned the phone around to give them an idea of what my ward looked like. Lydia was delighted to tell me that they had both worn my old T-shirts – for the smell apparently. Ali had my wedding ring fixed onto her necklace and Lydia wore my white gold chain, which was way too long for her slender neck. They had done the same when I had been holed up at Wexham Park Hospital just three months prior.

Lydia was a little spooked by the cannula that stuck out from my neck. I made light of it and said it wasn't too bad (but at the same time made a mental note to ask Lukas about removing it later in favour of the arm version).

Ali confirmed that she would make the trip into London the next day. She knew that although a call (video or normal) was always welcome, it was worlds away from proper physical contact. Unfortunately, there was a ridiculous situation at every petrol station around the UK at that time. Every garage either had no fuel, or there was a massive queue at the few that did. Ali said that the car dashboard told her she had 60 miles left in the tank. It should be enough to get to me and them back home. But she was off on her hotel break on Sunday, so she would need to find a garage eventually, and sweat it out with a wait to see if there was enough unleaded to go around – like the rest of the real world outside of my four walls. At least I didn't have that headache to worry about. Small mercies and all that.

I managed to convince them that I was fine. I almost convinced myself.

It took ages to end the call. None of us wanted it to finish, but there were only so many ways to express our love and to blow kisses. Ali begged me to look after myself and made me promise to do everything the doctors said, and to stay safe, and to get home quickly. I made all those promises and reluctantly I ended the call and found that I'd returned to the disturbing world of hospital life.

I had overdone the morphine. As soon as the bolus lit up green, I pressed the GO button. I'd repeated the pattern too many times.

It was either that or my eyes had gone seriously wrong.

I couldn't stay focussed on anything. I was looking at the phone in my hand and experienced a strange sort of drift sensation. No matter how hard I tried to look at the messages on the screen, my eyes simply drifted up and away and out of focus. After a second or so by clearing my vision with a few blinks, I managed to return to what I wanted to look at. But the sodding drifting sensation started again within moments. It was unnerving. I tried to read the words in my book. The same thing happened. I stared at the wall opposite me and found that even my long-distant sight couldn't stay fixed. I didn't feel high, but if I had to equate the situation to anything similar, I'd say it reminded me of a distant past event.

It wasn't one of my proudest moments, but when I was a young teenage lad my good friend Panda had shown me some super-strength car glue he'd taken from his dad's workshop. The fumes from the glue were powerful. Because we were immature and immortal, we continued to inhale the toxic vapours until we began to hallucinate. As a seasoned veteran, Panda seemed to be highly amused by the session and I was aware that he was in his own bubble, giggling away to himself. I, on the other hand, freaked out because the trip was so bloody frightening. It may as well have been LSD. I knew the sights my eyes told me were not real, but everything seemed so rational, so believable. I could see well enough, but everything repeated like a visual echo. I could see my hand touch the wall, but I couldn't feel it. Then I could see my hand touch the wall again. My world had become an unexplained repetitive glitch, like my brain had invented a dodgy Wi-Fi connection in the mid-Eighties. In a panic, I had looked at Panda to plead for some reassurance that the trip was normal and, more importantly, that the insanity would soon pass.

'Are you OK?' Panda asked me. 'Can you hear the echo?'

I wasn't in any fit state to hold a conversation. Instead, I found myself on my hands and knees and I crawled from my garage (where the solvent abuse had happened) to what I believed would be the safety of my house. I heard what Panda had called out, but his last word reverberated like a stuck record...

'...echo – echo – echo – echo...' Until the freaky sound faded out.

My ears, my eyes, and even my thoughts were all over the place. It was a horrible experience, and I made a vow to my poor chemically damaged brain that it would never happen again. It had been a one-off.

But the weird drifting away of my vision – it seemed so similar to that disturbing event that had happened to me thirty-five years earlier.

Although I couldn't control my eyes, my thoughts were normal. I managed to talk myself down in a rational way. I told myself that it was just the opiate-based drugs. That the chemicals would soon be absorbed and safely diluted by my body. All I had to do was to lay off the morphine bolus and wait.

It helped to shut my eyes. That way I couldn't tell if my vision was knackered or not.

I concentrated on my breathing. My chest still hurt. I refused to hit the pain relief button. Not until I felt that my eyes behaved normally. I kept my eyes shut. I drifted off, with the hope that when I was to wake, my eyeballs would agree to do as they were told.

When I did stir, the first thing I did was to check my eyesight. It was normal again. Thank Christ for that. I could see the time on my phone and discovered the day had approached midnight. I let Ali know that I was in good shape, that I was going to go to sleep, and – most importantly – I was not in any pain. I mentioned my eyes had been playing up, but they had returned to normality – I didn't give out any further details, as there was no need to worry my wife with tales of hallucinations, or potential madness. She came back with messages to wish me sweet dreams and a 'YES!' in response to my declaration of no pain. With an unusual (for her) fist-bump emoji. It put a smile on my face. I plugged my phone into the charger and adjusted the bed so I could lay flatter on my back. I hoped that despite the uncomfortable, unnatural (for me) position, sleep would come back to claim me again, quickly.

I must have been exhausted from such a long day of recovery because sleep did take me away. I hardly had to wait at all. I slept for two hours before something woke me. I couldn't wake up fully. Maybe the drugs or a combination of the medication and my extreme exhaustion. I'd been moved out from the bay. Although there was barely any light, I could tell I was not in the safety of my little ward, with the window and the view of the Wembley arch. It was strange that I hadn't stirred when they must have unlocked the wheel brakes of the heavy bed, and then re-engaged them because that was a noisy process. Instantly, I didn't like that new place.

I needed my adrenal glands to fire some adrenaline into my body because I detected danger.

Something must have happened to me.

I wasn't in pain – which, at least, was something positive to cling on to.

Why (why the fuck) were there doctors standing on either side of my bed? Two on each side. I couldn't see faces. The light was so bad for me that their masks might as well have covered their entire heads, but because of their aprons, I could tell they were a full surgical team. The lack of light was frustrating, and I couldn't make out any colours. All four of the doctors stood upright and they were either silent or my ears had been somehow disconnected. Their hands seemed to move in and out to the lower part of my body. All four of them took turns to work on me; it all looked robotic rather than frantic. I didn't think I'd 'done a Roy' because their attention seemed to be focussed too low down beyond my chest area and my operation didn't have a sense of urgency, which gave me a further sense of confusion. I couldn't physically feel what they were doing to me. I could sense it and made horrible assumptions. It was weird and as I began to take it all in, I realised that it was terrifying!

Fuck.

Shit.

Fucking shit!

What was going on? What on Earth had gone so wrong? If I was back in theatre – how come I was conscious? *Partly* conscious.

I thought about shouting out. I had to let everyone there know, immediately, that I was present. I was awake. What I found was more weirdness; my brain would not let me call out. I couldn't even move an arm. Shit, I was in serious trouble.

If I was back in theatre, wouldn't they have taped my eyes shut? How come I could see some of it? I'd heard stories before, where an anaesthetic had not worked, and patients were paralysed as they played witness to their own operation. Bollocks. That traumatic nightmare was happening to me.

One of the surgeons, the nearest one to my left, held a scalpel. Despite the poor light, I could make it out, gripped menacingly in that gloved hand – it looked clean and steely. It looked deadly. No blood on it. Why on earth were they operating on me in the dark? The scalpel seemed to just hang in the air, inches above my soft abdomen and below the line of my clean white dressings. I detected a pause; I don't know who was waiting for what – maybe they needed clearance from the anaesthetist...was Adam there?

My eyes remained fixed to the blade; there was no drifting sensation, I couldn't focus on anything else because I was magnetised to it. I had to know, had to see, what that knife was going to do next. Where it was destined to land. What level of pain was I about to experience?

I held my breath – the doctors remained silent. The movement of their gloved hands had stopped. They, like me, had become focussed on the scalpel.

More than ever before in my life, I needed to find my voice. One spoken word might save me.

The knife moved towards my belly. Fuck. Here we go.

I saw the metal touch my skin, and I anticipated the pain as the sharpness separated the cells on the surface.

'Arrgggh!'

Thank God my voice finally burst out from the darkness.

My scream had stopped everything.

More than that, it had *changed* everything. It had taken me far too long to work out why the light had been so poor and why the actions of the surgeons had been so robotic and weird. My scream had made me fully alert. It had woken me up.

My eyes and my ears had instantly become fully functional. My environment was back to what I recognised as familiar. The lighting was soft, for the night-time hours, the background sounds of machinery were, for that moment, a comfort rather than an annoyance. Most importantly, there were no surgeons – and no scalpel.

I was back in the safety of my bay; I was bathed in sweat. A proper full-blown night sweat. I must have held my breath for real during my nightmare because my breathing was all over the place.

I looked around. Fortunately, nobody had heard my outburst. Nobody, not even the ever-prowling Lukas, saw the quivering wreck that had become a scared little boy that was slick with sweat.

Shit. That was bloody awful.

It took me a while to come down. I gave myself a blast from the bolus even though I wasn't in any pain. My mind and my thoughts had raced away from me like I'd gone a touch insane. I considered that maybe I'd overdone the morphine. If that little blast of morphine triggered more insanity, maybe I should order the ketamine from the pain team's wonderful menu. Internally, I spoke to myself; I talked myself back down to planet Earth. I reasoned with myself that nightmares were perfectly normal and common. I was fine, I would be fine, there was no need to be scared or worried. I was perfectly safe.

It worked, and within the hour I fell asleep again.

Saturday - The Calm Before The Storm

I woke up on Saturday morning and felt pretty good. Apart from the unpleasantness of being laid out on a damp bedsheet and being clad in a gown that weighed four times more than it should, physically I felt well enough. I had no idea of the horrors that fate had planned for me to experience. Saint Fuck-Breath, the patron saint of awful days, sat somewhere in his shitty hovel, rubbing his hands together and chuckling to himself.

My day started well enough. Ignorance was bliss..

Lukas had disturbed me enough during his 6am visit so that I wasn't going to go back to sleep. The drip for the epidural had been changed. Lukas plumbed the other IV drip into my neck cannula.

'Do you have to use that?' I asked and offered my left arm up to him. 'Can't we use this one?'

'Vot? Ze Central Line? Yah. Ve have to use zis for a little vhile longer,' Lukas explained, sounding very German, serious and efficient. 'If zome-zink ver to happen unt vey needed to get you into ze operating room it is ze best unt ze qvickest vey to get vot vey need – drugs or votever – into your bloodst-veam. I know it is uncomfortable but it vill come out zoon enough.'

Lukas had referred to the neck cannula as the Central Line. That was a new one to me. The only Central Line I knew about was the red one on the London Underground. I'd always liked the Central Line, it never messed about, it cut straight through the middle of the capital, West to East, with great efficiency. I wasn't sure if Lukas' explanation was supposed to reassure me or scare me. It hadn't been discussed (well, not with me) that I would have such a violent breech of my jugular vein. However, I couldn't challenge its presence much further because it sounded reasonable to keep it jammed in there if there was any chance I might need to be whisked back into theatre. The idea that I *was* still a risk scared me.

After Lukas had been and done, I pondered more about that Central line. I understood what I'd been told, of course, that point of entry into my body would be a more efficient place to get all that life-saving stuff injected into me. Much better than wasting time with it creeping up my left arm first. My neck though, it was such a sensitive area of my body. It's no wonder why vampires went straight for the jugular – they certainly didn't piss about nibbling on a young victim's inner arm.

Breakfast was early and uneventful. My new soft diet resulted in the presentation of two Weetabix with tepid semi-skimmed milk. I rejected the sugar as I didn't want to test what was left of my pancreas until it had had a chance to convince me it could handle pure sugar. I was prepared to leave the diabetes medication out of the equation, as directed by Mr Chai, but I wasn't going to go crazy and get a membership to the Krispy Kreme club. I was a touch apprehensive because I wondered if my stomach would seize up and deny any access, so I took my time, and it went down without any issues. Slow and steady, I had worked out a winning formula. I washed it all down with a cup of milky coffee. With a successful breakfast in the bank, Saturday started off as a case of so far, so good.

What I craved was a freshen-up, especially after my night sweat, and if I could manage to get out of bed, I'd ask them to change the bedding. More than that, I'd ask the nurses if I could PLEASE have a normal bed, one that didn't move about, as my one had reached the point of getting right on my tits.

Two young women announced themselves at my bedside. I say young because anyone under thirty was young to my fifty-year-old eyeballs.

'Hi! I'm Kiki,' said the first one.

'Hi! I'm Becky,' said the second one.

They seemed ridiculously happy to be at my bedside. Maybe someone had played a joke on them and told them I was somebody famous, wealthy, or had some important status. Maybe it was just their usual demeanour.

'Er...hello. I'm Phil,' I replied with an air of suspicion as I looked from one to the other. I twigged straight away what they were there for. They wore identical white tunics so there was a possibility that they were beauticians that had come to give me my first-ever pedicure. Kiki stood nearest to me, and I read the badge on her chest. The badge confirmed her name as Kiki and below it was her job title, Physiotherapist.

'Hey, Phil. How are you today?' Kiki asked. It seemed that she was taking the lead.

'I'm OK, thanks. How are you?'

'I'm good, thank you, really good,' she confirmed with increasing enthusiasm.

Kiki and Becky were of similar height. About five foot two, so not tall. They were both blessed with a slim build, so they didn't look particularly powerful. I doubted that the two of them would be strong enough to support a big man like me through the first stages of physio as I had no idea how weak I was. Although I couldn't see her full face because of her mask, I could see a pair of pretty caramel-coloured eyes. Becky's eyes were electric sky-blue. Their physical differences made for an appealing double act. Kiki was a mixed-raced Londoner and styled her raven-black hair pulled back in a bun. Becky was white British with blonde hair tied back in a ponytail. If I had been James Bond, these two young ladies could have been an iconic pair of baddies to come and finish me off. Fortunately, I wasn't an incapacitated British spy; I was a spliced-together quantity surveyor.

Kiki stayed upbeat. 'We're your physio team and we're here to see if we can get you up and out of bed. And possibly see if you can come for a little walk with us.' Her last sentence was delivered coquettishly enough that no man could refuse her invitation.

I had been on strong painkillers since Mandy and her accomplice from the Pain Team had caused the peak of acute agony when they'd shifted my position the day before. My chest still ached, but I'd been relatively comfortable in the abdomen area, so I didn't want to upset that status. With great apprehension, I smiled and agreed to give her plan a whirl.

There were to be several stages that needed to be carefully achieved in a logical order so that the session could be considered a success. Luckily, Kiki and Becky had clocked up many successful first sessions before and their confidence and keenness were infectious. I'd been told how vital the physio process was to ensure the best possible recovery. I wanted to be able to get on my feet. I wanted to walk again. I was desperate to get out of that miserable bed. I was desperate to get home within the 7 days suggested by Mr Chai.

It wasn't all positive though. Some genuine fears were loud and present in my thoughts. Primarily, I was scared that physical activity was all a bit early. Yes, I was rigged up to a pain-reducing contraption but that was no guarantee that I wouldn't feel like the guy on the table in that old horror film - The Pit and the Pendulum. A move off the bed could be twice as painful as what I'd experienced at the hands of Mandy - if that was possible without passing out.

Added to the threat of searing agony was the worry that I could burst some of the many stitches that held me together. I'd been so worried about it, that I'd hardly moved at all since my operation. With the knowledge that I was supposed to be stood up, how could anyone be sure that the metal staples and stitches were tight enough to stay put when under the strain of moving in tandem with my big frame? I just had to take a sizeable leap of faith and assume they all knew what they were doing.

The final factor I was worried about was that I had no idea how strong I was. Could I support my own weight? Would my muscles support me? Would my nervous system behave? They'd only cut through nerves in the skin around my tummy, right? I could feel my toes and I could move them and move my legs (certainly from side to side on the bed) but I still wasn't totally confident. As keen as they were, how could Kiki and Becky catch me if the planned expedition went totally wrong and I ended up toppling over? If I were to fall, if I hit the deck - it would be so traumatic, and it could set me back days.

14 – SATURDAY - THE CALM BEFORE THE STORM

I had said that I would give their plan a go – but seconds later I wondered if it would be best to send them back and maybe try again tomorrow, after a further 24 hours' worth of healing time.

Kiki tilted her head and her determined eyes showed signs that she sensed my trepidation. 'Are you OK? Can you swing your legs around to the side?'

Sod it. Let's push on. If the plan falls apart (or if I fall apart), I was in the best place in the world to make it right. Or so I told myself.

One thing that I felt confident about was my modesty. I had a double-gown ensemble going on, so I was well covered. I was still commando, but as long as I didn't roll around on the floor like a beached beluga whale, the staff and patients of the hospital wouldn't get an eyeful of my genitals.

Stage one was to sit me up. I'd achieved that milestone a few times, but never on my own. The mechanics of the hospital bed usually did all the donkey work for me. The girls didn't want to wait for the slow motors and so, from my 45-degree angle, they grabbed an arm each and gently eased me up. Then, I gradually edged my red-socked feet to the right. I noticed that my legs seemed swollen, not outrageously so, but enough for me to take note. Kiki was poised, ready to grab me under my right armpit, whilst Becky was on drip and tube duty. She made sure that the two bags for the drains were clipped securely to my gown with a couple of blue plastic scissor-like clamps. Those two were a good little team. With the tubes and IV drips all sorted on the tall drip trolley, Becky unhooked my half-full bag of urine and carried that because, like it or not, it had to come with us. I'd successfully moved my legs around so that my feet dangled off the right-hand side. Kiki was on my right, Becky to my left. The drop wasn't exactly big, but I knew it would send shockwaves through me like an Exocet missile.

'Oh! Hang On!' Kiki said, and stopped me from jumping. She grabbed the bed remote control. She lowered the whole bed.

As I looked down at my toes, it also looked like the solid floor had risen up to where my feet were.

Now we're talking!

I held my breath (in anticipation of pain) and then followed Kiki's instructions. I leaned forward and then pushed up. The physio team helped me evenly on both sides.

Success!

I had managed to stand on my own two feet.

It felt good. Really good.

My posture was awful, I was stooped like an aged hunchback, but I didn't care about that. There was a psychological restriction that prevented me from stretching up to my full height. I felt that I had to protect my patched-up abdomen as much as I could, there was no way I would break into Sergeant Major mode and be bolt upright with my shoulders back. I was perfectly satisfied to ignore the strong, powerful appearance for one of pathetic, old, and wounded. I was just happy to know I could take my own weight. Well, my own weight with the help of two human crutches.

'Yeah! Well done!' Kiki chirped.

I let out a big breath that had built up inside my aching lungs.

I felt light-headed. *Don't you dare pass out, you twat.*

I took some breaths. No pain, there was a tightness across my middle, but no pain. Good. I think the team had let me take most of my own weight and were just there in case I couldn't handle it. Shit, I still felt light-headed *and* a bit woozy. Gravity seemed to have imprisoned most of my blood to the lower half of my body, and my brain wasn't happy about it.

Do. Not. Be. Sick.

'How is that? Is that OK?' Kiki quizzed. Maybe she sensed that I wasn't quite there yet.

I was still gathering everything together. 'Yep. That's OK.'

It was the truth. My body had done a decent enough job (albeit a tad later than I'd have liked) and managed to pump sufficient oxygenated blood up to my head. The swirling sensation had gone, and I stopped thoughts of fainting or being sick. My breaths seemed pretty normal to me.

I stood there for a few seconds as if to marvel at the minor miracle.

'Good job!' Kiki said and I wasn't sure if it was a little patronising.

Both Kiki and Becky maintained contact with my arms, but with no real support, I stood freely.

I puffed out my cheeks. Check me out! Cut in half two days ago and now standing strong.

A lot of my determination to get to my feet had come from what I'd seen Michael achieve when we were at Wexham Park Hospital together. I remembered back to when he'd been encouraged to get out of bed and get walking. He'd breezed through it, that scrawny lightweight. If he could do it – then so could I.

'Shall we try a few steps?' Kiki looked at me with intensity. No way would she accept a negative answer.

'OK.'

Kiki said, 'Great.'

Before I could change my mind, we were off. I shuffled my right foot forward. Then I shifted my balance ahead of me, so the right foot took most of my weight. I paused. My first step (half-step) was in the bank. I slid my left foot past my right and there was no pain. I was surprised because I expected muscles in my tummy to scream out as I moved my legs. My curled-over stoop was still there, alongside my apprehension that things could still go horribly wrong, but I did it; I walked.

The physio double-act were in attendance as I shuffled to the end of my bed. I took a sharp right, like a P&O ferry, and headed toward Stefano's bed. As I slowly stuttered past him, I sensed him watch me. My eyes were fixed forward; I didn't intend to start looking around.

'Wah-hey!' Stefano cheered. 'Bravo! Bravo!'

The smile that broke out on my face also broke my serious mood. 'Alright, alright! Don't put me off!'

The Italian laughed. 'Ha-ha!'

I maintained a slow, steady speed. We walked out of my bay and, after she checked with me, Kiki led me to the right and down the corridor toward the front desk. I felt pretty good. The whole recovery lark was OK. I kept my steps small and manageable, and as we approached the long reception desk the conversation between me and the two physios became chatty. Complacency had set in. I was asked what sort of a house I lived in (four bedrooms, ground and first floor) and if there were other people at home when I got out of hospital, to look after me. I couldn't be luckier on that front. Ali, Lydia, Harrison, Jayden and, if they were all out at work or school, I'd call my mum for back-up.

When we got to the end of the desk, I'd had enough. It was time to turn around and head back home. Kiki was satisfied with my answers about what to expect at home, but for them to sign me off, I had to prove that I could walk up a flight of stairs, unassisted. I bounced the idea inside my head. If I built myself up over the next couple of days, then I reckoned I'd be able to do a flight of stairs well before my planned 7-day target.

My feet must have moved twenty times to make my U-turn. I was happy to take my time and as I doddered my way past the desk, I dreamt of a well-deserved rest.

As I re-entered my bay, Stefano greeted me with another cheer.

'Yes! Yes! Bellisimo!'

Nothing, no reaction, or comment from boorish Dean, as he maintained his position in his bed and continued to mumble into his phone to some poor sod on the other end.

Roy was up and in his chair. I'd seen him move about quite freely earlier, and it was hard to believe that he had fully recovered from his near-death experience, yet there he was. Another miracle to behold.

'Well done, young man,' said Roy as I came near. 'How was that?'

'It was actually pretty good,' I replied truthfully.

He smiled. 'You'll be home before me if you keep that up.'

'Well look, Wednesday is day seven for me. You need to beat that because that is when I plan to leave.'

Kiki joined in. 'You've done well, no problems at all. I think they said they wanted to change your sheets whilst you were up and about. Are you OK to sit in the chair?'

'That should be alright, yeah,' I replied. The thought of being an anti-victim, and to have a spell sitting in a chair to read, eat, or whatever, seemed appealing. 'What would be good, if you know who

14 – SATURDAY - THE CALM BEFORE THE STORM | 119

to ask, is to see if they'll exchange my bed for a normal one. One without the moving air mattress.'

If you don't ask – you don't get.

Kiki seemed positive in her reply. 'Sure. OK, I'll see what they say.'

Becky was still in charge of tubes and bags, and she busied around me as I creeped past my bed toward the chair. There was a bag and some clothes to move and then they both helped me manoeuvre around so that I could just bend my knees and sit down.

It seemed so simple, but I had some mental block. Once again, I anticipated a massive rush of pain as I inevitably called upon muscles that had only just been mutilated. I remembered some words that my colleague at work, Tony with the prostate removal, had said to me. He'd advised me about using my arm muscles as much as I could to sit up in bed and that type of activity. To get over the fear in my head, I got my hands ready behind me to reach out and take the armrests of the chair. Then I bent my knees slowly until I was low enough to feel the chair with both hands. My upper body took over a lot of the weight. I felt the tightness in my tummy. The pain was beginning to brew, I could sense it. One wrong or sudden move and I would have been done for.

As I creaked lower and lower, the pain came. It hurt in several places. I expected my belly to feel it, but I also got sharp pains in my back and, because my breathing had increased from the exertion, my lungs ached more than before.

Under the watchful eyes of Becky, Kiki, and Roy from across the way, I managed to successfully plant myself in the armchair. The pain never got to the unmanageable level I'd been petrified of, and once established, I could sit back and relax a lot of different muscles that had been outrageously tensed up.

The physios neatened up my tubes and drips and Becky reinstated my urine bag to the side of the bed. They said their ultra-bubbly goodbyes and threatened a return visit to come and get me on Monday, as they weren't working on Sunday.

Fair play to Kiki, she must have had a word with the right person. Within a few minutes of sitting in my chair, Ami and another nurse went to town on my bed. I was impressed at their speed and their strength. They threw the crumpled sheets off in seconds, and discarded the pillowcases, and within moments there was a sizeable pile of laundry. Then, whilst the other nurse carried away the dirty, sweaty bedding, Ami wrestled with the mattress. She looked like a woman possessed. She activated some reverse pump that started to suck out all the air, but it wasn't like a beach lilo. The mattress was much thicker and had a considerable structure to it, so it was never going to go completely flat. Ami started at the bottom of the bed and rolled the mattress up. All that stiff plastic made a hell of a noise as it was forced into a compact bundle. I watched as Ami expertly held the coiled mattress with one hand and magically produced a strap with her free hand. Where had that come from? She used her body weight and expertly tied the mattress with the strap.

Wow, I doubted I could have ever done that on my own, at such speed. Ami looked like a formidable WWE wrestler.

The co-ordination was admirable. The other nurse returned with a trolley and fresh sheets. Whilst her colleague took the bedding off the trolley, Ami reached around the bundled-up mattress and hoisted it off the bed. I could see Ami was a big lady, but that mattress must have weighed a tonne. She walked it over to the trolley and banged it down. I felt like I had witnessed the NHS version of the World's Strongest Man competition. Ami wheeled the mattress away and the other nurse finished changing my bed sheets in less than sixty seconds.

I was exhausted just by watching them work so hard.

The fresh, crisp, and wonderfully stable bed looked incredibly inviting, but I wanted to feel normal in my chair for a bit longer. Anyway, there was no way I could get out of the chair and up on the bed without two or three weightlifters or, alternatively, one Ami. So, I remained in the chair, and waited for some help.

15

The Storm

Something was not right.

That something was me. Deep within me.

When you know, you know.

I did not feel *normal,* and I was caught between the need to get back into bed and not being able to move from the chair. I knew I wasn't physically paralysed, but there was some sort of fear that glued me to the chair.

I analysed my situation. For starters, I needed to calm down and think about what I had to do. One thing was for sure, I'd had enough of being stuck in that chair. That novelty had well and truly worn off.

Frustratingly, my bed was right next to me, waiting for me to climb on board and relax. The bed was within touching distance, but it might as well have been 100 yards away. I couldn't move. Not on my own – I needed help.

Perspiration built up beneath the surface of my skin. My body seemed to get warmer by the minute, and I could feel my pores preparing to open the flood gates, to douse me all over with the biological aim to cool me down. Maybe my physio excursion had been too much? No, that wasn't a healthy sweat brought on from exercise. I found myself in an incredibly uncomfortable position. Fear had caused this. Fear of excruciating pain had stopped me in my tracks. I was stuck with my weight shifted over on to my right side. My right arse cheek took all the weight that it usually shared equally with its identical left buttock. My right hand clung to the end of the wooden armrest, and I had tensed up as much as I could. I held myself locked in that position and I didn't seem to be able to let go. My left leg was bent, and it may have looked like it was in a sat-down position, but I had managed to rise up slightly, which is why my weight had shifted over onto my right. I had lifted my left foot to rest on top of the side of the right foot, which had twisted over.

The morphine bolus was on the other side of the bed. Fucking bollocks. I could have done with a blast of that and then maybe alleviate some of the inevitable agony.

I must have looked truly pathetic to Roy or anyone who may have seen me stuck there. The problem was, there was nobody around to see how pitiful I looked, and that meant I couldn't even ask for help. Roy had got up and gone for a walk. He wouldn't have known I was in any distress as he wasn't a mind-reader. The seconds turned into minutes and, still, I hadn't moved out from my twisted posture. The sweat broke out. I felt it seep out all over my body, but most noticeably from my forehead, my back, and my neck and chest. The hospital gown became heavier and strangely hotter as it soaked up the sweat.

I needed Ami or any other nurse. I hadn't seen her for ages, or so it had seemed. I felt abandoned and I had lost track of how long I'd been frozen in that state. A real sense of panic rose up as I had no idea how much more I could take. It felt like all my muscles were tensed up; it was painful and knackering. A nice little sit-down in the chair was supposed to have helped my recovery. It was doing the opposite and I just wanted to be in bed. That bed was next to me, with its clean white sheets mocking me from two feet away.

My catheter piss bag had filled up. My body temperature had jumped up a level. Jesus, I had been doing everything I could possibly do to get well and get sent home within a week. My rational thought processing deserted me when I needed it most, and I started to lose my shit. My pulse raced. My breathing had changed; it was harder and faster, like I had just finished a 100m sprint. Bollocks, my vitals are going to be all over the place. Where the hell was Ami? Wasn't she responsible for taking obs and vitals? She should be around. Maybe it was because it was Saturday? Was nobody else working the weekend? Where was the back up?

I tried to stop the panic from getting its claws deeper into me. *Get a grip, Phil*. I had never experienced a panic attack in my life, yet I had a feeling that I was about to lose my mind. I needed someone to help support me so I could rise out of the chair and somehow, fuck knows how, get me onto that sodding bed.

My left hand clasped on to my right so that both arms could share the burden of maintaining such an unnatural position. A position that may have been uncomfortable but was far better than the devasting pain I'd go through if I let go and moved only a few millimetres. My face was screwed up, all my body was screwed up, and I rested my forehead on top of my hands and waited for help. Sweaty head on top of sweaty hands. I prayed the horrible episode would finish soon and I would then reward myself with a hefty dose of morphine. I prayed for someone, anyone.

It wasn't help, not yet, but I heard voices. They weren't near enough for me to yell out. I didn't have any energy to scream out and that might have triggered the pain I was desperate to avoid. There were three, maybe even four voices. I couldn't calculate where they were, and I didn't recognise the voices either. I placed them either in the day room, which I hadn't even been in, but knew of its existence, or, possibly, the front desk. I tried to make out what they were talking about; however, I could not pick up full sentences. I hoped they were discussing me, and they would have decided who from their group would get off their arse and help the guy in Ward 21. Who would get him back into his bed because he'd been left to rot in his chair for bloody ages.

Laughter. That is what I could hear. Fucking laughter.

Not just one person but at least two, possibly three. Two women and a man. What the hell? It sounded like they were having a whale of a time. Whilst bent up, crippled me sat in a chair sweating my tits off, in dire need of some help. The situation was scandalous, but I was powerless to do anything about it. The distant chat and, more infuriatingly, the laughter, continued.

I was still stuck. I felt I might go insane. It took a hell of a lot to get me angry, but when I did lose it, I was like the Hulk on steroids.

I felt my temperature rise higher and higher, and it was possible that the increased heat was generated by the anger that I felt at being abandoned. I knew the NHS was short staffed and I knew it was Saturday afternoon, but come on, I could die on the floor, and nobody would have known. Imagine if I decided to 'do a Roy' and suffer a stomach tear; that would not be good for anyone. The idea flashed briefly - *Am I actually doing a Roy?*

That notion fell by the wayside as quickly as it had flared up. His symptoms included feeling cold and I was the polar opposite of that; I was hotter than Satan's bum crack.

Roy had been out, away from our bay, possibly watching TV or reading in the day room. I sensed him return to his bed. I didn't call out to him. I didn't call out for help, because I wasn't sure exactly what to say and I felt that I couldn't physically speak anyway. I thought, if Roy were to look over to me, he would see a twisted mess of a distressed man and he would not even have to ask, 'Are you ok? Do you need some help?' He'd know exactly what to do. He would go and get someone to help. I remained in my awkward position, and my muscles screamed to me as they fought to stay tensed up. It seemed the amount of energy produced in my legs, arms, and back was directly proportional to the amount of sweat those body parts excreted. My agitation and anxiety at those over-jovial voices were now compounded by the inactive Roy. I considered my options and realised that before much longer, I would have to embarrass myself and scream out for help. My situation had to stop, I was either going to need some help or I would collapse and pass out.

Roy got up and strode out of the bay and, I presumed, headed towards the laughter. I considered myself as someone up for a laugh, really, I did, and I believed any place, even a hospital, should be a place where laughter should be allowed. It is the best medicine, so they say. However, that amount of unashamed happiness was well beyond the realms of what was acceptable. It crossed my mind that their laughs and piss-taking might have been at my expense. Once the thought was there, then it started to gather momentum and maybe they wanted to see how long I could take being left in the chair before I cracked and begged for help. Christ! I knew I looked pathetic but to have those 'carers' make a joke out of me – that was bang out of order! Go on Roy, I thought, give them some shit!

A new male voice joined the conversation.

The giggles and the laughter stopped almost immediately.

I could tell that whatever was being said had instantly changed the mood of the conversation and there was now only the one stern voice that was not a rant, but it was at a volume and pace that I identified as a controlled bollocking. It was Roy, and he was obviously giving that bunch of jokers some home truths. I couldn't make out the exact words, despite me doing my best to focus on Roy's voice. I was sure he told them that to piss themselves with outrageously loud laughter for the last 10 minutes, in a place full of ill people, was a million miles away from what they should be doing. He didn't single out anyone, they were all guilty and they were all getting a piece of his mind. I wasn't 100% sure but he seemed to be reminding them of how important their duties were and that they needed to check up on the patient in Ward 21 that was suffering on his own and desperately needed some assistance – rather than being laughed at.

Thank you, Roy, you're my hero. A loud, firm voice is much more effective than those effing call-for-assistance buttons.

Roy wasn't with the jokers for long. He said his piece efficiently and then left them to dwell on his words. The group must have decided that Roy had a point as I could not hear any more laughing. It went quiet enough to hear the general sounds of the ward. After a while, the only voices I could hear were the soft mutters of general conversation, nothing loud and certainly not jovial and nothing inappropriate. At least they weren't laughing at me anymore.

When Roy marched back into our bay, I unstuck my sweaty forehead off from the back of my hands and looked up towards him.

'Roy.' I said, even though it was an effort to say his name with any volume.

He stopped between our beds, before doing his usual right turn to return to his quarters.

I noticed he was dressed smartly. The opposite of me being a sad, ill patient clothed in a sweaty gown with tubes and bags coming out of me, barely able to lift my head up.

'Yes?' answered Roy and looked at me through his spectacles.

'Did you just have a go at that lot?' I asked, with the intention of getting the important part of asking when they planned to rescue me from my frozen posture.

'No,' Roy said neutrally. Then, as cool as you like, he pivoted towards his bed and sat down on the chair next to it.

What? Did Roy just say *No*?

What?

He did – he'd said, no.

What a total mind-fuck.

I was confused. I was sure it was him that had spoken to the jokers, so he was either telling me the truth and he hadn't said a word to the group, or he was blatantly lying to me. If it wasn't him, then who the hell was it? I witnessed the man get up and walk towards the voices. It sounded too much like a coincidence that someone else arrived at the desk (I reasoned that the exchange happened at the desk as there were usually staff gathered there) at the exact same time that Roy would have got there, to bark out an effective reprimand, and then to see Roy return after the altercation when the timings were all there. The voice was his, I swear. Not that Roy had anything more distinct than an educated, middle-England accent. So, who was the mystery hero? Or, more likely, why was Roy denying that he said anything?

It was a Total Mind-fuck.

Confusion had now compounded my already distressed state. Just when I thought things were just getting worse and worse, my luck took a positive turn. Whether it was Roy or Mystery Man that had broken up the party, it didn't matter because I was visited straight after by a nurse. I don't think she was one of the pranksters as the voices were definitely British (London to be more exact) and the lady with an Asian accent gently asked me if I was OK.

Halle-fucking-lujah!

'No. I'm not,' I blubbered. 'I need to get up and get into bed and rest. I'm exhausted; I've been stuck here for ages.' I couldn't help my rant. 'I'm sorry, I know it's not your fault.'

'OK,' she said calmly, 'I'll go and get someone to help you up.'

She was true to her word. Help came in the form of a young, strong looking porter.

I hoped he had the strength of two men because I felt utterly drained of any power.

He asked me keenly, 'Are you ok? Do you need me to help?'

'I'm just trying to get into bed,' I confirmed wearily. He must have thought he was looking at a sad Great Dane at the end of its life, asking to be lifted to its final resting place. 'I need you to help with all these bags and tubes. If you can help me up out of this chair, I think I can get into bed.'

I wasn't sure at all if I could get into bed; I was exhausted, but it was him and me and, even though he looked as strong as an ox on Red Bull, there was no way he was picking me up like a groom carrying a new bride.

'OK. No problem,' the porter said. Strong and enthusiastic seemed a good combination for the task. Unfortunately, my hero, clad in his standard issue sky blue uniform, did not have much in the way of experience and that was going to cause us, and me in particular, a bit of a problem. Maybe we should have asked for back-up, but my determination to get into that bed would not give in to waiting any longer. My attitude was very much, '*Let's get this done.*'

My new porter friend stood to my left and he gathered up the bag of piss connected to me with his left hand and used his right hand to get behind my shoulder and under my left armpit. I made sure my smaller drainage bags were clipped on to my gown using the plastic scissors-cum-clip and gathered up the gown behind me with my left rather than holding on to my helper and prepared to release my right hand from the death-like grip it maintained on the armrest. I didn't communicate my intentions, but I wanted to stand up, and rose from the chair using my right arm and power from both legs and avoid (at all costs) using any abdominal muscles, most of which had been slashed deeply by Mr Chai only 48 hours before. Once up, I could shuffle to the bed and, well, simply jump onto the bed.

Easy. Yeah, right.

I looked seriously at StrongBoy the blue porter. 'On three, OK?'

StrongBoy nodded, 'On three.'

I corrected my feet so I was as square on as I could be and then commenced countdown to lift-off, 'One...two...three...' and it encouraged me to feel StrongBoy make a difference as I powered up through my legs and he balanced up the upper part of my left hand side as I supported my right as my right arm pushed down against the chair. A mixture of physical and psychological factors stopped me from standing fully upright; the stooped me was plenty good enough. Thank Christ, I was out of that chair. I was homeward bound. A peaceful rest that I was desperate for was in touching distance.

I shuffled towards the bed, but there was a crashing noise as StrongBoy stumbled. Somehow, he had got his feet caught up with the drip trolley because he'd been concentrating on just me. He managed to still hold me up and in those few seconds I managed to get both hands on to the side of the beautifully clean, welcoming, bed. StrongBoy failed to maintain his balance. He'd completed the difficult task of getting me up, but he staggered away to my left, taking my bag of piss with him.

His fall yanked the catheter tube out from my dick.

If I hadn't been drugged up to eyeballs on a cocktail of painkillers, the whole of Hammersmith would've heard my scream. Maybe the epidural was working its magic by neutralising acute pain, but whatever it was, I didn't scream. Unless shouting, 'Arrrghhh!' to everyone in earshot could be described as a scream. Alright, alright, I screamed like a stuck pig.

StrongBoy looked and sounded distraught.

He wheeled his arms around and reclaimed his balance. However, because his left arm still held onto the bag, his actions sent a jet of my warm, orange urine all over me, him, the bed and, mostly, the floor. If it wasn't so painful, and so God-damn awful, it would've been comical, like witnessing a fire extinguisher going off.

'It has come out!' he cried out and his eyes widened in horror.

I considered changing his nickname to State-The-Bleeding-Obvious-Boy.

15 – THE STORM

'How?' he asked the air around him, rather than directly to me.

I certainly couldn't answer him, but I thought that if the tubes were pulled hard enough, something had to give. I won't exaggerate and say I was suffering from continued excruciating pain; there wasn't, but the thought of what had just happened brought the sensation of nausea to the pit of my stomach. All I could do was stand there, with my palms on the bed and my head bowed waiting for the sickness and dizziness to pass. Being sick was going to be incredibly painful, that was something I did know. I considered how the catheters were built, how they worked, and that they were not supposed to come out easily. Like every man that had experienced an *incident* with their genitals, I wondered if my knob, or more likely, the plumbing to it, had been permanently damaged.

The crashes, bangs and my screams had been heard. A handful of nurses arrived.

Operation Clear Up began immediately.

Two new nurses had helped me get on to the bed. I was covered in sweat, splattered with my own piss, exhausted, and just wanted a blast of morphine to help take everything away. I wasn't sure about what was going on. The bed was low enough for me to place my arse on and, inch by inch, I managed to shuffle back. The nurses expertly moved my legs up and around so that I was in a sitting position, since the bed was already upright enough to support me. It hadn't been as painful as I'd feared. They had been quick and incredibly sensitive to my situation. Some other staff members cleared up the spillage in the aisle. I grabbed the bolus, and my thumb activated the release of a long-overdue morphine blast. I felt like shit.

Within a couple of minutes, I was alone again. I'd regained some composure, the relief of finally being at rest on the bed had helped. Or it might have been the drugs. My breathing had regulated, and the nausea had eased back. I used the bed remote to make myself less upright and I closed my eyes. I drifted off, grateful to my mind and body for not passing out.

A couple of minutes into my doze and Dr Haji appeared by my side. He announced that he was there to check out my catheter situation. Fuck me; I'd only just got my breath back. There truly was no peace or rest for the wicked. Once again, I found myself stuck between two options. I wanted to get all my plumbing business sorted, but at the same time, I just wanted to be left alone. I could handle the usual blood pressure rigmarole, but I dreaded to find out what had happened to my poor penis. At least there was no pain down there. Hang on, I realised, that nothingness might be a bad sign.

I was brave. So that Dr Haji could get a good look, I moved my gown to the right to expose my genitals to the both of us.

I was surprised by what I saw.

My little chap was looking short and fatter than its usual rested size, but no blood. What I noticed straight away was that my meat and two veg were not alone. A blue plastic adaptor was stationed in the end of my dick. There was an opening in the end of the adaptor, and I presumed that was where a tube would go, as I reckoned I could get the end of my little finger in it. I hadn't even felt the intruder since it had been rammed in me two days prior. I'd not been curious enough to look at it. Out of sight – out of mind. I had felt *something*, as occasionally there would be a little tug here and there from the tube, as I made slight movements. Upon seeing it, I instantly felt it in me. Although I couldn't tell how deep the plastic fitting was, it wasn't uncomfortable, it was just *there*.

It reminded me of my outside tap back home. The tap in the back garden with the Hozelock adaptor on it so it could easily connect to a hosepipe.

'Oh, Ok,' began Dr Haji. 'This is not so bad.'

What? So, it is still a little bit bad – was what I thought as I remained silent.

I guess he could tell I was one of those guys that wasn't up for a chat when their dick was on show. He was right; I can't stand guys that feel the need to strike up a conversation when stood next to me at the urinals. Just get your toilet business done and fuck off.

I didn't want to see anymore so I looked away. Dr Haji had brought along a sealed-up replacement catheter and, fortunately, he only needed the tube part of it. It didn't hurt me at all as he replaced the tube. He also repositioned my gown and went over to the bag, and he made sure that everything was tickety-boo.

'Thank you, Doctor,' I said grateful.

'You're welcome,' he replied. 'Rest up and take it easy, OK?'

I took the good doctor's advice. I fell asleep and felt a little better about myself, mainly because my penis hadn't been destroyed. It felt like every five minutes in hospital posed a different and increasingly stressful battle. I wondered what could possibly happen to me next.

When I woke, I found out it was bath time.

A young nurse, Shanice, had introduced herself and brought a washing-up bowl that was half-full of soapy water. She carefully placed it alongside my knees and didn't spill a drop. Shanice had also brought along some big paper towels and a new gown.

I was half asleep, but I knew that a freshen-up was something that I needed. There was no way I could drag myself into the shower room and do what I truly wanted, which was to stand under a powerful, hot shower and blast away all manner of sweat, dirt, piss and a lot of adhesive residue that was all over my body. I couldn't do that because I had to protect so many things on me that needed to stay dry. The big old dressing that covered 20% of my torso for starters – that would probably fall off me in seconds under a hot shower. Then there was the epidural and two other tubes that came out from my side. It made sense to keep all those entry points clean and dry.

Ali had sent me some messages earlier and was making the trip into London to come and visit me. Her time slot was due to start at 3:30pm, so the timing of my clean up couldn't have been any better. I wanted to give Ali the impression that I was perfectly well, even if I was struggling on the inside. It would have stressed me out more if I'd thought for a moment she was worried about me. There wasn't any point in her wasting energy, shitting herself about me. She had her birthday trip away with Lydia arranged for the following day – no way would I ruin that for her. What she would see before her would be her husband, sat up in bed, all freshly washed, looking his absolute best.

Suddenly, I had a minor moment of uncomfortable fear. *Am I supposed to lie here and watch this twenty-something nurse give me a bed bath?*

The fear wasn't aimed at me, it was for Shanice. What a horrible job, having to wash my stinky body. The poor thing would no doubt suffer PTSD if part of the routine was to scrub around my nether regions.

Then I had a *major* moment of uncomfortable fear. What if I enjoy a bed bath a little bit too much? As much as I could try and distance myself from a nice young lady being delicately attentive around my groin – what if I got an unplanned erection? The more I would try and NOT think about it, the more my animal brain would disobey me and think about nothing else. It wasn't always easy being a man.

Would a hard-on mess up the whole catheter thing? Would the catheter thing destroy up a hard-on? I pinged around bizarre questions that I had never had to even dream about before.

Shanice must have sensed all my fears. She cut off my distasteful train of thought before it ran away out of control. 'You can wash yourself. I'm not doing it.'

It was said with real purpose. Maybe with a hint of venom, as if, for her, there was no way on Earth she would get within six feet of my disgusting body.

'That's fine,' I said, relieved that I wouldn't find out the answers to my ridiculous questions at that moment in time.

'How do you want to do this?' she asked, as if I was a pro at the bed-bath game.

'Erm...I'm not sure.'

'Would it be easier if you were out of the bed?'

I didn't want my lovely clean bed to get soaked, so it seemed logical to get out of it. The only problem with that was that it was such an ordeal to get in and out of the bloody thing.

I made a decision. 'OK. Can you help me get up?'

'Yes, of course,' Shanice replied quickly.

Maybe I had got her wrong, and I sensed was that she was rushed off her feet. There was an urgency about her. She spoke fast and her actions were just as hurried. I guessed there was a lot happening out there in the ward and there weren't enough nurses to go around.

15 – THE STORM

The bed was still low down from my previous adventures and Shanice helped move my legs around to my left. I did my best to keep up with her pace. In a strange way it helped because I didn't pause to worry about pain. I got both feet on the floor, and she helped haul me out and I pushed up through my hips to get myself upright. It was a success. I didn't feel light-headed, Shanice had kept all my tubes out of the way and, apart from my stoop, I stood up unaided.

Shanice made sure the bowl was near, and the paper towels and the (not particularly fluffy) bath towel were all in easy reach. Then she told me she'd leave me to it and would see me soon. She closed the curtains all around my bed to give me privacy, then left to rejoin whatever nuttiness was happening in the rest of the ward.

It was an awkward, unconventional wash, but at least it was a wash. Fortunately for me, my hair was short, and the greasiness built up since Thursday morning was at an excusable level. A hair wash was not on the cards, so it was only ever going to be armpits and groin, oh, and my face to start with.

I didn't need to strip off to clean my face. I'd save that performance until it was necessary. I used one of the large disposable paper towels that Shanice had given me; they were industrial-strength ones that were good at absorbing water and didn't break up like an over-dunked Rich Tea biscuit. I sloshed one around the bowl and had to give it a good squeeze so that half the water didn't come with it as I lifted it to my face. It was a strange move for me. I supported myself with my left hand so I could bend over the bowl, and with my right hand I washed my face with the towel-come-flannel.

It felt pretty good.

The water was warm enough – it was never going to be great. I held the flannel over my face for several seconds and breathed through it. I circled it around all my face, my forehead, both ears, and right under my chin and back around my neck before I stopped short of the central line. Most of the excess water fell back into the bowl, and some of it ran down to my gown. I didn't care because that heavy sack was coming off next. The cleansing felt glorious. I hadn't realised how dirty my face was until it became clean. I returned the flannel back to the bowl and squeezed it, splashed it around the bowl and repeated the whole show. Yeah, that was bloody good.

I scrubbed off adhesive that I felt around my nose and mouth. No doubt it had been there since my operation on the Thursday, but I'd been oblivious as I had no mirror, and I hadn't given a shit about my appearance one iota. I left the flannel in the bowl as I didn't know where else to leave it. Next up, the body.

The flimsy curtains didn't offer the best privacy, but what could I do? I couldn't see out and presumed nobody could see in. Obviously, in the strip wash game, there would be a time when I would be stood up, stark-bollock naked. My plan was to reduce that time down to the smallest possible window, to minimise the chances of an uninvited peeper, or a strong gust of wind that might open the curtains to expose me and my tubed-up willy to all and sundry. I carefully took out some pants from my bag and laid them on the bed. I considered removing my red socks to avoid the inevitable soaking, but it wasn't going to happen. I couldn't bend down, but I could kick back each leg to reach the heel of each sock. It was a no-can-do situation because there was no way I'd be able to get the fuckers back on. I resigned to being a little bit more careful when the water started flying around. To take the brunt of the excess water, I dropped a bath towel on the floor and shuffled my feet around on it to get it in place.

With paper flannels, a second bath towel, and the new gown at the ready, I went for it.

If I hadn't been laden with so many tubes and drips, I would have got myself sorted in no time at all, but the tubes were there, so I had to be careful. I undid the gown, which seemed to have been tied up with double knots at about six different locations. I chucked it on the bed.

Apart from my red socks, I stood by my bed, naked.

I got to work on my armpits first. I didn't think they smelt of B.O., but I was probably only one sweaty ordeal away from it. A new disposable flannel got a dunking in the soapy bowl, a squeeze, and then it was a case of a few brisk rubs under my left arm. Then, following a switch of hands, my right armpit got exactly the same treatment. A fair amount of water ran down my flanks, but it didn't stop me, because I was determined to charge on through the torment.

I had enough flannels, so I made a final change over and used the third and final one between my legs. Betty Swollocks, as I like to say. I couldn't be too vigorous downstairs, because of the whole catheter set-up. I recharged the flannel and concluded matters with a gentle scrub of my bum crack, and my wish of easing out a fart did not come true. However, despite the obstacles, I did manage to give myself a half-decent freshen-up.

Conscious that I was still exposed, I swapped the flannel for a bath towel. I patted my face dry, quickly rubbed under my arms, and also dried my sides and chest. I was pleased that I'd been careful enough to keep my dressings fairly dry. Finally, I used the towel to dry between my legs. I knew I'd rushed it; just like getting changed after swimming.

I found that pulling on a pair of trunk-style underpants, when I couldn't bend down, and with a tube coming out of my knob, could have been a devious round on the Crystal Maze. I was certain there were better techniques, but I chose the one where you start off by lobbing your underwear on the floor. Then I stood on them with my left foot and fed my right foot into the leg hole. Then, I had to be nimble, and equally patient, because to feed my left foot through its leg hole was even trickier. Once both feet were in, I could move my pants north. I did it by kicking my lower leg back, so I could grab at my underwear and hoist them up from behind. I switched sides to help avoid over-stretching my knickers. Obviously, I had not dried my legs properly because my pants squeaked to a halt and ended up in some sort of reef knot under my scrotum. I tugged at them and finally won the battle. The tube poked out the top of my waistband but there was some give in the tube, so there was no uncomfortable tugging sensation. I was grateful that I hadn't fallen over or been seen.

The whole strip wash was such a performance that I began to overheat and sweat again. Fucking marvellous.

I waited a few moments to cool down before I donned the hospital gown. That gown, and everyone before it, had become the symbol of my imprisonment: the clothes handed to me, to signify that I was a victim, like all the other inmates around me. I hated it with a passion. I vowed to myself that, at the first opportunity, I would revert back to civilian clothes – a T-shirt and some jogging bottoms.

At that moment, with my central line still live and stuck in my neck, I thought I should be a good boy and comply. So, I put the bloody thing on.

As expected, I struggled with the ties behind my neck, but I'd managed to get myself covered up. As I fastened the sides, I felt a bit of a chump because I reasoned that I should have put the gown on first and then tackled the underwear? Ah, whatever, it was done now. I stood there and weighed up my options.

- Sit in the chair and wait for help to get back into bed.
- Stand where I was and wait for help to get back into bed.
- Try and get back into bed on my own.

I went with option 2, to stand there and wait for help. If it took too long (Shanice seemed exceptionally busy) then I could always revert to option 1. Option 3 was never going to happen.

My wait was not long at all.

Shanice soon appeared on the other side of the curtain. 'Are you OK? Have you finished?'

I was glad I hadn't attempted any chair or bed manoeuvres on my own. I would have pulled a muscle, popped a stitch, or yanked a tube out.

'Yes. I'm fine thanks and yes, I'm all done. Thanks. I just need a hand to get back into bed if that's OK?'

Shanice appeared from behind the curtain, said she would help, and moved all the wash stuff from the bed on to the chair to give me a totally free bed.

I was tired, but I had definitely got better at the technique of getting into bed. I did a one-eighty to get my bum on the edge of the bed and with the nurse's help, I swung my legs up and on to the bed. I used my arms and shuffled about until I was exactly where I wanted to be. Perfect.

Shanice finished her visit and cleared away all the paraphernalia. As she left, she said that she would check up on me later. I checked my watch. Later? Crikey, it already was later. It had gone 3pm and Ali was supposed to be with me within the next thirty minutes. I played with the bed's mechanisms and got myself as comfortable as I possibly could. I felt clean, and at ease with everything. My pain levels were all in check, so I lay back and waited for the highlight of my day, no, it was better than that, it was the highlight of my week.

An Oasis in a Desert of Despair

She was bang on time. I knew I could rely on Ali.

They'd made her dress up in full PPE, like she'd visited an Ebola ward. Facemask, gloves, disposable apron, blue overshoes. The works. A lot of it was all to do with Covid, but the truth was that there were far worse things flying around the hospital, or being brought in by the visitors. It made sense to protect everyone against nasty diseases and Ali was terrified that she could bring in a germ that might bring me down. With my spleen out, my whole immune system was well and truly knackered, so she complied with the rules without complaint.

'Hiya!' Ali cooed the moment we made eye contact. She followed it up with a cute wave.

'Hello, wifey,' was my standard response. It was said with a hint of an apology, as if what I meant to say was, *sorry for putting you through all this aggravation and worry.*

She wanted to express how thrilled she was to see me alive with a kiss, but her practical nature stopped her short as she came to sit in the armchair next to my bed.

What we both craved was a hug, a big cuddle, physical contact, and closeness. Reluctantly, we both accepted our second-best situation. We'd sent messages, and spoken on the phone, but nothing came close to being with the one I loved. Ali gave my leg a gentle, lasting rub. She was a little scared to touch me anywhere else, and my legs seemed a safe place to aim for.

16 – AN OASIS IN A DESERT OF DESPAIR

'How ya doin'?' Ali asked.

'Well,' I joked, 'I've been better.'

Ali scoffed and said, 'Are you OK? You look very white.'

'White? Do I?'

I was surprised by what Ali had noticed in me. I had been through the mill over the previous few hours, but since my wash, I thought I'd regathered my composure. *Good job you hadn't seen me earlier, you'd have freaked out.*

Ali was worried that I had no colour in my face, but even my hands looked starved of blood supply to her.

'Yes. Look at your hands. Don't they look white, *really white*, to you?'

I raised my hands up and turned them over and back again. 'Maybe. I hadn't noticed or thought about it. But I feel alright.'

'Do you? You'd say something if you didn't feel right, wouldn't you?'

'Of course. Don't worry, Ali. Honestly, I'm OK. Seven-day plan is still on track.'

Ali wanted to believe me, even though she thought I had the colour of a living corpse, but she didn't push her worries any deeper. After she told me that everyone sent their love and wished me a speedy recovery, Ali switched the conversation to everything other than my health situation and I was grateful for it. We spoke about the children, our parents, upcoming events like Ali's hotel trip, petrol shortages, the weather...normal shit. It was wonderful to be taken away into every day, some may say, boring, life. If laughter was the best medicine, then just listening to stories of what my family had been up to came a close second.

I knew it would happen. My allotted hour with Ali sped along ten times faster than any other hour of the week. I had told Ali all about Roy, so I made a point of introducing them to each other and they obliged with some small talk. I didn't introduce Ali to the other guys, Dean the Bore and Stefano the Farter.

Ali asked me what I was going to do about the trip I'd organised with our sons. I'd paid about £250 for three tickets to see my beloved New York Jets play in the NFL game in London. I had followed

American Football for years and the Jets were my team, but I hadn't seen them since my trip to New York in 1997. The game was only a fortnight away.

'You're not still going, are you?'

'Hmmm,' I mused. 'I may have to rethink it. When I booked it, I was going to drive there, so that is out. I can't expect the boys to drive, so we'll have to get a cab. Then there's all the walking, all the crowds, and what sort of state I'm going to be in with drains and bags and everything. I'll contact the stadium and see if they can change my ticket for a disabled person. Worst case scenario, we've still got Harri's wheelchair in the loft, they can wheel me there.'

'That's ridiculous,' Ali said, far from impressed.

'I know. But, at the moment, I'm OK, and if I can get out by Wednesday, I should be alright.'

I had previous history with that sort of thing.

Back in 2014, Queens Park Rangers made it to Wembley to play in the Championship Play-Off Final against Derby County. My entire family were QPR supporters, so we all got tickets, because it was a huge occasion. However, the week before, I managed to get myself booked in for a vasectomy. I made it to Wembley on the train, slowly walked to the stadium and found my seat without too much drama. I was generally well-behaved and didn't move from my position other than to sing up with all the chants. Mainly because Derby were all over us and we couldn't get out of our half. Once Rangers' Gary O'Neil got sent off in the second half it seemed inevitable that we would lose the game. But I was wrong. In the final minute of the game, our lone striker, Bobby Zamora, popped up with the only goal of the game. A last-minute winner! We were heading back to the Premier League!

The unbridled euphoria we all felt when our little team won something so important couldn't be replicated. Obviously, the blue and white half of Wembley erupted. Like everyone else, I blasted out of my seat like a lit firework. However, I didn't continue to jump about quite like everyone else around me. As I'd leapt up, I felt a crippling twang right where I'd had my operation. I feared that my internal stitches had blown apart. It was a different sort of feeling that I'd never experienced before or since; elation multiplied by panic. Despite being caught up in the moment with thousands of other fans, I managed to stop myself from uncontrolled bouncing about like a crazed maniac. I stood still and simply observed the expressions of joy all around me. The pain never got too bad, so I didn't go back to the clinic, and I remember that I took it nice and steady from that point on. I was fortunate that I had no complications to speak of.

As much as I was happy to discuss boring normality, I needed something special to aim for. Previously, when I'd received my diagnosis of a pancreatic tumour during my week-long hospital stay, I'd had an England-Germany football match to focus on. It seemed crucial for me to have such a real target to keep me upbeat and positive. I knew I couldn't beat my own toilet and a proper cup of tea, but I needed a unique treat like a holiday, or a special occasion on the horizon to keep me going. As I lay in that Hammersmith ward, it wasn't the call of my own bed, my family, and obviously not work, it was the call of my favourite sport and my favourite team that I hadn't seen live for twenty-four years that I found myself most excited about. I had always been a stubborn git, so there was no way I was going to miss that memorable event unless I was at serious risk of death.

Not for the first time, I apologised for destroying Ali's 50th birthday plans. Quite a milestone birthday that was due in just two days. I was more heartbroken than Ali that our big plans had been blown apart but at least she was still going away. We spoke about it for a while, and it was nice to do so. It helped me to think that Ali and Lydia would be able to distract themselves from worrying about my sorry arse. We made some new plans together, once I was out and all patched up, that we'd book another weekend away. It was all about having something exciting to look forward to. Reasons to be cheerful.

And then it was time up.

I had a genuine reason to explain why I hadn't been on top form.

Ali dismissed my apology and said that I had been fine, and she was just happy that she could see that I was alive and breathing. We didn't take the piss, we obeyed the rules, and when the hour was over, we said our emotional goodbyes. We blew each other some kisses. We both said that we loved each other.

'Can you call us later?' Ali asked as she got up and got ready to leave.

'Of course I will.'

'OK. See you soon.'

'Wednesday! I'll see you on Wednesday!' I declared with some morphine-laced confidence.

Ali wanted me home, of course she did. But, more than anything, she wanted me to be well, and if that meant spending more than a week at Hammersmith, then she would live with that. Her blue eyes never dropped their tinge of concern throughout her visit. 'Just get yourself better first, OK?'

'That is the plan. Have a great day tomorrow. Speak to you later.'

Ali moved away from my bed, and our time together was over. 'Thanks, Mr Gorgeous. I love you.'

'See you, Ali. I love you, too.'

And then she was gone. I saw Ali stop and turn to send me one last wave, and Ali blew a final kiss (even if it was through a facemask, it still counted).

After Ali left, I had a bit of a crash. Nothing major, but I'd definitely tired myself out. I didn't want to lie there half-asleep, so I'd made an effort to be as lively as I could – but there was a price to pay. Ami was back on observation duty, and she wasn't happy with my temperature or my oxygen levels. It had been a couple of hours since I'd nearly gone into a state of spontaneous human combustion when I'd got stuck in the armchair, and the freshen-up strip wash had helped lower my temperature – or so I thought. After making me lie back and take several deep breaths, Ami was happy that my oxygen level was satisfactory. She left me, with a red mark against my temperature on my record. I was worried that I might have caught Covid. That would be just marvellous. Spleen and immune system out – Covid-fucking-19 in. That was what an above-normal temperature meant back in those times. If the laser gun thermometer glowed a red 38 degrees, it meant strict isolation because I'd contracted Covid. It never rained; it just poured.

Roy and I carried on with our chats. It seemed like we were having the longest conversation I'd ever had. It was a possible contender for Guinness to consider in their next book. We'd started on Thursday morning, and although we'd been interrupted countless times (such as mealtimes, night time, doctors' rounds, and visits from our wives) we just seemed to pick up exactly from where we'd last dropped off. Although he was twenty years older than me, we had a similar outlook on life. We had a lot of mutual friends, colleagues and acquaintances. I knew his next-door neighbour; funnily enough his name was Roy as well. Ali's aunty Carol was Roy's local nurse at his GP surgery. His brother-in-law was possibly looking for someone to help with his property business…and I was looking for employment with the knowledge that redundancy was on the horizon. I didn't believe anything would come of it, but it was nice to chat about it.

We spoke about all sorts of things. Roy seemed to have recovered incredibly quickly. It was reassuring to have someone that I could talk to, someone I felt comfortable talking to that had experienced something similar to me. As usual, we were interrupted by the broken fire alarm, and it rang loudly for a good five minutes.

That bell was a fucking nuisance.

The Bizarre and the Ridiculous

I'd just sent a message to Ali to thank her for making the trip to see me and to apologise for me not being good company, when I overheard a conversation between Stefano and Ami to my right. I couldn't see through the curtains that had been drawn around them. I was grateful for that small mercy. I put my phone down and concentrated my right ear nearer to their voices. Roy had gone for a walk. It looked like Dean was asleep. It was just Stefano and Ami, with me listening in.

'Ahhh. That's a very good, Ami. Oh yes,' Stefano groaned with pleasure.

'Shall I touch you zhere, Pappy?' Ami seemed well on board with the game and was back to the whole *Pappy and Ami* conversation.

'Mais oui, mais oui,' the Italian sent out his encouragement in French.

Both voices stopped.

They must have been concentrating on something between them.

I could make out the rustle of bedsheets or clothing as they were being shifted about. I couldn't help but think there was something sexual going on a few feet from me.

Stefano broke the silence. 'Oh, Ami. C'est bon.'

'You are get-tin *very* excite-tid, Pappy,' Ami whispered loud enough for me to hear.

'Hmm,' he grunted in reply.

After another uncomfortable pause, Ami whispered something I could hardly believe.

'Pappy, I cannot get on ze bed, shall I use my mouth?'

What the hell was going on?

'Hmmm, yes,' was the pre-orgasmic yelp from Stefano.

Then more silence.

The nosy (slightly perverse) bastard within me wanted to know exactly what was going on. The angelic (slightly offended) person within me wanted the busted fire alarm to go off, or any interruption to break the spell. If I had owned some headphones, I wondered if I would have used them or not.

I heard Stefano's breathing. It got a fair bit louder, and it sounded like he'd been for a run. No run though, he was still flat on his back.

I couldn't hear Ami, but I couldn't help but detect a wet sort of clicking sound. It persisted at a steady rhythm.

It was the unmistakable sounds of a blow job.

Oh my God. In a hospital? An actual blow job? Jesus Christ, I thought I'd heard it all.

I thanked God above that my stomach was empty. My brain could not be stopped from conjuring up a mental image of the two of them engaging in oral sex. Ami was a big, strong African woman, possibly approaching 40 years old, and Stefano was a cross between Danny De Vito and Berlusconi. The scene on the other side of the flimsy curtain would have made for an extremely niche search on Pornhub.

It was difficult to gauge exactly how long Ami pleasured her patient.

The sounds of moist clicks and slurps were accompanied by heavy breathing. I did my best to be incredibly still. Both Stefano and I lay there, on our backs, for a good three or four minutes. The difference was that one of us wanted it to last forever and the other wanted it to end immediately.

As a finale, Stefano mumbled something quietly, that I couldn't quite make out. I was grateful that his orgasm was not one of the scream-inducing variants.

It sounded like Ami was on the move. 'Iz zat all better now, Pappy?'

'Mmm. Si, Si. Much better.'

'Let's clean you up.'

'Si, grazie.' Stefano hadn't forgotten his manners as the sounds of fabric being rubbed on fabric told me that the evidence of their tryst was being removed from the scene.

'Your-a money – it is-a under the fan, mon cher,' he said in a husky voice.

It made a little bit more sense to me. Payment from the pervy old guy. I wondered how much their agreed contract was, and I also wondered how long the weird, and quite frankly obscene, arrangement had gone on for.

'Zank you, Pappy!' Ami's manners were equally impeccable. 'I will check on you later, Pappy.'

'Yes,' said Stefano. 'See you later.'

I heard Ami leave. She opened the curtains up, so the Italian was exposed to the rest of the world. I couldn't even look over at him. I did my best to understand why they had done what they had. They both sounded so consensual. I guessed that Ami desperately needed the extra cash as much as Stefano desperately needed a blow job.

I stuck my nose into my book and kept myself to myself. Was I supposed to tell someone? I thought that the conversation might be too embarrassing. My toes were not built to take that amount of curling. Anyway, as much as I was sure what had happened, I hadn't actually *seen* anything.

I made a decision to keep the sordid business to myself; after all, there had been more than enough whistleblowing, so to speak, for one afternoon.

Half-way through reading a chapter, a new sensation had stirred within me. I needed a wee. Since the operation, the catheter had worked its magic, and I hadn't even had to think about a full bladder. But I felt the familiar ache caused by a bladder that bulged and demanded to be emptied. Dr Haji hadn't reconnected my plumbing exactly how it had been. It all *looked* OK down there, but the urine was not flowing freely like it should have been. I didn't think it was a psychological problem, although there was a possibility that I'd tensed up all the muscles that controlled my toilet business since the tube had been torn out from me. The more I thought about it, the more I needed a wee. It was not a case of getting up and going to the toilet, because I was tubed up, and a normal piss was off the menu. The longer I procrastinated, the more I needed a wee. Suddenly the situation got to the point of me becoming desperate to go. It was a new experience for me. I realised that I had to, somehow, consciously piss into a catheter.

It felt so unnatural, to be laid flat on a bed and to relax enough of my pelvic muscles to pass water. I was worried about two things, and they prevented me from just going for it. Firstly, I was concerned about the potential mess. If the bloody contraption wasn't working properly, who was to say that it wouldn't just leak, or come loose? I'd have been mortified if I had to tell the nurses that I'd pissed myself and needed another wash. I accepted that it wouldn't have been my fault, but I was the only one that knew that the catheter wasn't working. The other reason I couldn't simply let go was the fear of pain. I didn't know enough about the mechanics of the tube and what could have possibly gone wrong to prevent it from working properly. Would the action of urinating dislodge the already compromised tube or connecting parts? The stress made me heat up again. Shit, nothing was easy.

My situation was ridiculous.

Just bloody go, I told myself.

Talk about over-thinking. In preparation I made sure the tube that came out from my penis was as straight as possible, it then had a nice smooth curve over my left thigh and down towards the bag that hung onto the side of the bed. I had my gown on, but I pulled down my pants to fool my bladder into believing that it was a perfectly normal wee.

I went for it.

Then stopped. I wasn't sure how or why I stopped. Normally, once I started, that was it. For every other time in my life, when the floodgates opened, they stayed open.

No pain though. No piss either.

A bit more concentration was needed. As Yoda said, 'Do, or Do Not – There is No Try.'

I went for it again. I focussed completely on the task at hand. I looked up to the ceiling, and relaxed as much as I could.

Ahhh, yes! It worked.

Blissful relief started deep within my bladder and washed its way through and out of me. It took a bit of a push, but I managed to force the piss out of me. I had to get the pressure just right. I started off gently and became bolder as I sensed the urine flow. I felt a different and unusual tension around my lower belly, but there was no pain, so I pushed a little harder. I looked down and was relieved to see, and feel, dryness. I could see my amber piss fill the tube across my thigh. I maintained the force and emptied myself as much as I could. Going to the toilet had been exhausting. I'd started to sweat again.

I gave myself a metaphorical pat on the back. It had been the toughest, most stressful piss I could ever remember.

I'd been given some more attention. A nurse (not Ami) had taken my blood pressure, oxygen level, and temperature. Despite overheating from my wee, my internal temperature seemed to have come back down to a safe level. However, that didn't stop the nurse from ramming a Covid test swab down the back of my throat. Once again, I wondered how long I could keep my Covid-negative status.

Another nurse came by to give me new bags of clear liquids to enjoy. I lay there and let her go about her business. I didn't mention about my concerns about the efficiency of the catheter. I thought that, maybe, I had sorted it out by forcing that wee through it. Yeah, maybe.

My appetite hadn't returned. It was a strange situation where I wanted to eat but I just didn't feel hungry. I wanted to comply with Mr Chai's plans for me, so when my evening meal turned up, I struggled through it. A soft white roll accompanied the chicken and mushroom soup. The viscosity of the soup was somewhat different from the watery consistency I'd become used to. I'd been presented with a soup that was gelatinous to the point of being thick and gloopy. I needed plenty of water to help wash it down. It was strange that my stomach felt full so quickly. It behaved like it had been damaged even though, as far as I knew, it hadn't been touched during my surgery. I hadn't been warned about how my eating would go post-op. I thought that it should have been discussed, just so that I didn't stress about it. I had a small pot of vanilla ice cream to help take the taste of earthy mushrooms away. It half-worked. I was left with a taste of vanilla-flavoured earth.

Changeover between the nurses had happened and I hadn't even noticed. I must have dozed off after my meal because usually I could hear the teams as they discussed all their patients. It meant Lukas was back on the ward. He came to see me, and he refreshed my drips. The day before wasn't just a one-off, he still seemed ominous to me. I did my best to be friendly with him, and I tried to fit in with his sense of humour, but it wasn't easy. I felt that most of his jokes were a bit of a pop at me. Most of the time I would have been happy to be the butt of the odd joke or two, it was acceptable if it came from someone I knew well. I gave him the benefit of the doubt as I guessed he might have thought I was 'up for it' when it came to light-hearted small talk. It was just a general feeling and although his comments weren't that memorable, they were just a bit diggy. Too much of what he said to me were 'put-downs'.

I tried to like Lukas, but it was a struggle. He seemed to have a normal nurse/patient relationship with the other guys. Their conversations were brief and to the point. I always felt he was too curious about my life. There were too many questions that he shouldn't have asked. Maybe I should have nipped it all in the bud early. Except, I was a little bit scared of him. He liked playing doctors and nurses (for real) a little bit too much. I was totally in his hands throughout each nightshift, and it bothered me that he could inject anything into me. I hated the way I felt so vulnerable when I was in his care.

Dean had finally stopped his perpetual boring phone conversation. He was up on his feet. I had never seen him out of his bed before. Although the curtain between my bed and Stefano's was half-drawn, I saw diagonally into Dean's area. He stood about two feet away from his bed and Lukas was there, next to him. I could tell something was up because the tone of their conversation was different. It seemed weird as they were clearly trying to whisper, and at the same time, doing their best to seem like they weren't whispering at all to whoever might see them. Nothing could intrigue a nosy eavesdropper like me more than people whispering. I could just tell that they weren't being quiet for the sake of other patients, no, this seemed secretive.

I pretended that I wasn't the faintest bit interested. I turned away and closed my eyes. What they didn't know was that I had concentrated all my listening abilities to just them; all other noises had been shut out. For a split second I was worried that I might become witness again to another sexual encounter, but I soon discovered it was a conversation about drugs. Despite my intense efforts, I couldn't make out everything, but I sure as hell heard enough.

Boring Dean:	*(indistinct mumble)*
Lukas:	*...Yah. It iz very pure...the opiate...very effective.*
Boring Dean:	*(Indistinct mumble)*
Lukas:	*...So...vhich do you vant? Or do you vant both?*
Boring Dean:	*(indistinct mumble)*
Lukas:	*...Goot, goot. The opiate iz so goot. You von't regret it...*
Boring Dean:	*(Indistinct mumble)*
Lukas:	*...Yah. Ve can get as much as you vant, my friend...*
Boring Dean:	*(Indistinct mumble)*
Lukas:	*...Ze price? Zat depends on ze size of your order...*
Boring Dean:	*(Indistinct mumble)*
Lukas:	*...Goot, goot. I'll get zat all confirmed tonight...*
Boring Dean:	*(Indistinct mumble)*
Lukas:	*...No. Cash only...*
Boring Dean:	*(Indistinct mumble)*
Lukas:	*...OK. See you later...*

As I sensed the conversation end, I opened my eyes and moved to see Lukas turn and leave the bay. He headed back into the corridor and went right. I saw Dean get back into bed; he pulled the sheets over himself and within ten seconds was back on the phone to his girlfriend.

I was shell-shocked.

Completely stunned.

I found it hard to compute what I'd witnessed. I tried to dismiss the scene as a misunderstanding or a simple misinterpretation. I hadn't heard what Dean had said, but Lukas' words helped me fill in the blanks. Except my blanks were all sensational drug-dealing conspiracy blanks. I had no idea of the size of the problem. It was possible that Dean wanted an extra packet of pills for him or 'a friend', or maybe they had spoken about several kilos that were worth millions on the street.

I'd barely got over the Ami-Stefano situation and now I had a Lukas-Boring Dean issue to kick around in my knackered brain. Hammersmith Hospital seemed to be all Sex, Drugs, and Rock 'n' Roll – without any Rock 'n' Roll whatsoever.

Once again, I was faced with something serious that I couldn't talk to any authority about. I felt like I had plenty of first-hand evidence to satisfy *myself* that there was wrongdoing going on, but I doubted anyone else there would believe me. Had all that type of shit been going on forever? How naïve was I? I lay there feeling even more vulnerable, and lonely. What sort of people were looking after me? Had everyone got so desperate that they needed to resort to criminal activity to support themselves? I didn't want to go to sleep; I had an urge to see how things developed, and to see if I was going to witness anything else. I considered writing notes into my mobile, but quickly dismissed the idea as I thought that might not be a great idea if someone (a bad someone) found out about it.

How the fuck did I manage to get myself mixed up in such a horrible situation?

No matter how I replayed the conversation in my head, I couldn't shake the feeling that they had been arranging something they shouldn't have. Why the hushed tones and the mumbling? No, it was beyond suspicious, it sounded outrageously illegal to me. They weren't exchanging tips on their version of a spaghetti Bolognese. Opiate had been the key word. I was sure that Lukas had said it at least once.

Opiate meant Opium, which meant heroin. Just the thought of what they had spoken about scared the shit out of me, and it made me even more frantic to get the hell out of there.

I found it almost impossible to take my thoughts away from the disturbing things I'd heard. If I'd dwelled on all the bad shit happening around me, I think I would have gone crazy. I was tired, yet I refused to be overwhelmed by it all. I dug deep and thought back to times when positivity had helped me through.

I remembered the time, just three months prior, when I'd only just been told about the pancreatic tumour that had steadily grown to its frightening size. It was a Thursday, the day after I'd got back home from that first hospital stay, and I was taking the rest of the week off from work. I was up at my usual time, got washed and dressed, had a bowl of porridge, and then continued to get in Ali's way as she got ready to leave for work. Just as she'd gathered her bag and phone, I began to cry. It was the weirdest cry of my life.

At that time, I didn't know anything about the tumour other than its presence. I'd presumed it meant pancreatic cancer and the outlook for me was months rather than years. The tears were weird because they were genuinely happy ones. Ali saw me cry and smile in equal measure and it confused us both. I explained that I wasn't sad. I said that I was incredibly grateful for my fabulous life. Everything had been so fantastic, especially with Ali and the children. I could not have asked for anything more. In every sense, I was happy to go. I wasn't scared of death. I'd accepted my fate, and it made me cherish and value every last second I would be blessed with. I didn't think, *why me?* I wasn't plagued with any regrets or remorse. I stood there, a content and complete man, who was eternally grateful for all the wonderful memories and moments I'd experienced in my fifty years. I never found out where it came from, but the positivity that blossomed within me was ridiculous. I was so lucky that my thoughts went that way, rather than forcing me into a manic-depressive state. That would not have helped any of us. After a long cuddle, Ali went to work emotionally charged, thinking her husband had lost his marbles.

Despite a greater sense of apprehension about Lukas, I needed his help. My problem was that I didn't seem to have mastered the catheter after all. I thought I'd cracked it, but being prostrate was not the future for me. I had it in my head that I needed the help of gravity.

When Lukas came over and flushed through my cannula in his forceful manner, I asked him if he could help me go for a walk. He was more than happy to oblige. He couldn't get me up quick enough. He loved to show off his strength, and more than that, I think he loved the physical contact with me. We had a nice little technique worked out. He offered his meaty forearm; I accepted it, and we gripped each other's left arms at the elbow. He would pull me upright and then I'd soon be able to swing my legs around and using both my arms, I could help position my body to the edge of the bed and then get my weight onto my feet.

Once up, with Lukas acting as tube and bag holder, we shuffled past Stefano and Dean to the bay entrance. That is when I asked him to stop.

He waited next to me.

'I'm going to try and have a wee,' I said.

'Really? Here? Iz your catheter not vorking?'

'It is sort of. I just need to concentrate.'

'OK,' Lukas said, and he kept quiet whilst I focused on the job at hand.

I was right. Being upright made it easier for me. I still had to force the urine out, but at least it came out. We both marvelled as we watched the amber liquid move into the tube and trickle into the bag that Lukas held. It was a relatively long and satisfying piss. After our strangely intimate rendezvous, we headed back to my corner and Lukas helped me climb into bed.

After I'd emptied my bladder, I had a little morphine shot and felt comfortable enough to drift off. It wasn't a proper sleep, and I was disturbed by Lukas and Stefano as they were talking next to me. Once again, I felt like their voices were trying to be deliberately quiet. Not just out of respect for patients that were trying to rest, but there was more to it than that. I became immediately alert. Just like before, I had a sense that I needed to be switched on to the slightest thing. I'd just managed to calm myself down from all the evening commotion, only to find myself back in the thick of it again.

As I picked up more of their conversation, I realised that Lukas and Stefano had been talking about me. Once I'd discovered that, I had to instantly replay their words back to myself.

It was serious shit.

I heard Lukas say, 'No. Zey are only giving ze new stuff to *him*.'

But just the sneaky manner in how they were talking, and the way he said '*him*' – I just knew that the '*him*' was me.

I replayed as much as I could...

Stefano:	'And-a, iz it much stronger?'
Lukas:	'Ya. Very. Everyone sez so.'
Stefano:	'And-a, are they-a using it here?'
Lukas:	'Oh yah. Started ziz veek.'
Stefano:	'And-a, are we all on it now?'
Lukas:	'No. Zey are only giving ze new stuff to him.'

His words were spoken more quietly, but I still heard him. Stefano attempted to keep his volume down as well. He failed just as miserably.

Stefano:	'Oh. I see. I take it he-a doesn't know.'
Lukas:	'No. Of course not. Shush, say noth-zink more.'

Stefano did as he was told. If he had said anything more, I couldn't hear him. I did hear Lukas walk away – and I was left to, once again, process what I'd heard.

Fucking Hell. I felt I was in Hell. Hell could easily be something like that place. Somewhere I believed I was safe, but ever-so-slowly, my sanity had been tested bit by bit. Everyone had their limit, and I thought that I had finally reached mine.

There were versions of Hell that terrified me. The ancient one written about in the Bible never bothered me. I'd always considered an eternity in Heaven to be just as psychologically maddening as an eternity in Hell. Eternity was a long time. It was too long. Who on earth wanted to live forever? Everyone should be forced to watch Groundhog Day because it wasn't all laughs. Most people wouldn't get their heads around how long a million years truly was. People say, 'Oh, never in a million years!' and my slightly autistic brain would speak up with – do you know how long that actually is? I can't imagine how shit it would be to exist forever. It might be a strange thing to say, but death (and nothingness) didn't scare me, yet ever-lasting life did.

Whilst I endured hospital, I feared the versions of Hell conjured up by the makers of *Jacob's Ladder*, with haunting images of blood splattered on white tiled walls and unidentifiable body parts strewn on the floor. The only Tom Cruise film I've ever rated was *Born on The Fourth Of July*, the hospital scenes in that movie after he was shot were horrific and incredibly stressful to watch. Hell, for me, would look something like those hospitals where terror and pain were endless.

As I lay there, I felt so awake, and everything had seemed so real, but I questioned my sanity and, for a short while, considered that maybe I had died on that operating table after all. Was it not possible that I'd entered a world that was real to me because my brain told me so? Had my brain simply been shutting down? All the shit that I'd experienced, one dramatic thing after another, was either me experiencing death or, best case, I was in a coma.

If I wasn't dead, or rigged up to machinery in ICU, then it meant that I had actually been turned into a guinea pig. People in white coats were testing out a new drug on me. Whichever way I sliced it up, I was in serious shit.

And still the mindfuck continued further.

I couldn't believe I was dead or was dying someplace far away. I knew I hadn't suffered a series of lucid dreams, and I had experienced what an hallucination was like, so I had to assume everything was real. However, just like the Ami-Stefano Blow Job, and the Dean-Lukas Drug Deal, I had nowhere to go, and I had nobody to confide in. Ali was miles away and it seemed that all the staff were in on the big Phil Experiment. There was only one hope left for me.

Roy had returned from the TV room, or wherever he'd spent the previous hour. I was worried that once I'd started to spill my guts, he would think I'd gone stark raving mad.

That was the fourth option, and it wasn't beyond the realms of plausibility that I had gone absolutely, bat-shit crazy.

Once I'd decided not to suffer in silence, Roy seemed to be my only salvation. We'd got on so well and he seemed such a straight-up decent man that if anyone could help me, it would be him. I did have a niggling doubt since Bollocking-gate, when I was certain that he'd had a go at the staff that had been caught laughing. I still hadn't accepted that it wasn't Roy. It may have occurred a few hours prior, but so much had happened since then that it felt like a long time ago. I didn't feel quite so ill (or out of it) as I did back then, so I thought that an approach to Roy would be the right thing to do.

I looked over, but Roy didn't notice. He remained in his chair and read his book. After a while, I thought he'd never look over. I wasn't going to call out. I waited, and eventually he did put his book down and saw that I was staring back at him.

'Are you OK?' Roy asked, probably because I'd not looked away.

'Not really.'

'Oh?'

I beckoned Roy over with a couple of come-over-here waves. It would be a real effort for me to get up on my own, and I wasn't going to shout out my worries to all and sundry.

Roy came over. 'What's up? Are you alright?'

'Yeah, yeah. I think I'm OK, it's everyone else,' I whispered, and it forced Roy to come close to me.

Roy scoffed; he must have thought I was having a little joke, as people do.

I took a couple of seconds and a gulp because I wasn't sure how to start. 'Have you seen all the strange things going on here?'

'How do you mean?' Roy was quick to realise that I wasn't joking, so he joined my serious mood.

'All sorts of things. Lukas for starters. They've got some sort of drug thing going on here.' I was aware that I spoke with the same hushed tones that everyone else had been. Also, I had started to ramble and was probably not making much sense, but I couldn't help myself.

'Stefano. He's got some perverted arrangement with the nurses. It's awful. I don't know what to do. Do you know about any of this? This might sound crazy, but I think they're testing out a new drug on me.'

'What?' Roy drew away from me.

I thought I must have freaked him out.

'This place doesn't feel safe, Roy.' I wanted to ask him to look out for me, and I'd do the same for him.

'I would've thought you could have worked it out by now,' Roy said, totally deadpan.

Time paused for a brief moment.

Roy looked at me, exactly like he had done when he mind-fucked me earlier.

Our chat had spiralled into the Twilight Zone again. There was something to work out? What? I mean, there was serious shit happening all over the place, but I'd only just realised it – I hadn't had any time to understand any reason behind it.

'Worked what out?' I asked, but I sounded weak and pathetic.

'Money.'

'What...?' I hadn't expected a one-word answer.

'All of this, Phil,' Roy gestured with his hands to offer everything in the ward for my consideration, whilst he maintained eye contact with me. 'You do appreciate that the NHS is bankrupt? We are in desperate times, Phil. Desperate times. People have been forced to do almost anything just to put food on the table. Don't be so naïve.'

I had sought sympathy. What I got was a lecture.

Roy continued to surprise me. 'If there wasn't an injection of money here, *private* money, the whole thing falls down. The cost of *everything* here is extortionate. You got your operation for free, Phil. Think about that. Lucky for you, there are some very wealthy people that have a dark side to them.'

I struggled to keep up. Roy's words weren't fast at all, he was calm and steady, but every sentence was so weighty that I could have done with a pause between each one to process what he'd said. Each sentence required its own Q&A session. Wealthy people with a dark side? Where the fuck was this headed?

'You appreciate that everyone is different,' Roy said as a statement. 'We all have different wants and needs. What I'm trying to say is that there are some people that are prepared to pay a lot of money to receive the same level of care and attention that you have had.'

I did my best to catch up. I think I may have stopped breathing out of shock. My mouth was open, in anticipation of the restart of my breathing. Either that or my jaw stayed open because I'd worked out the clues Roy had given me.

It seemed that Roy knew about all the unbelievable scandalous events that went on and, even more worryingly, he appeared to accept the situation and was happy to justify it. It sounded like he knew about a weird underground movement where people paid a fortune to play an extreme adult version of *Doctors and Nurses*.

Naïve? I was glad to be ignorant of that sort of shit. I guessed if there were people that were deranged and sick enough to rape and kill, then anything was possible.

The revelation had put me in a spin. Was Boring Dean not ill at all and was just there to broker drug deals? Was Stefano just there to satisfy his sexual kinks? Surely Roy had been genuinely sick, because nobody could fake a bucket load of puked-up blood like he'd blasted out when I'd first arrived. Were all the staff in on the charade? So many questions; I didn't know where to begin.

'Are you joking with me?' I asked, with the slim hope that everything might return to boring normality if the answer was a positive one.

'No.'

We had a moment of staring at each other. I tried to determine if one of us was insane. I concluded that there was every chance that we both were.

Then Roy said something that blew me away. The mother of all mind-fucks.

'Think about it, Phil. How else could I have afforded to retire at 57?'

His words slapped me across my dumb face. It felt like all the outrageous behaviour I'd witnessed had suddenly became clear. My dead-turbot impression might have suggested otherwise, but all my activity had been in my brain, so the synapses that controlled my facial muscles had left their usual posts to join in with the main event.

Roy broke our eye contact, turned, and left me with my vacant expression. I watched him calmly return to his armchair. Light the blue touch paper and retire.

I understood everything, and yet, I couldn't believe anything either.

From that brief exchange, Roy had destroyed the straight-up, average nice-guy image that I had truly warmed to and genuinely liked. Within a minute he had become a money-obsessed, corrupted baron of pure evil. He'd spoken of all the wonderful holidays and city breaks he and his wife had enjoyed since his *retirement*. I tried to work out how long he had recklessly exploited desperate people. Talk about looks being deceiving. When it came to our outlooks on life, we had seemed so alike. I wondered what could have possibly happened to him so that he had ended up profiting from such a depraved underworld. We'd been made redundant together at the end of the eighties, but had such a stressful event actually turned him into a bitter and twisted criminal? Did sweet Grace know about his involvement with such criminal activity?

Rather than feeling sympathy for the countless victims that had been left in the riptide of Roy's perverse empire, I selfishly thought of myself. I'd never felt so lonely, or so defenceless and weak. Now that I knew everything (Christ – there couldn't be anything more, could there?) was I in danger?

Shit. I knew way too much already!

It wasn't a question of having seen too much violence on TV or films because the news was full of evil fuckers that would bump off their grandmother to continue living out their playboy lifestyles. They'd remove me from the equation in a heartbeat. And it would be dead easy to do it, I was a sitting duck.

I couldn't call or text Ali – she'd totally freak out and feel even more helpless than I did. I was on my own and I'd never been so frightened in all my life.

I tried to calm myself. I pressed the bolus for some morphine. I lay back and figured that my only escape would be to get well and get strong as soon as I possibly could. I knew it wasn't completely in my own power, but I had to find a way to stay alive. I had no idea what chemicals they were pumping into me. My plan to calm myself hadn't worked at all, and if anything, I had made myself more frantic. My normal calm, placid demeanour had been chewed up and spewed out.

Doctors.

They seemed like the last bastion of sanctuary for me. I played it over in my head and concluded that some of them (Mr Chai for starters) had to be genuine. They couldn't all be crooks on the fiddle. If they *were* experimenting on me, was it so bad? I mean, I seemed to be doing OK. Surely it was in their best interests to get me well, and essentially, keep me alive? They were qualified, trusted professionals. Either that or they were incredible actors.

It had become late. So much had happened within the forty square metres of my bay that I'd lost track of where Saturday evening had marched into Saturday night. Lukas had been stalking the ward for a while and I knew that the usual day staff were gone after handling all the planned operations and procedures. It meant only a skeleton crew of professionals were about to handle emergencies.

I was in the middle of an emergency.

I hadn't thought anything through, but I needed to get help.

I pushed the call button.

There was no big alarm. No song and dance. Just a little pink ceiling light came on between my bed and Roy's. I waited and anyone that saw me might have thought I was perfectly OK, but the truth was that on the inside, I was an anxious and terrified animal.

I might not have thought much through, but I did anticipate that Lukas would be the first to turn up, and if I wanted to get to a doctor, he was the gatekeeper.

I was right, Lukas walked up to my bed. Before he asked me what the problem was, he turned off the alarm light.

The big man leaned over me. 'Vot iz wrong? Iz ev-reezink OK?'

'I need to see a doctor,' I answered as calmly as I could.

'Do you need anuzzer valk, anuzzer pizz?' Lukas' words and tone were an attempt to see if the conversation was going to be like our regular light-hearted banter.

'No. No. I'd just like to see a doctor, please.' I stayed polite. I also stayed serious and intense. I had no physical presence, or at least I had no strength. All I was armed with was my voice and my attitude. I was determined that I would not be denied.

'Vot iz wrong?' Lukas asked for the second time, but he sounded harsh.

'I just don't feel very well.'

'In vot vey?'

'I feel a bit sick, and I can't sleep,' I said. Nothing wrong with half a lie, I mean I *was* sick – sick of being stuck in that fucking hospital bed surrounded by fucking monsters.

'OK. I vill see if ze night doctor can come unt check on you.'

'Thank you, Lukas,' I said to conclude the matter and I watched him leave. I was so frazzled that I had no idea if he was off to get me a doctor, or not.

Twenty long minutes went by. All seemed quiet with no further incidents. I was grateful for that. Roy had gone to bed and, from where I could see, he'd fallen asleep straight away. I think my other two campmates were also asleep because they'd been practically silent. Just Lukas and I remained. He came by to take the usual observations and said that he had passed on the message. He said it might take a while because there was only one guy covering the Saturday night shift.

Due to the sheer uncertainty, I had a picture in my head of the true story of Frank Abagnale in the Leonardo Di Caprio film *Catch Me If You Can*. At one point he faked it as a doctor and started off by taking the night-time shift on a quiet ward. His plan went smoothly until, inevitably, a patient needed help in the middle of the night, and he was called into action. I wondered if there even was a doctor. If there was, I don't think for one minute that they would have expected to hear what I was worried about.

When the doctor turned up on his own, he must have thought I was there because of rabies or I was an escapee from the psychiatric ward. I was rabid and sounded, even to myself, like I had gone insane. He was mid-to-late twenties, olive-skinned and with neatly cropped dark hair, he could easily have had Mediterranean roots. He introduced himself and said he was the doctor responsible for the ward, but I immediately forgot his name. The doctor bent down to hear my frightened plea.

'I'm really scared,' I began. 'I don't know what is going on here, but it isn't right.'

He looked at me. He didn't say anything, and he waited for me to carry on. Which I did.

'I'm worried about the drugs they're giving me. Can you check that they are correct? And...erm...the people here, I don't know...they aren't doing the right things.'

'OK,' he replied, like he was having a chat with a toddler or a geriatric.

'I don't feel safe here.' I didn't want to sing like the proverbial canary, so I tried to stick to the headlines and avoid any details.

'In what way?'

Ami had been so lovely to me, so I did not want to incriminate her and say that she'd sucked a patient's dick for money. Anyway, why would that have had anything to do with me? I didn't give a shit about Lukas; he seemed like bad news. But, if I named him, and it ended up being a game of his word against mine – where would that leave me afterwards? Under his power, that's where.

Then there was Roy, the Big Boss. I couldn't implicate him, he was untouchable. If I'd bleated on about Roy and all the horrible atrocities he'd been controlling, then there was every chance I wouldn't make it through the night. Rock and a hard place.

I saw the doctor's brown eyes focus on my wild left eye, then move to my right one, then back again. Somehow, I had to trust the new arrival. I used to be a good judge of people's character, but not anymore. He had kind, intelligent eyes, but what the hell did that count for in my crazy new world?

'I just...don't feel safe,' was my pathetic answer. I didn't have the strength to spill my guts, even if I wanted to.

17 – THE BIZARRE AND THE RIDICULOUS

'OK,' the doctor said sympathetically. 'What would you like me to do for you?'

It was a great question.

I mulled it over for just a few moments. I should have given it minutes and written up a whole list.

'I...just want you...to check up on me...throughout the night. Make sure I'm alive. Make sure I'm safe.'

'Ok. Ok. I can do that for you,' the doctor reassured me.

'Good,' I said as we continued to chase each other's gaze from one eyeball to the other. 'Thank you, doctor.'

'I'll check your medication. Try and get some rest.'

'OK. I'll try. Thanks.'

The doctor (with a name I couldn't remember) left me to stew. I felt a tiny bit better because I had spoken out. I had roped someone into my situation, and it meant that if I was to die in the night, then my death would be on their conscience. Even if they were a baddie, they'd have to feel some remorse, wouldn't they?

Sunday, Please Save Me

Despite it being the most eventful Saturday of my life, I was more wired than weary. I barely slept a wink on that Saturday night. I stirred at every sound or any change in light. I watched Lukas like a hawk whenever he changed a bag or took his obs. Those fuckers weren't going to get me without a fight.

I was proud of myself that I'd made it through the night but there were no more scandals and no more dramas. When the dawn light of Sunday morning started to push through the gaps between the roller blinds, I was overcome with relief. Obviously, I was exhausted, but I'd achieved something incredible. I'd survived.

And that effing doctor never checked on me once. What a wanker. I vowed to make a complaint at the first opportunity. All I had to do was work out if he worked for Mr Chai, Chris Witty, or Roy.

When I say that I was proud of myself because I'd made it through the night, what I was most proud of was that I'd regained my sanity. I'd worked it all out. Nobody would ever know the true extent of the battle that went on inside my brain during that horrible Saturday. Sanity versus insanity.

For such a long time, I had totally lost it.

As I thought back, I considered that it started to go pear-shaped when I was stuck in that chair, sweating my tits off. Or, possibly earlier, when my eyes wouldn't stay focussed. Then, when Ali had come to visit, I seemed to have regained some composure and, although

I might have looked like death-warmed-up, I felt OK and didn't experience any weird or outrageous thoughts. However, once Ali had left, she must have taken my sanity with her because soon after, I'd lost my grip on reality.

I had spent all of Saturday evening and most of the night feeling crazy and utterly paranoid.

It was the paranoia that came close to finishing me off. Luckily, just when I was at my most desperate, I managed to take a step back and unlock the truth.

I'd experienced manic paranoia like it once before.

Many years ago, I was at Sean and Donna's fancy dress party at their local village hall. With a hero and villain theme, I dressed up as Captain Hook with a huge hat and Ali went as Dorothy from the Wizard of Oz. To spice up the fun, Panda had baked some delicious cakes, and I made a poor decision to start tucking into them. They were Space Cakes, generously laced with cannabis and within half an hour, I became a raging lunatic.

Back then I realised that I was in big trouble, so I searched out two seasoned party animals to, hopefully, talk me down. GaryMan and Matt were best qualified to anchor me back to terra firma.

GaryMan thought it was hilarious, and because he was as equally bollocksed as me, said, 'Hey, Phil. Just because you're paranoid, it doesn't mean that they're not out to get you.' Then he pointed out a couple of people in a far-off corner of the hall and added, 'Those people over there. They're talking about you. And about how fucked you are.'

It was a strange state of mind to be stuck in. I knew why GaryMan laughed at his own joke because I could tell that it was funny. But the madness overpowered the rational part of my brain. Fortunately, Matt was far more sympathetic, and he succeeded to talk me down and stayed with me until enough time lapsed for the THC to wear itself out. After a while, I could join in with GaryMan and laugh about it, but at the time, I was in bits.

That old reckless experience helped me with my Hammersmith House of Horror ordeal.

I'd recognised the anxiety, the madness, and the different way my mind worked. I didn't have my good friends to help me (or laugh at me), but once I'd managed to question the reality of my predicament, the illusion started to crack.

It must have been the morphine. That formidable opiate-based painkiller. I had gorged on it to the max. The bolus had a built-in automatic delay to stop me overdosing, but throughout the day I'd waited and watched intently and had pushed that button the instant the green light came back on. I realised that I had drugged myself to the absolute limit.

I'd mastered the physical pain aspect of my recovery, but by overcompensating, I'd done so at the expense of my mental well-being.

I wrestled internally with myself in those early hours of Sunday morning. All those outrageous events must have been distorted by my drugged-up brain. I looked over at Roy as he slept. Sweet, innocent, gentle, and kind Roy. He *had* come over to see me before I slept, but he couldn't have said those awful things to me. I wondered what he had *really* said.

I still wouldn't have put it past Stefano, but would Ami have had sex, like I had believed? I never saw anything. My ears – or more likely, my brain – must have concocted a sensationalised version of the sounds that were real. I satisfied myself that she had probably just put some more cream on his sore arse cheeks, like she'd done before. Surely that was far more likely?

Then there was Lukas and his drug deals and experiments on me. As intimidated as I felt, I put all of it down to a complete manic episode. Everything had exploded in a crazy, uncontrollable couple of hours. It seemed logical that EVERYTHING had been distorted.

I'd made it through the night, so that had to be a good sign that my fears of mortal danger had been way over the top. Or so I believed.

My anxiety levels had receded to what I considered normal. I'd abstained from the suggestive lure of the bolus. I made a pact to only call upon the morphine if the physical pain got to be unbearable. After I'd suffered confusion and distress for so long, it had become far more important to stay compos mentis. I could easily handle moderate pain over being terrified.

Even without the intoxication of the bolus boost, I found that I wasn't doing too badly that morning. My ribs, and therefore my breathing, had moved a step in the right direction and had eased. However, my new foe seemed to be phlegm. I was scared to clear my throat and airways in my usual way because of the pain that would accompany a simple cough. I'd developed a weird quarter-cough that I could control, but they were so gently controlled that I needed about four of them to do the job of a proper man-sized cough. It was more of a growl than a cough.

I considered myself extremely lucky that after 72 hours post-op, my chest and abdomen hadn't been fully tested by the random spasms that filled me with dread. I'd avoided sneezes, coughs, and hiccups, and unlike Roy, I'd dodged vomiting. Most notably, despite being sent some hilarious WhatsApp messages from the guys, I'd also managed to contain my laughter. I'd normally be in the camp that believed that laughter was the best medicine – well, it was not the case when I'd recently been spliced back together.

I scrolled through some of the ridiculous messages I'd received. They were what I asked for, and they'd be the sort of shit that I would dish out as well. They lifted my spirits in direct proportion to how childish or offensive they were.

> Sean: Have you got a disabled blue badge for your car?

> Panda: Have you had a wank yet?

> Richard: I can categorically tell you that Phil has definitely had a wank.

> GaryMan: Ask one of the nurses for a hand job. If not, Panda will pop by and help out.

> Panda: Soz. I'm in Portugal.

> GaryMan: What drugs are you on today, Phil?

> Me: Morphine yesterday. Could be Ketamine or Meth today.

> GaryMan: You can't beat a bit of crystal. It makes your teeth fall out. Which is much better for sucking off your dealer for a free hit.

I sent a text message to Ali, to let her know I was OK. It was before my breakfast time, so still quite early. I kept it brief; it wasn't the time to type out the magnitude of my craziness since she'd last heard from me.

> Phil: Survived another night x!!x
> Hope this rain stops for you.

It had started as a dreary, rainy day. Not that it affected me because I was confined to the hospital with no chance of parole. From my bed, I saw the ominous dark grey clouds that looked like they were too laden with rain to move on quickly. I felt bad for the girls as their weekend away would have been so much better if the sun was there to brighten up the occasion.

Breakfast was a quiet affair. One Weetabix softened by some full-fat (almost chilled) milk. It was still a strange meal for me. My appetite was not raging like it would have normally been and I still had to take my time as I felt a degree of sensitivity in my stomach. No way would I force it down. I took baby-sized portions from my spoon. Gently does it. The coffee was milky and that suited me just fine. I checked my phone and found that Ali had replied to my texts. She always loved a lie-in that girl, it must have been the earliest she'd been up on a Sunday in years. I guess that was what being at home crapping yourself about your loved one's health was all about.

> Ali: How was it, did you get any good sleep? x
> Not raining here (yet). So much for a lovely weekend hey?!

18 – SUNDAY, PLEASE SAVE ME | 169

> Phil: Bit rubbish - too noisy and getting disturbed every 15 minutes for a test of some sort. Slept some though, so hopefully strong enough to be up and about soon. xx You ok? Wish I was there!

I enjoyed the flurry of messages we sent each other over the hour. It wasn't constant as we both had things to do. I'd moved to my chair and Ali needed to get ready for her trip. I told her that I was giving up on the morphine as if I had some unbreakable habit. She did ask me to explain further when I said that I was treading a thin line between pain and insanity, but I kept it vague and made the decision to tell her another time so she wouldn't worry unnecessarily. It was good to have some normal messages, like I had to forward the Runnymede Hotel confirmation to Ali's email address so she could see (and prove if challenged) that breakfast and their evening meal was included in the deal. I confessed that I still hadn't farted, and Ali was worried for anyone within a mile radius for when I finally managed it. To end the exchange, I told Ali I'd let her know what the doctors' update would be. She seemed satisfied about how I felt, and just like my milky coffee, that suited me just fine.

Mr Chai and his little team of doctors, Haji and Christakis, were still pleased with me. Or so he said.

They didn't hang about for long, and I was OK about that, it was Sunday after all. We covered plenty of issues and I learnt something new.

I asked about my catheter situation. Although Dr Haji had connected me again the day before, I had to tell him that it wasn't exactly perfect. Yes, I could empty my bladder, but it was a bit of an effort. With a vast amount of trepidation, I asked if they could have another go at re-fitting it properly. That got quashed in a heartbeat. In a word – no. That was never going to happen. For starters there was no plan to put me under a general anaesthetic any time soon, and the alternative was to have Dr Haji attempt to force a different tube into my urethra which would be an extremely unpleasant experience for me. He recalled how my enlarged prostate gland had restricted my tube diameter and he recalled that he'd needed to give it some extra welly the first time, to push on through that obstruction.

OK, alright, enough! I decided to put up with how things had evolved in my toilet department.

We agreed to see how things would pan out over the day. Maybe, if I stayed on the path of good recovery, the catheter could be removed soon.

'How soon?' I asked, desperate to get the bloody thing out of me.

'Soon. We're not ready just yet. But soon, OK?' Dr Haji didn't commit to revealing the precise moment in history that I craved.

Ali and I had a friend, Caroline, who had been in and out of hospital. Caroline had messaged Ali several times to see how I was doing. Her advice was to ask how my CBC levels were behaving as this was a good indicator to see if there were any cancer tracers in my blood. At the time I didn't know that CBC simply stood for complete blood count. The problem was that Ali passed on Caroline's advice to me on the day when I'd completely lost my marbles. To compound my confusion further, it was also at a time when my colleague from work, Tony, gave me his advice to get my PSA (Prostate Specific Antigen) levels checked. Not that I was worried about prostate cancer, but at the time I thought a PSA level referred to any cancer.

My question to the specialists ended up being a mash-up of everyone's input. 'Do you know what my PCSA levels are?'

Mr Chai and Dr Haji didn't move.

Dr Christakis, with hands on hips, slightly shook her head and with a bemused look asked, 'PCSA?'

I instantly felt stupid. It was true that I was ignorant of what CBC and PSA actually stood for and I'd essentially asked about a PCSA, which was a construction industry form of contract (Pre-Construction Services Agreement). Maybe my brain had still been a bit mashed.

'Oh, I don't know. I thought these were some sort of test to see how I was doing.'

The men remained indifferent, but Dr Christakis continued with her dismissive look, and she shook her head a little bit more. She looked clueless, like I'd just told her who had won The Derby in 1976.

'Sorry,' I said and rather than getting all hostile and asking them to fill in the blanks and figure out what I had meant (I knew they knew), instead, I asked them if they'd had the biopsy results back from the tumour.

Mr Chai had previously told me that the initial biopsy I'd had a few weeks back was encouraging, insofar as it indicated a low-grade non-aggressive lump. He had followed that positive news with the caveat that he wouldn't know the full character of the lump until it had been removed in its entirety and pathology had sliced it up for full analysis.

The others waited for Mr Chai to answer me.

'No, we won't get the results back for a little while.'

'OK,' I said to all of them. I suspected that I might not know exactly how ill I was until the dealing was done. They'd explained to me that the pathology team would take some time and they wouldn't report back until they were one hundred percent certain of their results. My query was at least a week premature.

Mr Chai waited to see if I was going to say anything more than two syllables. I didn't. Eventually, he asked, 'Was there anything else bothering you?'

'Yes, sort of. My legs seem very swollen. They're not painful, but they are definitely bigger.'

Mr Chai didn't seem overly concerned and offered a reasonable explanation. 'Yes, this sometimes happens after surgery. It is quite common for the cells of the body to react after significant trauma. Surgery, or a car accident perhaps. The cells react and retain water in a state of self-defence. It is your body's natural response that helps recovery. That is why your legs seem swollen. Your blood tests and your urine samples seem normal, so you don't need to worry. We'll monitor the liquids going in and coming out and if you're still uncomfortable we can give you some medicine to help lose some of the water.'

I accepted the information. It was bizarre how my body had behaved. I was fascinated, but I stopped short of asking further questions like; *how much longer would this retention go on for?* Or, *how big will I eventually balloon up to be?*

I nodded to him as I wondered if I should've been warned beforehand of such a possible phenomenon. Maybe there would never be enough time to tell every patient about every possible outcome. I reasoned that we were all on a need-to-know basis.

'We have booked you in for an X-ray later today,' Mr Chai announced.

'An X-ray? What is that for?'

'A chest X-ray. Just to make sure things are exactly as they should be.'

Again, I just took whatever they dished out to me. I was in their hands, and I just had to comply. There wasn't an alternative.

Before they left, I had one more metaphorical itch to scratch. 'One last thing. Sorry, but last night I was really struggling. I got myself in a bit of a state, and I asked for the doctor to come and check on me throughout the night. Maybe he was busy, or there was an emergency or something, because he didn't come and see me at all.'

It wasn't a huge deal, but I was a bit miffed that when I felt at my most vulnerable, the guardian angel I'd called upon never showed up. Good job I hadn't died in the night, otherwise he would've been right in the shit.

Dr Christakis responded first; she seemed to be the one that picked up on complaints. 'Oh, really? OK, we will check on that and see what happened there.'

Her intensity was a bit scary. I guessed the night doctor was younger and therefore junior to her and would probably get a right bollocking. *Accountability, sunshine – you should've popped down at least once.*

Their visit was a punchy one rather than a rushed one. They'd come in, bang-bang-bang, and then left me to enjoy my Sunday. Other than a trip to radiology, they told me to expect a visit from the pain team (oh God no) and one of the nurses would be by to check out my dressing. It wasn't going to be a totally relaxing Sunday after all, but it was all good positive stuff. We parted company on good terms. Sunday morning had started off a million times better than the way Saturday ended.

A Target to Aim For

Two weeks.

I had a massive event to get fit for, and I had a fortnight to get myself ready. I looked down at my mangled body and the practical side of my brain gave me no chance of making it whatsoever. Fortunately, the stubborn, determined side was much louder and, well, more determined. A faint glimmer of hope that I could make it to the Jets game was all I needed to cling to.

I reasoned that if Mr Chai was OK to discharge me within the next week, then I would also be alright to make it to the game the week after. My initial Plan A was already compromised. Firstly, there was no way I would be able to drive there. Unfortunately, public transport was not going to be easy for the crippled person I'd become. Even if I could get Harri to drive us, I'd need to contact someone at the stadium to reserve a dedicated parking space because a long walk was out of the question. Moving about in a vast crowd of eighty thousand people didn't sound appetising at the best of times, but especially intimidating when I knew my movements would be so limited. Then the normally simple feat of getting to my seat, which was high up in the upper tier, was another challenge that might prove to be a bridge too far.

What I needed was to exchange my tickets so that I could sit in the disabled area. It was a credible thought, and I did have access to a wheelchair. There was one in our loft, a leftover from when Harri was ill as a youngster. It sent shudders down my spine whenever I thought back to those dark times, but I'd kept the wheelchair because I was a bit of a hoarder. It had helped us out a few times, so maybe it could be used one last time?

I spent most of Sunday morning on my phone as I frantically searched for contact details to reach Ticketmaster, the Jets, and Tottenham Hotspur Stadium. I emailed and called every organisation I could. I didn't get far. It was Sunday. My calls weren't answered and if they were it was by an automated helpline that was no help whatsoever. I saw that my emails had been sent, but I had no idea as to when they'd be seen or ultimately responded to. No problem for stubborn Phil – I'd try again the next day. And every day from then on until I got the result I wanted. If things got too desperate, I contemplated that I might have to bury my pig-headedness and possibly open up a Twitter account to beg to utter strangers on the internet for their help. When it came to the importance of the game, I was prepared to ditch all my dignity and beg.

I should have resigned to a convalescence period at home that involved doing sweet FA, but I seemed to have parked that idea into its own disabled bay and carried on with the notion that everything would be OK, much to Ali's apprehension.

So that my little dream could come true, I had to remain positive. It was out of my control, but I had to assume I'd be released within a week and that there wouldn't be any complications. Dr Haji had suggested the bags and drains would be removed *soon*, and I kept my fingers crossed for that because I didn't fancy taking bags of piss and pancreatic juice to the game.

Before lunch, Mandy from the pain team came to visit me. She once again apologised for the previous time we'd met. In her Aussie twang, she told me how awful she'd felt, and I told her that I had been totally fine after a minute or two, that she was not to beat herself up about it, and that she had been forgiven for the Bedsheet-Gate scandal.

We spoke about how I had coped with the pain. I confessed to overuse of the morphine and that my plan was to wean myself off it, as if I had been some hardened junkie. Obviously, I would not be able to take an IV drip set-up home with me, so before long they would be feeding me pills to make sure I was comfortable. She suggested two or three drugs that I'd never heard of before. It was a whole new world for me. They were opiate based, which happened to be my favourite, so I was open to any ideas. It would be a case of trial and error, to find out what worked for me and what didn't. I would have said suck it and see, but I knew I wouldn't be sucking anything.

Mandy asked me how the epidural was. I gave her an honest reply and said that I wasn't convinced it had been as effective as it had been. My right-hand side felt alright, but if I was getting twinges and pains it all seemed to come from my left.

She got me to lean forward, and we lifted up my gown so she could get to my spine. She did exactly the same as she did before. She got her head right up close and gently tapped where the needle was, and also just around it. After a little pause, she said that the needle may have moved, she couldn't be too sure. She said I shouldn't worry, she'd monitor the situation, and if things changed, I was to let her, or someone from the team, know immediately. It was tricky to not be nervous when people spoke about matters of the central nervous system.

Whilst we spoke, I had the sensation that I needed a wee. The catheter was broken, or at least it was not draining effortlessly like it had been. I felt it go past the point of *I think I need to go soon*, and had moved swiftly to – *I have to go right now*.

'I'm sorry to ask Mandy, but can you help me get up please?'

'Yeah, sure I can. Are you goin' for a wander?'

'Not exactly. Slightly embarrassing, my catheter isn't working as it should, and I need to stand up to go.'

'Oh, OK. Come on then.' Mandy didn't seem too fazed by the request.

I didn't have time to waste. I performed my bed shuffle and she positioned herself to catch me. It was a weird situation for me, and I wasn't sure how many times she'd been asked to keep a man upright while he took a piss in front of her. As I stood (stooped) before her I left the urine collection bag where it was and clung onto the side of the bed. I needed the physics of the world around me to do me a massive favour. The altitude of my bladder had become a good foot above the height of the bag, so gravity, and whatever syphon effect I could muster, was all on my side.

Mandy continued to speak to me about pain relief, or something or other. I failed to give her any attention as I was only focussed on my connection with the correct sphincter muscles that I had used before. It wasn't natural to call upon those different muscles, but I had mastered it before so I was certain I could do it again. It felt rather like trying to operate three locks along the Grand Union Canal, at the same time, using only the power of telekinesis.

I looked up from the floor and said, 'I'm sorry about this.'

'No, no. Not at all,' Mandy said with genuine sympathy.

I looked back at the floor again; it wasn't the done thing to maintain eye contact with a stranger whilst urinating. I tried to recreate what had worked for me before. I relaxed in some places and tensed up and pushed out in others.

Come on, before your bladder bursts.

I went beyond feeling like an idiot, and I'd gone past the point of worrying what she thought of me. My next destination: Panic City.

Oh. Hang on. That's it. Cracked it. Thank God.

Something unlocked and my bladder emptied. The relief felt magnificent.

'Ah. Finally!' I announced as I exhaled. I hadn't been aware that I'd held my breath whilst I concentrated on the task at hand. I could see the orange-coloured liquid flow through the tube that snaked from under my gown and looped up and into the collection bag. It was a strangely intimate moment for me and Mandy.

Mandy, as chatty as she naturally was, didn't interrupt my flow.

I checked out the bag. It filled at a steady pace.

The wee kept coming. The level in the bag fast approached the top.

My God. It never rained, but it poured.

It had taken a big effort to open the floodgates, and there was no way I could possibly stop what I had started.

Both Mandy and I watched the level of piss continue to rise in the bag.

19 - A TARGET TO AIM FOR | 177

I couldn't judge if we were about to see an overflow situation.

Usually, when it came to the operation of emptying the bag, there was a fancy little door that could be opened and then the bag could be tipped to pour excess liquid into another vessel. I'd witnessed Lukas, Ami, and others do it many times. I figured it was too late to get a nurse to empty it. I wondered what would happen when it reached the top. Would it leak out of the flap, or would the mechanics of the syphon stop and result in a pushback all the way back to my bladder? Would the tube pop out again? Was I about to experience a searing jolt of agony right where I didn't want it?

I felt my flow ease up. It had been an exceptionally long wee, and I calculated that I was down to the last 10% of it. The power behind continued to decrease with every second.

The only problem was that because of the length of tube, there was a bit of a delay in the fluid reaching the bag, so the level in the bag rose higher and higher. It looked more like John Smith's bitter rather than shandy. If I'd been out on the razzle on the Saturday night, I would've said it was the colour of a proper hangover piss.

After what felt like the longest slash I'd had in years, I finally finished up. Fascinated, I watched the bag.

The liquid reached the top of the bag. The tube leading to it was full.

Could it take any more?

Thank the Lord that I was a lucky bastard.

With everything full up to the max, it stopped.

I let out another gasp of relief. 'Phew!'

Mandy looked up from the amazingly full bag and said, 'Are you OK?'

'Yeah, yeah. I am now. Thanks for the help.'

'No worries,' she said.

Mandy helped me get back into bed and made sure I was nicely tucked in and went off in search of Shanice, my weekend nurse, to empty the ridiculously full bag. What I wanted was the catheter out, but they wouldn't do that until all of us were happy that I could use a toilet on my own. The simple task of taking a wee had been an ordeal, and I lay back, exhausted.

Shanice did come by and tipped out a big serving of urine into a measuring vessel. It was all part of monitoring how much liquid went in and how much came out. I took some interest, but the tiredness had got to me, and I let myself drift off into a deliciously comfortable sleep.

On the other side of a satisfying nap, I was served a lunch that was surprisingly pleasant. I never would have thought I'd say that about an egg sandwich, but there we are. It felt like the first substantial food I'd eaten in ages. It felt like that because it was the truth, I hadn't eaten since the previous Wednesday evening, which meant I'd lasted almost four days without a proper meal. Yes, I'd had soup, but I couldn't count that.

I appreciated and enjoyed every morsel. The white bread was soft. The butter wasn't too thick or over-powering, but it was salty and complimented the bread perfectly. The egg seemed incredibly tasty. There was some mayonnaise present and with the black pepper, and the filling simply worked. I didn't wolf it down; I took my time and savoured each small bite. My stomach handled the change-up in the carefully managed diet. It felt good. I had never enjoyed a simple egg mayonnaise sandwich half as much as the one given to me on that Sunday lunchtime.

I welcomed the idea of a change of dressing. I hadn't wanted anyone to go near my belly since the operation, but I also appreciated that the dressings had a limited time before they needed replacement. As I'd suspected, they'd left me well alone for the first 48 hours so that the wound had a chance to knit together. The waterproof polythene cover had done a great job to keep the dressing from getting wet and there was no way through for bacteria or other nasties to start up an infection. But I could see enough dried blood where the incisions had crossed, and the adhesive power of the covering was failing. If the initial protection wasn't removed soon, I knew there'd be a wet, mushy manky mess underneath. It was definitely time for a change.

Shanice arrived in full PPE regalia and with a trolley that had about a dozen drawers in it. On top of it she already had everything she needed, or so it looked to me. There were packets of gauze stacked on top of each other, rolls of bandages, hermetically sealed plastic sheets and strips, surgical tape, scissors, clips, and Christ knows what else that lurked beneath the pile.

Shanice closed the curtains around us and seemed to be far less stressed than the day before. I could tell from her calmer demeanour, and to be fair to us both, Saturday had been a bad day for us all. I thought it would be best to kick off with an apology, and maybe we could start anew.

'I'm sorry if I came across as rude yesterday.'

Shanice was sweet. Even if she had thought I'd been an absolute drama queen, or an arrogant prick, she didn't show it. 'No, no. Not at all.' Her brown eyes that looked like they were smiling along with her mouth that hid under her mask. She sounded convincing, but it could have been a grimace.

'Bad day for me yesterday,' I confessed.

'Yes. You weren't on your own there. Don't worry, how have you been today?'

'Much better thanks. I'm getting there.'

'Good. That's good.'

Shanice then helped me get settled into a comfortable position on the bed. I opened up the gown to expose the area whilst Shanice stood to my left and began to arrange things on her trolley.

I was truly frightened to see my wound. Out of sight was out of mind. Obviously, the big white dressing was an undeniable reminder, but I was ignorant of the ugliness and brutal mutilation that hid underneath. I wasn't mentally ready to see. I wasn't squeamish; it was a case that I had a choice to watch, or not to watch. I looked to my right, although there wasn't much to see apart from the computerised machinery that controlled the morphine for my epidural. I was sure that boring view was a hundred times more appealing than the scene that Shanice was about to see.

Shanice quietly went to work. I felt her pick and tug at the sticky clear covering. I had assumed it would be the ultimate body wax sensation, but when she managed to get a gloved nail under an edge and pulled, it wasn't at all painful. I guessed I'd been saved by a combination of the pre-operation shave and the loss of sensitivity from cut nerve endings. It didn't all come off in one go, and there were a few layers and a bit a patchwork to deal with.

Shanice stripped the area clear. The final act was to gently lift off the blanket of gauze where some rogue fibres had broken out like little fabric fingers that clung on to the sticky liquid skin along the entire length of the wound. I couldn't see it, but I felt it and knew from experience what it was like to pull bandages away from my broken skin. From the edge of my peripheral vision, I saw her bundle up all the dressings and dispose of them in the medical waste bin that was fixed to the side of her trolley. The entire two feet of the incision was exposed to the air.

Shanice turned back to me, and then I heard her gasp. 'Oh!'

I didn't like the sound of that *Oh*.

What I liked even less was that she left me and her trolley behind and took off. She'd brushed around the curtain without saying another word and, I guessed, dashed down the corridor.

She'd left me confused and worried.

What the hell was that all about?

What could she have possibly seen that resulted in such immediate action? I thought her trolley was the equivalent of Batman's utility belt. It had everything on it, all those slender drawers, surely every tool, dressing, lotion and potion she could need for little old me?

It wasn't a question of lack of equipment because it was obvious to me that Shanice had seen something that had instantly triggered her flight reaction.

I considered that maybe I should take a quick peek at the war zone.

It didn't take long to bottle out of that idea. Shanice was able to run away from the horror scene, but I couldn't.

Just how bad was it?

Shanice was young, mid-to-late twenties, but she must have seen worse in her career?

I remained motionless, with my head turned to my right, and contemplated what could possibly have gone wrong.

Out of control infection, maybe early gangrene? Was I bleeding? Had some of the staples broken or opened up? Had an important organ or a clump of tissue begun to poke out? If the flesh had started to rot, surely I would have been able to smell it?

I wondered what the next steps would be for me. A sprint to the operating theatre? A painful re-stitch? More powerful drugs?

I checked myself. I realised that I was panicking and making up scary thoughts. *Stay positive, Phil. Just keep doing what has been working for you.* What had worked for me previously was to not worry about the unknown, and to not go to dark places that didn't need to be visited.

So, I lay there. Quiet and alone. I tried to distance my thoughts from anything related to the exposed gash that had frightened the nurse away.

It wasn't easy. I felt sorry for myself. Why couldn't things be straightforward? My plans for leaving Hammersmith within the week seemed to be at major risk. Forget about recuperation at home with Ali and the children around me, and don't even think about going to the Jets.

The moment got to me. A solitary tear defied my resolve and I felt it trace down my cheek on to my pillow.

Hold it together, Phil. Even if your staples can't.

I had been left alone for at least five minutes. Each minute had ticked by slightly longer than the previous one. I had kept a lid on my emotions, to a degree. Well, there were no more tears. However, in that time, I'd resigned to the fact that I was in a pretty dire state, and it was purely a question of how serious. I didn't think Shanice had gone for as long as ten minutes, but if I was forced to put a tenner on it, I'd bet on seven and a half minutes.

'Sorry about that,' Shanice announced as she casually re-entered my bay.

Stay cool, Phil. Stay cool.

Sometimes the wait could be worse than the actual event. I prayed that that was the case with whatever my event was to be. I was petrified to ask, but not knowing felt worse. I took a leaf out of Ali's book of dealing with serious shit and came out with a Hollywood-or-bust question.

'How bad is it?'

Shanice seemed taken aback with my straightforward approach. 'Sorry?'

'It's just that you took one look at me, and then you ran off without saying anything. I'm assuming it's serious.' I'd craned around to address Shanice with eye contact to show I intended to be told my fate directly. No way would I be fobbed off. I resisted the urge to look down at the damage below my chest.

'Oh. No. Sorry,' Shanice said whilst she patted my arm. 'No. Oh my God, no. Oh, is that what you thought?'

I didn't answer and just maintained eye contact.

Yes, that is what I thought, what else was I supposed to effing well think?

Shanice let out a gasp. 'No. Oh, I am so sorry.'

Sorry about what exactly?

'I just had a really bad coughing and sneezing fit. I could sense it coming. Sorry, I actually couldn't speak as I was trying to hold it all in. I thought it best to get myself away from you rather than spray my germs everywhere.'

I processed the 'It's me - not you' explanation.

By the sounds of it, it had all been a big misunderstanding, and the Grim Reaper's visit had been postponed for yet another day. I wanted to accept her word, but needed clarity before I allowed the sensation of relief to wash through me.

'So, I haven't got some flesh-eating bacterial infection that will kill me off in the next 24 hours?'

Shanice laughed at my question which had been half jokey and half serious. 'Of course not! Is that what you thought?'

'Well, I did wonder. You left me here long enough for me to think some bad thoughts.'

'Oh no. I'm really sorry,' she repeated.

'It's alright, it's not a problem,' I said. At the same time, I allowed relief that had been waiting patiently at the front door, to come in and de-stress my uptight mental condition.

Jesus, that was a close one.

I counselled myself to make sure that in the future, I wouldn't jump to such wild conclusions. If the situation had truly gone catastrophic, I was in the best place in the world, and they would have taken me into theatre or confined me to the Intensive Care Unit. That central line was in place in my neck, and it was ready to be called into action at the drop of a hat.

The rest of Shanice's visit was a success. Not that I watched any of it. I had to assume that she carefully cleaned away the blood, pus, and the breakaway fibres and gunky adhesive from the dressings. It felt good that someone qualified had finally taken a considered look at how the healing process was shaping up. I didn't interrupt the silence as Shanice gently used some antiseptic wipes to make sure the whole area was clear and as sterile as it could be. Then the cover up began. I heard the packets being ripped open. Virgin white dressings were cut to size and softly laid in place. There were a lot of them. I guessed that nurses had to be good at arts and crafts, and equally good at wrapping presents. Shanice had to work her scissors around the sticky waterproof cover so that it was the correct size and shape to hold the dressing in place, with enough border to cling on to my skin. I let her do her magic without commentary, and Shanice cracked it at the first attempt.

'All done,' Shanice announced.

I looked down and was delighted to see the new protection in place. 'Thank you, so much.'

'You're welcome,' she chirped, equally as pleased with her handiwork as I was.

Shanice left me to put my gown back on and drew back the curtains so that I was fully back in the room. It should have been a simple task of changing a bandage, yet I'd managed to put myself through mental torture where I'd condemned myself to a quick, gangrenous death. I wasn't normally quite so neurotic, so I told myself that I might have been tinged with the after-effects of the morphine that had sent me loopy the night before.

Why did everything have to be such a pantomime? I wished for the rest of Sunday to be a calm one. Please can I have an hour (or two, if that isn't pushing my luck) with no drama?

Just when I had settled down and spent thirty minutes on my phone, I suffered a flashback to my Saturday nightmare. It came from nowhere and manifested as a man.

A young doctor, in his mid-twenties, with cropped dark hair came to see me. He didn't shut the curtains. I didn't know his name, but after a moment or two, I recognised him. He was the doctor that had been on night duty throughout my darkest hours on Saturday through to Sunday morning. His next shift must have started up again.

In my most desperate time, he was the man that I had relied upon to check up on me. All I had asked for was for him to check on me and he hadn't shown up once. Luckily for both of us that I had made it through that treacherous night.

He had some explaining to do, so I let him.

'Hello, Philip. How are you today?'

'I'm OK. Much better than when I last saw you.' I hoped there was a good reason why he had never helped me. I wasn't going to let him off the hook until I heard it, so I remained on the border between friendly and civil.

'Good, good. You look much better,' he said with positivity, possibly to cement that there was no issue between us because, as people say, all's well that ends well.

I nodded. 'What happened last night? I thought you were going to check up on me?'

'Ah, yes.' He seemed to be edging towards embarrassment. Maybe Dr Christakis had given him the bollocking I'd predicted. 'You said that I didn't check up on you.'

I paused before confirming that, as far as I was concerned, he hadn't. It looked like the doctor had something more to say, so I let him finish his speech.

'I did come and see you. Four times in fact. You were asleep every time, and you looked so peaceful that I decided to let you sleep.'

I looked at him. He hadn't displayed embarrassment, but instead it was awkwardness. It sounded feasible. With the knowledge that I'd been off my nut, his story sounded far more credible than mine. I shared the awkwardness. I felt bad that I had potentially got him into trouble.

'Oh,' I mumbled. There wasn't much else I could say, so I apologised. 'Sorry.'

It was his turn to nod. 'That's OK.'

'I hope I haven't got you into trouble.'

He didn't reply, so I got the impression that he had been challenged on it but didn't want to make a big deal out of it.

All I could do was apologise again. 'Sorry. And...err...thanks.'

'No problem,' he said firmly.

I got the impression that he wanted us both to end the conclusion to the misunderstanding. I thought that I could offer to speak to his boss and say that I might have accused the young man without any evidence, but it also might be better for him if I just said nothing.

We said our goodbyes and he left me to mull over the situation that I'd caused for him. I did feel guilty, but it wasn't entirely my fault. I truly believed he'd failed to monitor me. Granted, I should have given him the benefit of the doubt, but I was confident that I had barely slept as I believed I'd spent the entire night terrified that my life was in danger. It wasn't anyone else's fault. No doubt it would prove to be the most insignificant blip on that young doctor's career. I made a mental note to not throw people under a bus that were trying to help me.

Away From the Bay

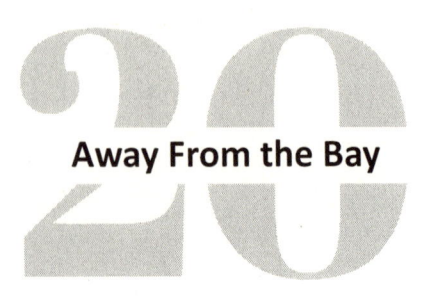

A porter came to take me away for an X-ray.

He was a young Asian man, and he was friendly and helpful. I took my time to climb down from the bed and with the bag of wee and the epidural IV drip as my ever-present attachments, I managed to get into the wheelchair without being tripped or strangled.

Apart from the little waddle I'd performed for the physio team, and the walk I'd had with Lukas to tease out a wee, it was my first proper excursion. The porter trundled me out of the bay. Both Roy and Stefano called out a goodbye, and as expected, I got nothing back from Dean after I called out, 'See ya later!' to all of them.

We carried on past the long reception desk on my left. I noticed that nobody was in attendance. On the opposite sides we drove past a ward, which I assumed was the female equivalent of my bay, because I could see a couple of women in there. There were also a couple of private rooms, and I couldn't resist taking a peep inside as we rolled by. Nothing much to report other than an ancient looking man who was asleep and a gowned woman who stood next to a machine that looked like it might be pumping milk into her via a tube. There seemed to be about ten to twelve patients in the ward. I wondered where I ranked in their hierarchy of illness. They still had Thursday as the exit date on my whiteboard, so I figured, despite all my trials and tribulations, that I must have been one of their non-critical patients.

We entered the lift that I hadn't seen since I went down for surgery on Thursday morning. I couldn't gauge whether it felt like a long, or a short, time had passed. My little hospital existence, my parallel universe, had taken on a time duration of its own.

The porter took us down to the ground floor and after a right turn out of the lobby, we went on a long journey. Radiology seemed miles away, and by the time we arrived, I'd been chugged and jumbled into an uncomfortable position. Not that the porter drove me there carelessly, but it was just a long, exhausting trip.

The porter parked the wheelchair and left me facing three doors that led to individual X-ray rooms. My back was against a big set of windows and glass doors. It was still raining outside, but it felt good to have daylight all around me. The doors to the outside world, my old universe, were just there. Freedom was less than ten feet away. In theory, I could get up and leave. It was a delicious thought. But the bubble burst as soon as it appeared because the bags, drains and tubes were the equivalent of electronic tags. Escape was not going to happen.

The queue for the photo studio was four deep, including me. It felt like the most miserable, sombre queue I'd ever had the misfortune to be a part of. Four wheelchairs, four men, and all looking sad, as though they only had a week and a half left to live. And they were going to spend most of those remaining days in hospital.

The starting line-up for the race for the X-ray machine looked like this:-

Lane One: Chunky Grandad; 11/10 favourite; Top Weight; 80 year-old; well-backed grey due to his advantageous lane draw, and age.

Lane Two: Phil the Powerless; 10/1; 50-year-old; came into the line-up behind Chunky Grandad and Original Rasta, so that horse would be an unfancied outsider to reach the line first.

Lane Three: Original Rasta; 5/2 second favourite; 80-year-old and second favourite because of his inferior lane draw. Looks tired and disinterested in the paddock, although could jump ahead of Chunky Grandad if tiredness was reclassified as an illness. The only one wearing a facemask.

Lane Four: European Handyman; 50/1; last to enter; youngest runner by ten years, looks too well to be considered for a first-place finish. The only reason punters could back him would be because of the bag of urine strapped to his calf.

I couldn't stand the sadness any longer. I turned to my right, to address Chunky Grandad because he looked more alert than Original Rasta. 'Is anyone actually working here today?'

The old boy suddenly sparked into life. 'D'you know what? I was finkin' exactly the same fing!'

He was a proper Londoner. He also sounded like his throat had suffered at least 20 cigarettes a day for most of his life. His swift reply was so friendly and lively that it instantly changed the mood of the waiting area. Encouraged, I continued with the sarcastic and light-hearted tone of our conversation.

'I thought that I'd been wheeled down here because they were ready and waiting for me.'

'No, mate,' my new friend confirmed. 'They brought you dahn 'ere to rot wiv' the rest of us.' He followed his joke up with a mischievous chuckle.

At least, I assumed it was a joke. So I showed a smile. 'Don't say that. How long have you been waiting?'

His chuckles continued. 'Ha-ha. I've only been here for five minutes.' He pointed over to Original Rasta. 'But he's been here for nearly an hour. He's already been seen; he's just waiting for a ride home.'

I turned to my left, but the ancient black gent didn't respond. His eyes didn't want to connect with me. I didn't take offence; it seemed that he didn't want to communicate with anyone. Maybe he was completely pissed off after such a long wait. I would have been fuming, too.

I waited just to see if he was going to join the conversation, but he didn't.

Instead, the Eastern European guy in the next chair piped up. 'Oh, great! If I'd known there was a wait, I would have gone to the toilet.'

He had a catheter, complete with a bag. He had sandy-coloured, cropped hair, and looked like a rugged Polish handyman to me. His accent was strong, but his English was good. He delivered the words in monotone, yet he had a cheeky expression on his face, so I couldn't tell if he was joking or not.

The temptation of a wind-up was irresistible. 'Sorry, mate. We're all going to be ages.'

He nodded back at me. 'Yes, I can see that.'

We smiled at each other.

I was surprised at how quickly the mood in the room had switched. Two minutes before and we had stayed silent in our private bubbles and, as a result, we'd become the most depressed bunch of victims I'd ever been a part of. Then something magical happened. Just the tiniest spark of human interaction had changed everything. All we had done was talk. I had no idea how ill the gang was, but it didn't matter. We discussed how long we had been inside, what we were having X-rayed, and how shit the food was. What was more amazing was that despite our totally different backgrounds we shared the same sense of humour. The conversation flowed between us, although Original Rasta seemed content to just listen to the three of us jabber on – maybe he felt like a fraud as he was the only out-patient. I laughed to myself as I thought about the term gallows humour. That was exactly what we had experienced. If we had been lined up, about to face the hangman, I reckoned that we would have coped with that terrible situation in just the same way.

It made the wait enjoyable. As a self-confessed sociopath and hater of the human plague, it was quite a revelation. Without that spark, it would've been a boring wait that would've felt even longer. Maybe I had got the average person completely wrong.

The doors to radiology finally opened and they wheeled a hospital bed out. There was a frail old man on board; I figured that the team must have been extra careful and taken their time with him. As he was taken away, a young nurse came out with a clipboard to announce the winner of the Sunday X-ray Stakes. There were no shocks, Chunky Grandad was the winner. He celebrated with a little cheer as his name was read out, and I wished him good luck and a speedy recovery. He returned the same message to me. Whilst he was gone, a casually dressed Asian man claimed to be a cab driver for the oldest living

Rastafarian. He held a piece of paper, yet still had no idea where he was supposed to be taking his patient. After we'd heard a few grunted mumbles from the old man, the driver claimed to know precisely where the destination was. I thought it was incredible that there was such a place called Mmoober mmottin mi Mmansin.

With the group whittled down to the final two, I carried on joking with the upbeat Polish man. We compared urine bags, and he told me about how much he had loved having his bag strapped to his leg for almost a month. He said *loved,* but it translated as detested. A month? Christ, I hoped I would be able to ditch my one by the end of the day.

Chunky G's visit to radiology was a quick one. He gave me a thumbs up as he was trundled back to his ward that catered for those suffering from respiratory problems. Off he went, back to reality.

The nurse called out my name before my new European friend. I turned to him, and in an act of silent celebration, I raised my eyebrows and then gave a wink as if to say, 'I've done you, son.'

He responded with a defeated bow of his head and a couple of hand claps to acknowledge that the race was officially over.

As I'd expected, the room did have a big bed situated dead centre. Above it loomed some hefty equipment. On the far side, there was the little glazed booth, which I knew they'd be hiding in when all the harmful radiation started to blast out.

The radiologist came out from behind the screen and as the nurse handed him the clipboard he said, 'Hello.'

I returned the greeting and, when prompted, I confirmed my name and my date of birth.

'We're doing a chest X-ray today, so it would be best if we could get you to stand up over here. Are you OK to stand?'

He had indicated the machine on the side wall. It was familiar to me; I'd had a stand-up X-ray before. I also knew that it would be easier and quicker than if I had to get onto the big bed. My only reservation was that I hadn't successfully managed to stand up completely straight. Oh, hang on – I also had enough metal across my belly to make up a snazzy belt – had that been considered?

'Yes. I'm alright to stand up for you. One question though, I've got a whole load of metal staples in me, is that going to give you a problem?'

'No. It might be different if we were doing an MRI, but we'll be OK today.'

The two of them were a good little team. They wheeled me right up close, so all I had to do was get up and stand. They supported me from both sides and made sure all my tubes were out of the way. I used the muscles in my legs and my arms as much as I could to avoid straining my midriff. It was a smooth transition, and I was pleased that my technique was improving each time. There were handles attached to the sides of the big metal square in front of me and I gratefully made a grab for them. The main guy adjusted the height upwards because, even with my stoop, I seemed to be considerably taller than the previous patient. Once they were satisfied with my position, we were all set, and bang on cue, they dashed off to hide in their bomb-proof kiosk.

The radiographer called out for me to breathe in and to hold it.

I did as I was told. It still hurt to fill my lungs beyond three-quarters capacity. There was a dull ache that got me high up at the top of my rib cage and also my lower ribs reminded me that they were still sore.

I heard more instructions called from behind me. 'And keep your chest pressed against the plate in front of you, please.'

There were no noises, and no flashes, but the call came out that they were all done.

How wonderfully efficient. My previous experience involved at least three or four takes to get a shot that everyone was happy with.

Before I knew it, they'd helped me back into my wheelchair, spun me around and pushed me out of the room to be queued up, again, to wait for my Uber-porter. There was nobody else there, everyone had been done or they were being seen to. Fortunately, my porter only made me wait a couple of minutes and we made the long trip back.

Stefano and Roy welcomed me back. The change of scenery had been a good thing, it had taken me away from the cabin fever I'd suffered and had broken up the afternoon. It had taken a chunk off my sentence. I was a tiny step nearer to recovery, and ultimately, to escape.

Whilst I'd returned to my prison cell, my girls *had* escaped.

Ali and Lydia had arrived at the Runnymede Hotel. After they'd settled into the room, they had got themselves ready and went out to enjoy dinner which was all part of Ali's birthday treat. Lydia shared a picture of their table in the restaurant where there was a spare seat. How I would have loved to have shared that meal with them.

I returned the message, with a picture of me as I scraped the bottom of a pot of strawberry jelly with a plastic spoon. I told them that the jelly was my main course, and my dessert was a Covid test. As the crow flies, we were about thirty miles away. The way I felt, I might as well have been on another planet.

Although I felt sorry for myself, I was delighted that Ali and our daughter were away. They had been under immense stress, sat at home, full of worry and dread over what I was going through. In order to be strong enough to support me, Ali needed her respite.

When they got back to their bedroom, and before they settled down to watch a film whilst they gorged on Maltesers and popcorn, we connected with a video call. As rubbish as my phone battery continued to be, it lasted long enough to enjoy ten minutes of their mini break. Lydia gave me a guided tour of their room. It was a generously sized double room, but she had managed to throw most of her clothes over the bed and floor already. Who needed wardrobes?

It was an uplifting and joyous call. I updated them with my antics for that day, and I told them about my plan for Monday which was to convince the doctors to get all my bloody tubes out of me. They both wanted to know how I was coping, but I didn't want to talk about me. I answered their questions as briefly as I could because I wanted to forget about everything I had been through. They were all smiles and full of love for me. It was a magic moment. I thanked them for being so lovely and happy, and it felt fabulous to share Ali's birthday with them, even if it was from a hospital bed.

They told me that they were about to get themselves into some comfy PJs and snuggle up to watch Godzilla Vs Kong. I wished them good luck with what sounded like the most terrible film choice. I would've loved to have stayed on that call for a lot longer, but the battery life of my phone would not allow it. We said our goodbyes, and I told Ali that I would think of her as the clock struck midnight, as that was when her 50th birthday officially started. We ended the call with a lot of kisses.

It was the best, and most positive, I'd felt about the future since I'd woken up from the darkness of the anaesthetic.

At midnight I had recharged my phone enough to send out a message:-

> Phil: Happy 50th Birthday you incredible woman. Can't wait to give you that kiss and that hug xxx enjoy your special day off xxx

21

A New Week for the Weak

The old-fashioned-style mattress had given me the best night's sleep since I'd arrived. Yes, I had woken up early and had to endure the usual disturbances from Lukas throughout his nightshift, but I felt I'd truly added some percentage points to my health bar. I must have slipped into a deep sleep at some point. There had been a tangible move forward in my recovery. Maybe it was psychological because it was Ali's big day, or possibly just the fact that I could breathe without feeling like my lungs had been repeatedly bayonetted.

Three times that night I'd needed Lukas to help me up, walk to the corridor, have a wee and then return to my bed. Between us, we had worked out the routine and we had it down pat. My relationship with Lukas had softened a little over time. I still couldn't work him out. He kept up his air of arrogance, and I sensed that he looked down on practically everyone around him. I might have been wrong, but I couldn't help but feel he was disgusted by his pathetic patients. He never said anything directly; it was just a feeling. It stopped me from liking him, but I did manage to accept him and work with him because we were a little two-man team with the same aim of fixing me up. I must have been tired because I fell back to sleep without delay in between my Lukas-walks.

Roy was up and about.

His healing process had been even more remarkable than my own. Anyone that didn't know his history would have thought there had been nothing wrong with him. They certainly wouldn't have guessed that four days prior, he'd stared death in the face. By the time I'd stirred he was already washed and dressed, and somehow, his stomach seemed perfectly capable of taking on a reasonably sized breakfast. Not a full English, but he'd ordered some toast and a bowl of cornflakes. He appeared mobile to me. Granted, he wasn't sprinting around, but he was agile enough to get in and out of bed unassisted, and he frequently took himself to the bathroom or the TV room with a steady, confident pace. I was impressed.

Like me, he was on a mission to prove his wellness to the authorities, so he could get the hell out of Dodge.

I gave in my order of Weetabix (banana variant) to the catering lady. She wrote it down and then, after checking her notes, said that I wasn't allowed anything.

'Eh?' I said. 'Are you sure? Why is that?'

She double-checked the notes on her trolley. 'Sorry, I will have to check with the doctors.'

Then she scooted off, presumably to find out if her notes were either current or possibly hadn't been updated with all the superb progress I'd made over the weekend.

Roy must have spotted that I was awake as he called over. 'Morning, Phil.'

'Morning, Roy. How are you this morning? I see you're already up and about.'

'Yes. I'm doing very well, thanks. You?'

'So far, so good,' I replied. 'Although, they've just said that I'm not allowed breakfast.'

'That doesn't sound right. It's probably just an admin thing.'

'It had better be. Unless they're not telling me something.'

Roy tried to reassure me. 'Try not to jump to any conclusions in this place. I'm sure everything is fine. Dr Haji seemed quite happy with you yesterday.'

'Yeah, that's what I thought.'

My mini panic only lasted two minutes. The catering lady was back with a tray. She apologised for the misunderstanding in her broken

English, and I smiled back and said that there was no problem at all. Obviously, the opposite would have been true had she come back empty-handed.

She'd placed the tray on my adjustable trolley-shelf thing and left me to it.

As it was the start of a new week, I'd already made the decision to get positive about my situation. What I had prayed for was to be freed from the bondage of plastic tubes. For that to happen I would need buy-in from the specialists. To get them onside, I needed to do my bit. There wasn't a great deal I could influence, but it seemed possible to achieve a few simple goals.

To get things started I got down from my bed and, after positioning the trolley within reach, I sat in my armchair. Although my mobility had improved, I couldn't help but worry about the continued bloating of my legs and all around my hips and lower back areas. The tops of my red socks looked tight against my expanded ankles. With the catheter being such a problem, was the water retention putting additional stress on my kidneys? That was all I needed, bloody kidney failure. I made a note to ask Mr Chai on his morning visit.

With my worries pushed to one side, I pulled the trolley over to me. I had been given a pill of Omeprazole which was designed to help my stomach accept the slap-up breakfast that I drooled over. I say slap-up; however, in reality, it was a bowl with one biscuit of banana-infused Weetabix lying in a splash of tepid milk, a foil-sealed pot of orange juice, and a cup of tea. Not exactly the Breakfast of Champions, but I was not going to complain.

I took my time. My appetite was different – it had become timid. I knew my stomach was going to take a while to get back to what it could take. At that moment, it was nothing hard, nothing big, and only bland food. I hadn't tested it, but I knew, like a Gremlin, there'd be consequences if I failed to obey the simple rules.

My taste buds seemed to be more active than normal. I took a tentative sip, and they immediately alerted me as the orange juice zinged all over my tongue. I had been starved of anything sweet for such a long time. Fortunately, the more I drank, the less radioactive the vitamin C felt. The tea was a bit weak and milky for me. I gave it 4 out of 10.

With breakfast done, it was all about getting my shit together for when the doctors did their morning rounds. I needed them to see exactly how well I was. I pushed the trolley away and was about to get up when something quite unexpected happened.

I recognised the internal rumblings of a fart.

I'd had experienced many rumblings over the previous few days, but that one was different, it felt lower down. I'd almost forgotten *how* to fart. I tried to concentrate to make sure it didn't go shy on me and shoot back up my colon. God, I desperately needed the trapped gas to escape from the depths of my bowels. In many ways, that little guff was a representation of me and my mission to escape the bowels of Hammersmith Hospital.

I lent to my right and lifted my left butt cheek off the chair.

A quiet, half-fart escaped.

That was good enough for me. It wasn't the spectacular Jaws theme that I'd been expecting, but it was a modest and much-welcome start. The physical relief wasn't completely sated, as I still felt like there was a hell of a lot more gas stored up. Psychologically, it was a relief because there was no pain, and it was great to know that everything in that area of my body had stirred back into life after being redundant for four days. I had an unpleasant history of blowing off the most fowl-smelling farts, but that one, as far as I could tell, was odourless.

Stefano was well aware of my wind constipation. It was our favoured topic of conversation, and he knew how jealous I was of his flatulence. It was finally time to announce that I'd broken the seal. I couldn't see his face because he was partly hidden by the bunched-up curtain divider, but I could tell he was in his bed.

'Stefano? Are you there?'

'Yes-a, ma friend. Are you-a alright?'

'I'm better than alright. I've finally, FINALLY, managed to fart.'

'Did you-a? Maybe I'm a goin' deaf. I didn't 'ear eet.'

'It was a silent one. But it still counts.'

'Well, I'm-a very 'appy for you-a. Bravo, bravo!' Stefano gave me a couple of claps.

I didn't look over at Roy. I guessed he wouldn't have been quite as impressed as our Italian inmate and, undoubtedly, he was far from delighted to know there was another farter in the ward.

My mission to get ready for the rounds continued. I felt well enough to attempt a wash and found that I had a brief window of opportunity in between drip renewal, so was free from the machines that I would have had to otherwise drag with me into the bathroom.

It was never going to be the full Monty. Although my hair was fairly short, it had managed to get greasy enough to make itself known and annoy me. It would be an exaggeration to call it dirty, but after 4 days, I was more than ready for a shower. The strip wash I'd attempted on Saturday had at least helped me feel slightly normal, but other than that I'd been too ill to even contemplate the idea of a full-blown hot shower. Having made a notable improvement since that day, I knew that another freshen-up would do me the power of good. My hair could wait, but my face, armpits, and groin – they could not.

I slowly gathered up a change of pants, trackie bottoms, and a clean T-shirt. I had made the bold decision to ditch the dreaded gown and dress like a normal person. Bollocks to it. I was on the home straight. As much as I knew I was a sick man in recovery, I also knew that I didn't have to play that role. There was nothing that stopped me from acting like everything was A-OK.

It was a tough challenge to move in the first place. It was made harder by the additional luggage allowance that included three fluid bags, a washbag, a towel, and my clothes. The two bags for the drains had always been attached to my gown with the simple but effective scissor clips, so they weren't much of a problem. Bag three, the bag of wee, had to be carried because it was considerably heavier than the juice bags, so that was going to be the final thing as I needed both hands to load myself up. I slung the towel over my shoulder. I considered wearing my joggers to the bathroom, but with the knowledge that I'd have to do a dance to take them straight off again to change my pants, I dismissed the idea. I wedged a clean pair of undercrackers into the pocket of my joggers (good thinking, Phil), but didn't bother with replacement socks as the red ones provided by the hospital were all the rage. I balanced the joggers on my shoulder, on top of the towel, and then I was able to carry my washbag in one hand and my urine bag in the other.

Once I eventually crept my way into the bathroom, I used about a dozen steps more than usual to turn around and locked the door. There was nothing quick about my quick wash - every movement was measured and deliberate. I chuckled to myself as I considered my efforts as doddery as an infirm 90-year-old.

The wet room was designed for patients to have a good splash around under the shower. Unfortunately, I had too much body area that needed to be kept dry for a while longer, so I had to stick with the basin. The task was slightly less clumsy than the wash I'd attempted while stood next to my bed with the washing-up bowl and big paper towels.

I completely stripped and stood on the discarded gown. It wasn't ideal, but I worked up a decent enough lather with some shower gel and warm water from the basin. Face - armpits - groin (including bum crack) all got some treatment. I wasn't soapy for long - I cupped my hands under the mixer tap, and after several sploshes I towelled myself dry.

I brushed my teeth, jabbed contact lenses into my eyes, and gave both armpits a blast of deodorant. The final act was to put on my clean clothes.

It was a great feeling to be stood there, clean and in fresh pants. Washed and dressed, I felt refreshed and ready to take on the world.

Albeit with greasy hair and a stoop.

I returned to my corner and unloaded all my gear. Every slight movement I made had to consider the tubes. I was paranoid about getting them caught or snagged on something. The thought of any of them being yanked unexpectedly shot a chill through me. Coupled with that was the constant threat of a ruptured wound caused by moving about. I was sure that the staples were doing a sound job, but what about the weak points around them? I didn't want to feel fragile, but it was nigh on impossible to forget that I was.

I lowered myself into my armchair as gently as I could. I knew that the doctors would soon arrive. I couldn't have been better prepared.

I checked my phone for messages. The Birthday Girl had sent me her film review.

> Ali: Watched the shittiest film ever. Poor choice. Kong VS Godzilla, utter crap. We could hardly keep our eyes open! Love you, Phil xxx

I chuckled to myself. I mean, who would want to watch such an abomination of a film?

> Phil: Oh well...so much for chick flicks

> Ali: My stupid choice, I thought it would be good. Worst film by a mile!

> Phil: Day 4 at Hotel Hammersmith. They reckon there's a chance epidural and catheter and maybe drains out today - oral pain relief from here on maybe.

> Ali: If that happens, it'll be my birthday wish xx

Our exchange was cut short. The doctors were in town. I put my phone down on the trolley-tray. I sat up and attempted to look fully fit and well. Ali's wish had been multiplied by my own.

They drew the curtains and I noticed there had been a slight change to the Monday line-up.

Mr Chai was there, as was his trusty right-hand-man Dr Haji, but Dr Christakis had been subbed off in favour of a young student doctor. Young Dr Colin Woo was in tow, with a clipboard and he did his best to keep up. He had a friendly face and spoke with a middle-England accent that brimmed with intelligence and an immaculate education. I instantly liked him.

The fourth member of the team was a nurse that was new to me.

Her name was Anika, and her uniform was a deep enough blue to suggest to me that she was more than capable of looking after me. I guessed she had some Eastern European roots, as her name and accent gave that away. She was tall and slim, and she came across as both friendly and efficient. I warmed to both the new recruits.

Mr Chai began proceedings in his usual positive way. 'Good morning, Philip. How are you doing this morning?'

'Pretty good,' I said. 'Better than yesterday and I managed to get some sleep in between the fire alarm sounding off every hour.'

'Sorry about that. But it is good that you're feeling better.'

'Yes. So, do you think I qualify to get these tubes removed today?'

Dr Haji was the tubes guy. He was already inspecting the bags of juices to my left and he jumped in before Mr Chai had a chance to respond. 'Yes. We've spoken about that. We'll be taking out the catheter and this drain.' He held up one of the bags that didn't have much liquid in it. It resembled the plastic bag I would hold after removing a beef joint to get it ready for a Sunday roast. There was maybe a spoonful of blood in there.

Dr Haji carried on with the news I craved. 'Then we will remove the epidural today.'

He then mumbled something to his colleagues. It sounded like he also thought that the drain he held wasn't doing much good anymore, or at least, the volume inside hadn't changed. There was a but, and I twigged that Dr Haji had suggested that the other drain was still needed. Mr Chai nodded whilst Dr Woo wrote notes on his clipboard. Anika followed suit by making notes on a palm-sized note pad.

'We may need to keep that last drain in for a little while longer,' said Mr Chai.

Bollocks, I thought. That could scupper my escape plans. 'Oh no. Really?' I couldn't help but show my disappointment.

Mr Chai's cheeks grew chubbier behind his facemask. It was a smile. 'Don't worry. You are doing very well. Your temperature seems to be under control. How has the eating been?'

The truth was that it had been frustrating, painful, and the fact that something so basic was not working properly bothered me. 'It's been

OK. Slow. I'm assuming all of that will get better in time.'

'Yes, of course,' Mr Chai said. 'And have the physio team been to see you?'

'Er, not today. But I'm sure they'll be by to drag me out of here soon enough.'

'Ha. Yes. Good, good. You're doing really well.'

It was time to push for the answer to the $64,000 question.

'And...am I still on track to be out of here by Thursday?'

Mr Chai's brown eyes remained locked on mine.

I felt the truth was on its merry way.

'You are doing very well. If you keep it up, and you're moving about, and eating and drinking, then I can't see why not.'

'Really?'

He checked himself. 'Well, certainly by the weekend.'

Home by the weekend? His words were beautiful and, better than that, they sounded believable.

'That sounds good to me,' I said as calmly as I could because on the inside I was jumping for joy.

Then Mr Chai walked over to me, raised his right hand towards me and said something I wasn't expecting. 'High five?'

I was happy to accept the offer, so I smiled some more and slapped his palm with my own right hand.

The bond between doctor and patient had been officially sealed.

'Out *before* the weekend. THAT is a deal,' I said to underline what we had physically agreed to.

Mr Chai seemed OK with our deal, and he retreated to his team. Their catch up with me seemed to have come to a pleasant end. Mr Chai said his goodbye and the full team left. As a veteran, I knew that they would be teaming up out of my earshot so they could discuss me and my case a little more.

I had hoped the tubes would come out there and then, but I was delighted to bank the outcome of their visit, as long as they came out at some point.

Find a Happy Place

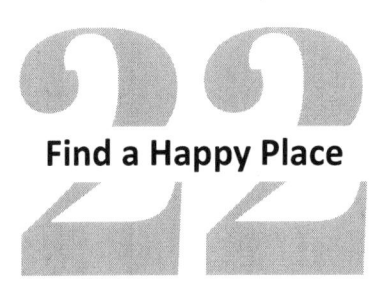

After drooling over pictures of the full English breakfast that Ali and Lydia were being treated to, I had a visit from nurse Anika. She was armed with medication that I was supposed to inhale via the nebuliser. It had been quite some time since I'd been tasked with that rigmarole, and because my lungs still gave me some gyp, I was happy to go along with the full treatment. My oxygen levels hadn't been great over the weekend; the nurses always seemed to have a minor panic if I went below 94%. I needed to make every effort at every opportunity to get well as quickly as I could.

I gave Anika my battle-cry to demonstrate that I was her most willing patient. 'OK. Let's fire it up!'

Before long, I had the mask strapped to my face and I inhaled the cool misty vapours like an old man in a Shisha lounge. Anika left me to it, as there was no need for her to sit and watch, although I wondered if it was on my notes that I'd dodged the mask-business previously.

The oxygen-enriched gas that magically came out in tubes from the wall sounded noisy enough to cut off any other stimulus around me. The medicine fizzed and bubbled in the reservoir at the base of the mask, and I inhaled as deeply as my 94% capacity lungs would allow. I held in the menthol flavoured air for as long as possible, and then I exhaled slowly through my mouth, well before any coughing fits threatened to ruin my life. I had no idea how effective the treatment was, as the entire set up could have been a placebo for all I knew, but the act of concentrating on my breathing was therapeutic on its own.

It took me a good ten minutes to complete the nebuliser task. It sounds disgusting, but I had to regularly spit out phlegm into a plastic cup, which I did as discretely as I could. Slightly more pleasant was the thoughts I had during the imposed meditation session. I wasn't envious of the girls' luxury trip away; I found a lot of comfort in the knowledge that they were distracted from my situation. I knew that one day, or as soon as I was well enough, I would take Ali away and celebrate her birthday all over again. I had always loved hotels that maxed things out at breakfast, and I just had to get my whole digestive system back to normal so I could enjoy the event more than ever before.

Another person I did have time to think about was my dad. I thought back to the time he had been ill and spent time in hospital.

We never had the best father-son relationship, and it would be easy for me to blame him, as he left the family home when I was six. However, even as a young boy I was pragmatic and accepted the situation for what it was. Financially, he was always there and time wise, he tried his best. Visits drifted from every-other-weekend to once a month, and eventually every few months, but I understood that we simply had other things in our lives, and totally different families that didn't mix. Over the years we never fell out, and we always managed to catch up every so often, so we just coasted along. Both of us accepted the deal for what it had become. I never felt any resentment, and it was true that my single-parent mum had covered the role of both parents to more than make up for any shortcomings.

Then, about ten years ago he got sick. Because of our lack of closeness, he never relayed how serious his health situation was, and he kept all of his symptoms and troubles to himself. I knew that he suffered without any help or support from me, his youngest son, because he simply didn't want to bother me. It would have been true to say that I couldn't have helped cure him, but it might have been nice to have appreciated what he had gone through.

Eventually, he ended up in hospital and had to undergo surgery to remove part of his bowel that had become cancerous. He had always hated and feared hospitals and, knowing that, I think he must have been petrified. Just before he was due to have his general anaesthetic, he wrote me a letter. It was a few pages long, so I don't remember everything, but it was somewhat confessional and was also fairly complimentary towards me. He said how he admired how I had managed to gain a true balance of my time between work and with my family. It was true, he'd been a classic case of spending too much time at work, or at work-related functions, when his own family were young – the trade-off for his commitment to make his marketing business a success. He had worked out what was truly important a little bit too late. As a consequence, it had made me a more determined father by always putting the family first in every big decision that Ali and I made. We'd been fortunate to have jobs that meant we could spend evenings, weekends and holidays with the people we dearly loved.

As I had sucked in my percolating medication, I felt massive pangs of guilt. I had offered him no comfort or help at a time when he had needed it the most. I had only just realised (I was four days in) how serious major surgery was. I'd found out the hard way that it was an absolute bastard. And it would have been even worse for my dad, who would have been in his late 60's and riddled with a genuine phobia of hospitals. I felt awful because not only had I given him nothing in the way of support, much worse than that, I hadn't shown him much love either.

My indifference towards my dad had suddenly become an ugly part of what made me who I was. I felt the need to speak to my dad about his illness and his surgery. I vowed to apologise for not being there for him at the first opportunity I could get.

After my gas mask treatment, I was faced with my familiar role as lab rat.

Anika impressed me with her efficiency. She didn't say much, and that was fine with me. If I'd had a choice, I would've voted for smashing through the prods, pokes, and pricks as quickly as possible anyway. She could have possibly got herself an alternative job as an F1 pitstop team member.

Observation trolley rolled in position.

Oxygen monitor clipped onto index finger.

Blood pressure cuff Velcro-ed onto bicep.

Blood pressure machine switched on.

Temperature gun fired into earhole.

Oxygen monitor unclipped.

Cuff ripped off.

Trolley rolled away.

Syringe inserted into canula.

Blood drawn into vial.

Sticker written up on vial (in tiny handwriting).

Covid swab scraped around back of throat.

Covid swab housed in separate vial (more tiny writing).

Anti-clotting injection stabbed into left thigh.

Juice bag 1 measured and noted.

Juice bag 2 measured and noted.

Urine bag measured and noted.

Old IV drip bag removed.

Saline flushed through cannula.

New IV bag hoisted and connected.

Drip valve adjusted and set to steady.

All done in 26.7 seconds. Very impressive.

'Thank you,' I said.

'You're welcome,' Anika replied sweetly and then raced off with all her paraphernalia to keep her World Record attempt on track.

Twenty minutes later (or straight after Anika had serviced everyone else on the entire wing), she was back. She brandished some virgin white dressings and asked me if I wouldn't mind climbing back onto the bed so that she could make the change. I was more than happy to oblige and between us we worked together as a great team. The drip had stopped as the bag was done and Anika swiftly de-rigged everything. Then, with her help, I raised myself from the armchair, spun around to get my arse on the bed before grunting my way into a comfortable position. Anika had lowered the bed to make life as easy as possible and was on hand to elevate me back up and then adjusted all the pillows and sheets, giving me five-star treatment. I could tell we were a great team because we barely spoke; we just instinctively knew what to do for each other.

As predicted, the dressing change went as clockwork. Anika removed the old dressings, and I hardly felt a thing. It was strange to witness her *not* whizz through the cleaning up of my wounds. I assumed she did everything at break-neck speed, but I was wrong. I don't think she could have been slower, or more tender if she'd tried. I wasn't brave enough to watch and I barely felt the touch of her wipes and swabs as she ensured the healing process had the maximum chance of success. Her ministrations were so gentle and so caring that her actions bordered on the loving, and almost caressed their way into the erotic.

Before I got too carried away, the sterilisation of my belly had been completed. And if the thought of that alone wasn't enough to kill the mood, Anika returned to super-efficient mode and soon had new dressings cut up, applied, and stuck down. It felt so good to be all bandaged up with the knowledge that I was clean and had been looked after so expertly. Anika had done such a wonderful job on me that I didn't crave the comforting blast from the bolus that had sorted me out so many times before. In fact, it must have been around that time that I was sure I had kicked my opium addiction.

The fun and games continued. Anika left to be replaced by a double-team of Dr Haji and his young assistant, Dr Colin Woo. That privacy curtain was sure getting a lot of action. Both were suitably PPE'd with additional goggles and aprons.

I guessed it was time for my de-bagging.

Dr Haji started proceedings. 'Hello again, Philip.'

'Hello,' I responded, with the hope that I was about to witness actions and not just words from those two. I felt like he was about to get straight to business because he moved towards me, but then he suddenly checked himself.

He stopped short, like a voice had told him to stop. He looked back at me. 'How are you? Are you OK?'

I smiled. 'Yes, thanks. I'm fine. And you?' I figured that maybe he added in that extra layer of patient check because he had young Dr Woo in tow.

'I'm good, thank you.'

'And you?' I said and turned my attention to Dr Woo.

'I'm good too, thanks,' he replied.

Bless him; he was about the same age as my Harrison. He had such a likeable aura, and, mixed with his obvious intelligence and the young man's confidence, it made me feel uplifted to think that the younger generations weren't so doomed after all. I had always said that the best thing about millennials was that we wouldn't get another batch of them for another thousand years. Maybe I'd been too harsh.

Dr Haji took control and let me know what they were there for. Dr Woo was about to receive a practical lesson in the removal of an internal drain.

I was an expert as I'd been through it once before, although I'd conveniently forgotten if it had been painful or not. The skin and tissue around both entry points – or, technically, exit points – had grown a lot sorer and irritating with each day. I just wanted them out, but I knew only one tube was being freed.

I did my bit to expose the area of attack, lifted up my T-shirt and pulled down my trackies a few inches to offer them a nice, clean site to work with. Plus, I didn't fancy getting unwanted juices on my clothes. I turned to my right as the entry point into my body was on the left.

I didn't look. If I watched, I knew I would feel more pain.

Dr Haji's voice lowered as he chatted to both Dr Woo and me. I gathered he was using the power of distraction on me, maybe even attempting to hypnotise me, but surely not Dr Woo? As he spoke, he peeled off the sticky plasters that had protected the opening for the previous four days. That pull on an area of sensitive skin was something I could feel. It took him a few tugs because I'd kept the whole area dry and, if anything, the glue had got stronger each day.

Once the plasters had been ripped free and dumped on the trolley that Dr Woo stood by, I sensed that he had hold of the tube. Any movement aggravated the bullet wound.

22 – FIND A HAPPY PLACE

Go on, just get this fucking over with.

I couldn't tell if there was much, if any, resistance from my end, but Dr Haji won his tug-of-war. He drew out the invasive drain from the depths of my body. I felt it, but because it wasn't painful, I diverted my eyes left to steal a rubber-necked gawp at the crash scene.

I thought the snake would be six inches at most, but oh no, that fucker seemed to be about three feet long. It must have grown since they first attached it. It came out relatively cleanly. It had some smeared blood or a mixture of other fluids I didn't want to think about along some of its length. No sooner had Dr Haji delivered my offspring, he'd coiled it up and rushed it over to the trolley. Presumably to weigh it, prior to allowing me to bond with it or name it. Nope, I watched him wrap it up with the old plasters, wrappings, paper towels, and even his disposable apron and he walked the newborn over to the pedal bin with the yellow liners. The yellow bin liners were strictly medical waste destined for the incinerator. He stamped on the pedal and chucked everything inside and then released his foot, so the hungry lid clanged shut. Oh, goodbye then.

It was out. Thank God. Yes, there were still a few foreign objects stuck in me, but it was a lovely little victory to have one of the annoying bastards removed.

I saw that the bullet hole was substantial. I wondered if it would need stitches.

I didn't need to ask. Dr Woo had exchanged places with his senior and cleaned the sad-looking wound before he carefully covered it up with a fresh square-shaped plaster.

Job done. No mess. I thanked them both as they cleared their shit away.

In the absence of stitches, I wondered if I would be left with a proper scar. Not an ugly one, but one that had intrigue and a story attached to it. One for the grandkids to hear a horror story about. Yeah, that would be cool.

I barely had time to let my lunchtime vegetable soup and white roll go down before my next visitor arrived. Pain Team Mandy breezed in, but she didn't greet me with a 'G'day.'

'Hey, Philip. How ya doin' t'day?'

My family was used to me speaking with an Australian accent, but I checked myself from sounding like a piss-taking prick to those that didn't know me well.

'Hello. Yes, I'm doing OK, thanks. How are you?'

'Pretty good, thanks.' Mandy looked at my tray. 'Oh sorry, are you in the middle of ya lunch?'

'No. You're OK. I'm all done and ready for you.'

'Great! How's that epidural been?'

'It was working well, but the last day or so I'm not so sure. My right side feels good but my left is nagging me a bit and the imbalance makes me wonder if everything is OK back there.'

'OK. Well, I'll have to take a look because I'm here to remove it anyway.'

It was good news, it was something that I wanted, yet it was laced with some fearful thoughts. Had I been numbed from all pain the whole time? Was I soon about to feel what real excruciating agony truly felt like? I told myself to get a grip. Ali had suffered an epidural once in childbirth and a second time to repair the damage caused by the first. If the realities of pain were too much, I could always ask them to stick it back in. Couldn't I?

'Oh right. Good. What, right now?' It must have sounded like I wanted a few extra seconds of comfort and no pain. Because that was the truth.

'Yep,' she said, with intensity in her brown eyes that probably hadn't needed any words at all. And with her confirmation, we got straight down to business. She helped pull me forwards and whilst I sat upright, she used the remote control to flatten the bed behind me. It gave her maximum access to my spine. Between us we lifted up my T-shirt to expose my back, and more importantly the entry point of that ridiculously long needle.

Mandy did her trademark finger-pat around the entry-point and cooed that it all seemed fine. She didn't offer an explanation as to why it hadn't been as effective, but that didn't matter anymore. She asked me to lower my head and to try and curve my spine. It seemed logical to do the same thing I'd done back on day one, when Dr Adam and his team had inserted the epidural in the first place.

There was a bit of a pause, but with my head bowed, I couldn't see what was going on. The sounds gave me the impression that she had put on some fresh gloves and had taken some time to line up some cleaning gear and a fresh dressing. One place I didn't fancy falling foul to an infection was the route straight into my spinal cord. So, although I was uncomfortable and feeling vulnerable where my belly had become compressed by my position, I accepted that it was all part of the bigger picture and respected that maintaining strict sterilisation protocol was imperative.

I did my best to find a happy place. It wasn't that easy when I had my head between my knees in the crash position, whilst my central nervous system was exposed to the elements. I thought back to the night when Harrison had been born, our first child. He was so perfect and before midnight, I left him and Ali at the hospital and drove home. I was so ecstatic that I believed I would never, ever top that moment for sheer happiness. From that pinnacle, I clearly remember thinking that I was prepared to die as my life felt so complete. It seemed weird to say that the birth of my son not only gave me a purpose to live and a reason to succeed in life, but his arrival also simultaneously extinguished all fear. That was my happy place, a place where there was no fear. No fear of failure, no fear of death, because life could not possibly get any better than that moment.

That emotion must have made me an optimist as a true pessimist would argue that my life could have only got worse from that point.

Whilst I mulled over if I was both an optimist and a pessimist, Mandy went about her work. The strips that held the tube in place and the big plasters that fixed the needle came off gently enough. There was none of that ripping off the Band-Aid business.

'If you could keep dead still, that would be great,' she said firmly.

I didn't reply, as I wanted to do my bit by not taking a breath, let alone talk.

I couldn't see, but I knew she had the needle held between her right thumb and index finger. I was completely, and literally, in her hands.

Please don't paralyse me...

But, if you are going to paralyse me, from the chest down, can you get it over with because the suspense of the dramatic pause is also killing me.

Mandy's voice sounded triumphant. 'There you go, sweetie. That needle is out now.'

I exhaled, relieved that there was still a chance that, one day, I would be able to walk Lydia down the aisle.

She wasn't quite finished.

I let her clean the small wound left behind. Yes, I could feel my toes, but I wasn't out of the woods just yet. As she cleaned and patched me up, she reminded me of the contents of the leaflet she had previously handed me. For the next two weeks I had to be mindful of what had happened to my spine. Any problems, such as pain, numbness, or loss of bladder or bowel control and I was to raise the alarm immediately.

So, fingers crossed tightly for a full fortnight then, as I didn't fancy any of those delightful complications.

When she had finished, I let my T-shirt fall down and she elevated the bed so I could sit back at a better angle. I had felt self-conscious about lying on my back with an epidural jammed there, yet I still wasn't totally comfortable because I knew I was putting pressure on the tiny wound that was trying to heal underneath all my weight.

'All done!' she confirmed, and I thanked her as she cleared away all her bits and bobs. She checked if I wanted the curtains left closed, and I said that I'd rather have them open, so she gathered them up to my right and we exchanged goodbyes.

A successful result. Another drain out, and epidural out. Progress, progress, progress.

Soon after being detached from my bolus, I reflected on its role. It had helped me through some tough times, but I had probably over-used it. I was convinced that it had driven me insane as a consequence of the battle against pain that might strike, rather than coping with it as, and when, it occurred. I was fearful that once the epidural was out, the real pain would find its path the way nature intended. I was pleased to find out that there was no crippling agony, and my heightened levels of distress and pain were much the same.

Although, that might have been because I had been given morphine via pills.

Whatever it was that was doing the trick, my body or the pills, I rested comfortably. I had decided against any form of sit-ups or stomach crunches for the time being.

The afternoon sped by. I read, I played some chess and some poker on my phone, and I also scrolled away a massive chunk of time on the bloody thing. I also managed to exchange some messages with Ali, and similarly with my brother and the guys. I'd even managed to squeak out a few farts. Everything looked promising, and the positivity with being on programme and doing well was fixed in my mindset.

Dr Woo popped by with a magic pill. He told me that it was designed to help unlock my water retention. It had been on my mind that I had kept on getting bigger and bigger. I felt how swollen my legs were and all around my pelvis. Was that what women complained about so often? I took the pill with a gulp of water and hoped that I would soon be filling up several urine bags via the catheter, just like having the plug removed from a paddling pool. In reality, it was not an instant remedy.

I had separate chats with Roy and Stefano. The more I spoke to Roy, the more we got on. We were so similar in many ways, particularly in the way we thought and our calm, placid demeanours. Stefano was pure amusement for me. I never worked out why they barely spoke to each other, but in a place where human contact was so beneficial, they seemed pleased that I was there to act as a mediator for them. Obviously, Boring Dean continued to self-isolate and that was fine. Horses for courses. I thought about solitary confinement, and how effective it seemed as a punishment. It was one of those things that I struggled to imagine, because I needed to appreciate and comprehend a vast amount of time. It must have been sheer torture for hostages like Terry Waite and John McCarthy all those years ago.

I could have gone private and had my own room. I think if I'd only been in for a day I would've gone for it, but I was content that I'd chosen the NHS route, and to be stuck with those old bastards, who were chatty and helped me feel better about my traumatic situation. I surprised myself (as a self-confessed sociopath), that when the chips were down, I needed contact with other people. Maybe I'd been wrong about myself all along.

The bonds of my imprisonment were being cut loose one by one and I welcomed each release with gratitude and relief. The two that I wanted out were the central line and the fucking catheter. I can call it a fucking catheter because it was literally doing that to me.

It was still Ali's 50th birthday, but my personal highlight was when Dr Haji turned up to finally relieve me of my personal nemesis.

I'd returned from a little walk around with the physio team. They had promised me the stair challenge the next day, so it was, essentially, training for that final stage. During my walk down the corridor, I had to stop twice and force out a wee. As much as I had mastered the process, it was still uncomfortable and extremely undignified to be stood in the middle of the ward and have people watch as I filled up my urine bag. Granted, my genitals weren't exposed to all and sundry, but being stood there with people milling about made me feel infirm and well placed on the humiliation spectrum. I felt my face redden as I concentrated on the task at hand. I must have looked like a toddler filling its nappy. I desperately wanted to lose that medieval contraption that had been essential but was no longer fit for purpose.

Dr Haji appeared, and I noticed the sleeves of his checked shirt were rolled up, and with a facemask and latex gloves on, I could tell he meant business. The disposable apron was a dead giveaway as that meant, like earlier that day, he would be expecting some unwanted splashes.

'Hello again, Philip,' he said as he swept the curtain around us.

It was great to see him, especially as I guessed that he was there to rid me from my restrictive binding. I think my enthusiasm was evident in the way I greeted him.

'Oh, hello, Doctor! Nice to see you.'

'If you're feeling ready, I've come by to remove your catheter.'

As eager as I was to get the catheter out, I was equally as scared that the process of removal was not going to be straight forward – especially after the StrongBoy incident. I hadn't discussed my fears with anyone. It had remained locked up within me for some time. I realised that the time to cross that dreaded bridge was nigh. What a horrible bridge. The Kidney Harbour Bridge, Golden Wee Gate Bridge, maybe Waterpoo Bridge. I struggled to think of other toilet themed bridges to take my mind off the thought that the invasive plastic tube was about to be drawn out from my dick.

'Ready? I've been ready for days,' I countered like an excited bunny. Dr Haji was quite a serious character, but I felt the need to make the process of correcting my internal plumbing as light-hearted as I could. The truth was that, to me, it was a serious matter, and I didn't want to put him off his stroke, so to speak. I put a lid on any further jokes. As a result, Dr Haji and I got straight down to business.

I was already on the bed, so my first action was to drag my trackies and pants down in stages. I'd bent my knees, and dug my heels in, but I couldn't raise my bum completely off the bed. At least things weren't so bad that the doctor had to do the undressing for me. I lay back, and after a final glance at the blue plastic adapter rammed into the end of my distorted penis, I looked away to my right. I had no idea how painful the removal process was going to be. My logic remained that if I saw something horrific happen, then the pain would be far worse. It was the fear of the unknown and the added anxiety of how delicate the area of attack was, that was responsible for me trying to cope with the stress by pretending I wasn't at all bothered. The truth was that I was scared enough to shit a brick.

Dr Haji used his favoured technique of distraction whilst he freed my penis from its internal noose. He talked about how they would leave the final drain for a little while longer, but it should still allow me to go home with it. The distraction might have worked had I not felt my dick being manhandled. I tried to not think about it, but it was incredibly hard. The task, not my dick. I couldn't help my lower muscles' involuntary contractions. It was virtually impossible to relax.

I had no idea if there was some special tool being used. A tool for a tool. The thought wasn't the best idea as I conjured up images of an angler using a disgorger on the mouth of a freshly caught carp.

The doctor was fiddling about, but there was no pain.

Keep looking away, Phil. Keep looking away.

Whatever he had done to unlock the catheter seemed to have been a success. He pulled the tube that had been nestled deep within my bladder, like an artificial tapeworm. I was so happy to get rid of the bloody thing that had been taking the piss out of me for days.

'There you go,' he announced.

I exhaled. I hadn't realised that I had stopped breathing. 'Ah. Thank you so much, Doctor.'

'OK. Good. You can pull your pants back up.'

I was more than happy to cover up my poor, poor willy.

I'm so sorry you had to go through all of that, mate. You're safe now.

'You should be able to go to the toilet perfectly normally now. It is not uncommon to notice a small amount of blood in your urine at first. If that gets worse, or you have any problems you will have to let us know, OK?'

Expect blood, and if going to the toilet doesn't work – scream for help. Got it.

'Yep, all good,' I confirmed, still in a state of amazement that there had been no pain. The dormant pessimist in me couldn't help but throw up the thought that maybe the vitally important nerves that served my groin had been severed during surgery.

So, all good, if the assumption was that I never wanted to experience sex ever again.

Monday, Get Behind Me

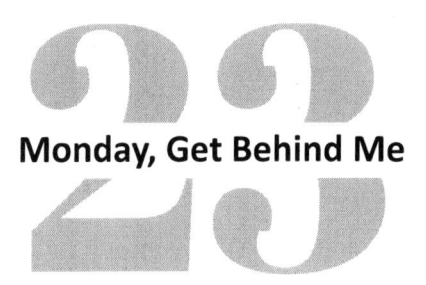

Monday had been full-on. My evening meal punctuated what had been relentless attention. The child-sized Shepherd's pie wasn't tasty, and my stomach still forced me to eat at a pedestrian speed. It seized up at every mouthful. I wasn't hungry, but I did crave the nutrition. I could have given up and pushed the bland meal away, but I persevered, and I got through it, like I had done all the other ones. Another step closer to my goal.

Lukas was still on night duty. He had replaced Anika, who had been non-stop since the moment I first saw her that morning. I found it incredible that she (and other nurses and doctors like her) could maintain their intense speed and energy and remain so focussed all-day. Every day, no matter how tough or challenging that day became.

Lukas didn't offer the same speed as his colleagues. Slowed by his sheer bulk, he did however give me the impression that he was an unstoppable force. He probably took as many breaks as his contract allowed, but it would be fair of me to say that whenever I saw him, albeit during every night shift, he was busy doing something. My attitude warmed towards him. Maybe it was a male/female thing, but he just wasn't as gentle as the female nurses. I'd had to get used to his direct, no-nonsense style. I was a little surprised when he announced on his first visit that he was going to remove the central line.

I was not at a crossroads; I was at a T-junction. I had wished for my neck cannula to be removed, so I should have been ecstatic to race down that path of acceptance. But I wasn't ecstatic at all. I wasn't convinced that Lukas had the authority or the qualifications to play around with my jugular vein. Changing an IV bag over or flushing through cannulas was one thing, but surely, insertion or extraction of such a critically important bit of equipment was a different matter altogether. My second option was therefore to object and question if he was the right person for such a vital procedure. Lukas' announcement had come out of nowhere. Dr Haji hadn't mentioned it earlier when he had several chances to. Yes, I'd made everyone know how much I hated the bloody thing, so I would have thought that the doctors would have been the ones to remove it at the right time during their daily rounds. I hated the way it felt like a big plastic leech that clicked and clacked whenever I moved. I was forever conscious about knocking or pulling it even though it was stuck down in place.

I remembered I was British. So, I let Lukas carry on.

If he was the sadistic maniac that I once believed he was, I was about to find out just how demented he truly was. I gifted my neck to him, like I was the Bride of Dracula.

He stood to the right of my bed and laid out some gauze and a big square plaster on my chest. Then, with a little too much force, he used his powerful right hand on top of my head to turn it away from him, to my left, to expose the right side of my neck.

I don't think I'd ever kept my head and neck so still.

Petrified means to be scared stiff, right? I'd turned myself to stone.

I looked out of the big window. I saw the Wembley Arch. A pleasant last view to have as my hot blood started to gush and pump out from just under my right ear. I wondered if I'd feel the heat or the wetness first...maybe I'd see a huge red jet perform its own arch...

Lukas released my head and used both hands on my neck.

I felt his big fingers under my jawline and above my collarbone.

He didn't hang about. He tore the plasters off that had held the needle in place for so many days. In one swift motion Lukas had grabbed the gauze from my chest and shoved it at the exact place where he had removed the cannula. He held the pad there so firmly, and I thought that it was the clamping of the jugular vein that was his method of claiming his victims.

'Here. Hold ziz in place,' he instructed.

I didn't reply. Fortunately, I did manage to cross my left hand up to the gauze and held it there so that Lukas could release his pressure and leave himself free to use both hands.

I'd done something similar many times over in the crook of my elbow when I'd donated blood or had a blood test, but that moment was different. It was a bloody great vein that connected my brain to my vascular system. I didn't have a clue how hard to press.

Too hard and there was every chance I'd pass out, but too loose and I was worried that my blood would find a way around that white cotton dam.

Before I had time to pass out (I had decided to press hard), Lukas' hands were back.

'OK. Sank you.' He had opened up the square plaster and in a dexterous movement, he covered the gauze with it, without trapping either of our fingers. 'Zhere. Zat iz all done for you.'

All done? Wow, I'd survived.

If he wasn't a psychopath, then he was excellent at pretending that he was.

'Thanks for that,' I said. I didn't add, *and thanks for not killing me.*

'No problem.'

Lukas packed up the debris caused by his work and left me there to lie in a shallow pool of my own sweat.

Thank fuck that went well.

Tuesday. Hopefully Not a Newsday

I woke from the best sleep since my arrival in paradise.

It was still bloody awful, but it was a notable improvement. I had got a little more used to sleeping on my back, and because I'd been relieved of so many tubes, it had reduced my levels of anxiety and irritation. With the dodgy catheter gone, I felt much more at home in the toilet department. The bedtime bathroom routine had become easier, with just one last bag clipped to my T-shirt. I'd successfully negotiated a normal wee, which was a polite ladies' sit-down one, as a manly stand-up version would have been a complete gamble with an unpredictable spray. I'd pictured something like putting my thumb over the end of a full-power garden hose, and the inevitable clean-up afterwards.

I still had familiar obstacles to overcome, such as the broken fire alarm and the regular observations, but with all that considered, it was a sleep that *nearly* qualified as deep and I woke up *almost* feeling refreshed.

My throat was 95% back to normal. The soothing spray I'd been given was something I'd self-administered regularly. Every swallow had hurt, but I'd realised that it must have improved because I'd forgotten about it. I took a gulp. OK, the soreness was still present, but it was a discomfort that was manageable and on its way out.

I sent Ali a message at 6:44am to let her know about the great news surrounding the removal of my drain, central line, and catheter and how it had all contributed to my successful sleep, despite the fire alarm going off three times between 3am and 5am. She woke up for a normal day of work half an hour later and replied.

> Ali: Morning gorgeous.
> What a wonderful message to wake up to.
> This is fantastic news.
> I hope today brings even more positive news. I hope you can enjoy some breakfast and even perhaps do a poo xx

The message made me smile. I still hadn't managed a number two, and it niggled me that I might not be allowed home until I had. I'd get there, of that I was certain. I gathered my washbag, towel, and a change of underwear and made my way to the bathroom. I sat on the toilet and waited for gravity to entice something out of me. The force of gravity was on its own; there was absolutely no way I was going to attempt a push. I was too scared of the inevitable pain. After a couple of minutes, although I'd emptied my bladder, I conceded that I'd drawn a blank. I decided I would just have to wait until I was so full of shit it would fall out of me, or I'd wait a few more weeks when I'd recovered enough to push. I couldn't help but check the bowl as I stood up. The liquid was more orange than yellow. I concluded that I wasn't dehydrated because I'd never been so pumped full of fluid thanks to the IV drips, so it must have been the presence of blood. Dr Haji had warned me, but what I saw was more dirty brown than an attractive Cabernet Sauvignon. I noted the colour as *expected* and made an additional sidenote to chirp up if the colour looked more worrying at the next visit.

The rest of my morning bathroom routine went smoothly. Everything was so much easier with only one drain and the one cannula on my left forearm. My speed had improved and even my little dance to change my pants had got better, so I'd pretty much nailed that choreography. Practice made perfect.

Being able to walk about and freshen up independently made a world of difference to me. I knew my midriff was doing its best to knit itself back together and I did what I could to protect that process by moving slowly and deliberately. It seemed to be working, as I hadn't experienced any sharp pains for a while, but instead, just the rumbling dull ache that remained a constant presence.

I returned to the bay and exchanged good mornings with Stefano as he was in pole position, awake, and sitting up. He seemed to be impressed with my rate of recovery.

He beamed and said, 'Look-a at you. You're-a gonna be da first-a one outta here.'

'That is my plan,' I joked back as I trundled past.

I half-ignored Dean. He was unbelievable. I checked over to see if he wanted to acknowledge a good morning and saw that he was already back on his bloody mobile. He must have been aware of my presence, yet he chose to look away and continue his boring mumble that must have been approaching a British record of 38 hours straight. *Your loss, you ignorant tit.*

I arrived between my bed and Roy's. He was already dressed and lay on top of the bed, reading. Like he was relaxing on holiday. He agreed with the Italian.

'You're doing well,' he said.

'Thanks, Roy. I do feel a bit better.'

He nodded to mark his approval. 'It helps being young, most of the people in here don't get out of bed for two weeks after what we've been through.'

I was stooped, and shuffled along like a 90-year-old, but I was happy to accept Roy's definition of young.

'And you? How are you doing? When are they chucking you out?'

Roy nodded a bit more. 'I'm OK, thanks. With a bit of luck, I might be home tomorrow.'

'Really? Wow. That is fantastic news. Well done, I'll keep my fingers crossed for you.'

I was pleased for Roy. He'd been through so much and he fully deserved the all-clear to be discharged and sent home. After I'd seen what had happened to him when he was first given freedom, I was worried that it had not been that long ago. I wasn't going to rain on his parade and ask him if he thought it was too soon. I was sure that the experts looking out for him would not even consider a discharge if they thought there was a risk that Roy was going to put in a repeat performance of his exploding stomach routine.

It would be a shame to see him leave me with just Stefano, and because I was a tad jealous, I had another metaphorical set of fingers crossed that I would follow him out of the automatic doors soon after him.

I carefully got myself back on to the bed. Over previous days, I'd had enough time to play with and master the remote control that adjusted the height and configuration of the bed. I got myself nicely comfortable and looked forward to breakfast.

As I paced myself through my (just above room temperature) porridge, I thought about what more the doctors could possibly serve up for me that day. Surely, I was on the home straight, with the wind behind me? All I had to do was take my medicine and my painkillers, keep eating the food, and not fall off the bed.

The three wise men came to visit me. Doctors Woo, Haji, and Chai.

The visit was positive, friendly, and brief. They had decided that my recovery was on track, but they wanted to make sure they hadn't missed anything. Despite the regular blood tests and the recent chest X-ray, they still needed more from me. They said that my temperature, although it seemed stable now, had caused them some concern. I remembered that infection following surgery was one of the dangers that Mr Chai warned me about. A high temperature suggested infection. My day would therefore involve a trip downstairs to undergo a CT scan, as that would help them know what was happening. Mr Chai told me that they also wanted a urine sample, so the nurses would help me out with that.

I accepted my duties for the day. They didn't seem too taxing. The three of them left me to my devices. When I say devices, I mean my phone and my book.

Nurse Anika was back on shift, which was great news. If anyone could race me through a day of recovery it would be her. First up, she handed me a small, clear plastic bag so I could see the gubbings of a urine test kit inside. I'd been warned it was due, so I'd stopped myself from going to the toilet earlier. When she handed me the bag, my bladder was painfully swollen. I assessed the small tube and thought I'd be able to fill at least a dozen of them.

Fortunately, the kit contained a natty shallow plastic jug thing. I didn't know its official or technical name, but an NSPJT was exactly what I needed. Equally as fortunate was that there weren't any CCTV cameras in the toilet to record my awkward attempt at a urine sample. At least I didn't think there were. I mean, I had a good look around the ceiling and there were vents, lights, and alarms, but I didn't think there were cameras. Mild paranoia had a word with me – *I was in hospital; wouldn't it be a good idea to have cameras in the toilets? What about that thing up there, is that hiding a camera?*

At that point, I shook my head; I was beyond caring about privacy and dignity. If some weird fucker wanted to perv over me going to the toilet, then let them go for it. It wasn't going to be the most erotic thing ever seen on a TV screen. Whatever floats your boat, I say.

Inside the locked room I set up the kit on the basin, next to the toilet. Concealed cisterns behind the laminated back panels meant I had no other choice (except the floor or an uneven plastic chair). I unscrewed the cap to the sample tube and carefully placed it on the sink. I took the shallow collection vessel (NSPJT) and put it next to the tube, all ready for me to grab when in mid-flow.

I went slightly off-piste with my undressing. In my bout of paranoia, I decided to out-perv any voyeurs. I completely stripped off my bottom half. My boldness meant that I'd totally regained all power over any potential on-lookers who usually fed off the weak, the timid, and the shy. It was also practical to be half-naked because I had no idea where the trajectory of my piss, or any ricochets, were headed.

I kept my red Totes on because I wasn't a weirdo.

I lowered myself, as best as I could, over the bowl. I couldn't sit down comfortably because I wouldn't have been able to feed my hand and the jug between my legs when the time came. I had to rely on my unused thigh muscles to hold me in a hover position. I held my T-shirt up and tried to look down at the business end, but my agility was shot to pieces, and the padded bandages caused my view to be more obscured than the cheap seats at Loftus Road. I was uptight and despite my bladder screaming out that it was ready to be emptied, I simply couldn't go.

Come on, just go.

No.

Why not?

Don't want to.

Come on, my legs are actually shaking now.

No.

I gave in and sat down. Plan B was to start to wee in the more traditional manner, and then I would rise up to resume the hover position, to reveal a golden stream that could then be tapped into.

Plan B started off OK. After a wait (that caused pins and needles in my feet) my internal plumbing complied, and I finally felt the relief of urination. Despite the prickles and sharp pains in my soles, my legs did manage to get me off the seat. The handsome, golden stream I'd expected had been replaced by an unimpressive amber trickle.

My left hand kept my T-shirt up, and out of harm's way, while the other grabbed the small jug. I'd already lost precious seconds and couldn't tell if my body was still pranking me, and it might stop the flow at any given moment. I felt like I had no control over the show.

I couldn't see what I was doing.

I was forced to use my ears. It sounded like I'd interrupted the trickle with the jug.

The trickle had mysteriously turned into a multi-directional spray.

I hadn't intended to, but I also used my sense of touch. I felt splashes of piss hit the skin of my fingers and hand.

Marvellous.

I collected more in the jug than on my hand, which was a bonus. I lifted it up and out of the danger zone. I relaxed and sat back down on the toilet, with the jug held high. To complete its joke, my body then proceeded to complete what ended up being an exceptionally long wee as if there had never been a problem.

If I'd been more agile, I might have been able to lean over and grab the tube on the basin, but I had to stand up and keep all my movements slow and deliberate. My urine still looked too dark to me. Carefully, I poured it into the tube. There was more than enough to get between the two lines marked on the side of the tube that indicated a minimum and maximum. The perfectionist in me tried to get the level right in the middle. I set the tube down as precisely as I could and with only one hand free, I couldn't screw the top on.

I tipped the excess into the toilet bowl and moved to the pedal bin to dispose of the redundant wee jug. I was pleased with my decision to strip off as I had avoided the need to waddle over to the bin like a six-foot penguin with trousers and pants wrapped around my ankles.

With both hands free, I screwed the lid on the sample tube and slipped it back into the bag.

All done. Job's a good 'un.

Well, all done – bar the clean-up.

Someone (alright, it was me) had sprinkled piss all over the shop. I hoped my unruly rogue jet was just one of those random things and it was not my new normal caused by catheter damage.

I got dressed and used a combination of paper towels and toilet paper to mop up what I could. Hopefully, the cleaners would be in attendance soon enough with some decent disinfectant to keep everyone safe from whatever germs had been sprayed around.

I washed my hands twice, left the bathroom and only had to wait about two seconds before Anika whizzed by, so I flagged her down and handed her my sample. I used up a small wish, one that related to that tube of wee – please don't let the test results stop my release date.

I lay comfortably on my bed and focussed on sorting out my one-off trip to see my beloved New York Jets. The distraction was welcome; I forgot all about where I was and looked to the future. I used my phone to check and send emails out to every organisation associated with the game next Sunday. I had contacted the stadium, Ticketmaster, the NFL, and the Jets, as I attempted to get new tickets that would cater for my new disabled status. I got lucky. Not only did I manage to get new tickets in the disabled section, but I'd also saved about £100 as I could get one of my sons in as my carer. That saving went towards the transport costs to get me safely to and from the stadium. My intensity had paid off. All I had to do was qualify for hospital discharge and to stay physically well enough to get there for high noon on that Sunday. Result.

Kiki and Becky bounced their way over to me. It was to be my third and final session with them. They'd told me before that all I had to do was to show them that I could walk up and down a flight of stairs, and then they would sign me off. They had previously quizzed me about my situation at home and were happy enough with my answers that I had family there to look after me. Some poor buggers got sent home with no help.

I felt strong enough and I was certainly up for the challenge. They weren't going to take no for an answer anyway.

I surprised myself. Everything had come together to achieve one of my best sporting achievements – the flight of stairs walk of freedom.

A few things gave away my otherwise civilian-like appearance. The final drain bag, clipped to my T-shirt, my stoop, the cannula, and the half a dozen cotton swabs dotted about my body gave away my true identity as I walked unassisted out of the bay and into the corridor.

The physio team gave me some gentle encouragement and also just chatted generally as if we were having a nice little stroll down to the shops. Kiki was the chatty one and Becky was the listener. The walk was slow, but more importantly, it was pain-free. Once again, I walked past the doors to the other bays and private rooms – *Hello, you lot. It's me again. Why aren't you lot up and stood by your door, clapping me as a guard of honour? Look at me, I'm walking!*

I had no idea what they were in for. I wondered if, after everything I'd been through, I was in better shape than everyone else in the ward. If the test was a success, I might be allowed home before anyone else.

The three of us passed the reception desk and took a left turn toward the lift lobby and the door to the emergency staircase. Becky stepped forward and pushed the doors open for me. Kiki stayed behind me as I entered the staircase. It was a back-of-house staircase, not usually seen by anyone unless it was an emergency. The stairs were bare concrete, and the walls were unplastered blockwork. There were no windows, so the lighting appeared unnatural and didn't lift the all-round grey mood of the place. The only colours I detected were the faded yellow nosing strips painted on each stair tread and the bright red tubular handrails. As I prepared to make the ascent, I checked with Kiki if it was still a pass if I used the handrail. She confirmed that it would be fine if I needed it.

I stood at the first step and looked up. The journey seemed to be twice as high as my flight of stairs at home. No doubt the storey height was greater than a domestic measurement and for a moment I wondered if they'd let me get away with reaching the half-landing that I could see before me.

Concrete Kilimanjaro and the two women beside me waited for me to get on with it.

Whatever sport I've played, I've always thought that the first thing I've ever done is to set my feet properly. I attacked the stair climb in a sportsmanlike manner – as though I was about to perform a record-breaking deadlift or setting myself up behind a quarterback ready to take a touchdown-scoring handoff, and I made sure my feet were completely square on to that first step. To give myself the best shot, everything had to be evenly balanced. I'd only shuffled about up to that point because I'd been taking baby steps. It was time to engage my whole body to perform something quite strenuous. If my core proved to be a total wreck then my arms would have to haul me up, so I took a firm hold of the handrail with my left hand because the stairs went up on the right and down on the left.

It made sense to do the ascent first, whilst my energy levels were good.

Let's do this.

I trusted my right leg more than my left, so I led with that one as it would be called upon for that first push up.

Oh God, please don't let this be painful.

I had a second where I thought that the whole thing was ridiculous. If I failed the test, it might equate to a trip or a fall. I was a big guy, there would be no way Kiki and Becky could catch me if things went bandy. The fear of tumbling down a set of concrete stairs kept my mind channelled on the task ahead.

I maintained the most even balance I could and avoided any twists or unnecessary bends – like a robot, with my left leg taking my weight, I lifted my right foot up and onto the first step. Then, in one motion, I shifted my weight forward and to my right and I pushed through and up with a force that I felt confident would be just right. At the same time, I pulled at the handrail with my left arm with a similar power to pull myself upwards. My theory was that my damaged core muscles could be by-passed.

I landed my left foot next to my right.

Success!

It had worked. I stood still. I'd made it to step one, with no pain. Well, apart from the constant buzz. No sharp, searing agony to stop me in my tracks.

'That's it. Well done. Just keep doing that,' said Kiki from the landing behind me.

'Thanks,' I replied.

And I went on my way. Onwards and upwards. I thought about and planned every step, synchronised with my left arm and right leg, and each step became a mini triumph. I took my time, and we took a rest at the half-landing. I had nailed the technique straight away. My left arm suffered a bit of fatigue, but I wasn't going to let up and get complacent. I waddled around to attack the second half.

I impressed myself. Confident that my method and execution was painless, I drove on and climbed the second half mechanically, and kept a pace that worked for me. The staircase had been cool compared with the rest of the building, but I was conscious that I had worked up a sweat.

That final step, to conquer the full flight of stairs, was a fantastic one.

It signified recovery.

It represented a gateway that led to home.

All I had to do was to take my time, turn around, and walk downstairs.

Not quite as simple as it sounded. The methodology was similar. I switched arms (which was fine with my aching left arm) and slightly different leg muscles took my bulk in a controlled manner. I stayed square and precise in my movements. I didn't take any chances.

The two physios encouraged me all the way and I made it back to where I'd started.

'Well done, you,' said Becky.

'Great job,' said Kiki. 'How was that? All OK?'

I thanked them both and confirmed that I was OK and was happy that I wouldn't have to perform any more tasks for them.

They led me back to my bed. My victory lap was slow and steady, and I was a little disappointed that the crowds hadn't turned up in their droves to cheer me back home. Clearly there was a lot of jealousy from my fellow inmates as they knew I'd secured a Get-Out-Of-Jail-Free Card.

To be fair to my bay family, they showed me some love when they saw me return. They were pleased for me, and Roy and Stefano both asked me how I'd got on and congratulated me on my successful mission. As I was escorted back into bed, the guys made me feel a little like their child that had taken their first steps. The thought made me chuckle to myself. I was tired and sweaty, but it was all in a positive way, like a session at the gym or after a football match. I said my goodbyes to the physio team and thanked them for all their help. They countered with their own goodbyes and were exceptionally complimentary about my brilliant stair-walking. Then they left me there to recover as one satisfied customer.

Second Half, Downhill, Surely?

Anika continued her tests on me throughout the day. I'd always ask her if the readings were OK, and she would always tell me that they were. I took her word for it, as I hadn't got neurotic enough to start worrying about what my blood pressure was up to. The important thing was that I felt OK.

Unfortunately, saying that I felt OK wasn't enough. They'd booked me in for a CT scan.

How they loved those bloody scans. They couldn't leave those machines stood there gathering dust for more than a couple of minutes. Maybe someone, somewhere, was on a commission-only job.

Despite proving that I could handle stairs, a porter arrived to make sure I kept my date with the machine. I had become a professional patient. I'd come such a long way since my first scan just three months before. I knew the deal so well. That is not to say that it didn't bother me, because it did, but at least the process was familiar and predictable. The only doubt I had was that X-rays were one thing, but I'd not had the dye-injection-scan treatment since my insides had been mutilated and stapled back together.

When I was wheeled into the spacious scanning room, and as soon as our introductions were complete, I did have to question the main man. 'And it's quite safe with all these staples in me?'

'Yes. This scan is safe. It isn't based on powerful magnets if that is what you're worried about.'

Well, yes, as it happens, I was worried about powerful magnets that might rip all 48 staples out of my body, thank you. Every time I'd had one of those things before, they made sure my wedding ring and my chain are removed. Shit, they even hated zips and buttons enough to make me take off my trousers...oh bollocks, maybe I wasn't the pro that I believed I was.

'OK. Just double-checking,' I said to him, his two assistants, and myself. A little voice inside me nearly asked whether the iodine-based dye was going to screw me up, but I shut it down before it squeaked out.

I powered through and got the job done. I acted cool and calm throughout. Any observers would have thought – that guy isn't even in any pain. He's taking everything in his stride. The truth was that I put myself in the zone. It wasn't a case of finding a happy place; I just knew it would only be ten minutes of being uncomfortable mixed with spells of pain. That's exactly what it was.

The two assistants did everything they could to make the ordeal easier for me. I let them move me about, which must have been a challenge as I was completely tensed up. They must have thought I had rigor mortis.

As I entered the hoop of the machine I had to keep my arms above my head. It was awkward and my pain receptors pinged off. My lungs and my ribs weren't happy about the stretch. Any nerves that had remained uncut around my belly didn't scream out exactly, but they were not shy about letting me know that they were at their limit and anything more would cause a loud roar of objection. I concentrated on my breathing, which seemed the best (only) thing I could do to keep a lid on my emotions.

Something that had started off as disturbing, but had been downgraded to annoying, was the sensation of the liquids being injected via the cannula. The experience of the flushing through of the cool saline and then the iodine had become almost negligible to me. I lay there and waited for the rush.

When it came, I rode it. I recognised the warm feeling as it spread and raced around my vascular system. Despite the many scans, I still didn't like it much. I went through a few seconds of the familiar feeling that I was about to wet myself as the chemicals were pumped around my groin.

The table/bed pushed me in and trundled me out of the big hoop, and I breathed in and out as instructed. After ten minutes I'd finished my performance of the medical hokey-cokey.

When it was done, the main man who had hidden himself behind the glazed screens announced that they had everything they needed. As I was helped back into the wheelchair, I saw inside his recording studio. I prayed that whatever had been laid down on tape had been good enough to convince the doctors that I was safe to be released back into the community as planned.

We all thanked and congratulated one another for such a successful session. One assistant held the door open, and the other one wheeled me out into the corridor. I was pleased to see that my faithful porter had waited patiently for me, and he took the reins (the handles) of the wheelchair. We scooted off down corridors, rode the lift, and arrived back to the haven of my bay.

It had been a tiring outing. Straight after I'd climbed back into bed and got myself comfortable, I couldn't stop the sleep from claiming me. The gentle rush I felt as I drifted off was a far more natural one. My energy levels were spent, I was asleep in moments, and I was out for the count for two hours.

My Tuesday evening session was uneventful, which was perfect for me.

Because I had proven to everyone, including myself, that I was supremely mobile, I took an excursion to the communal day room. I had known of its existence, and I'd been wheeled or guided past it several times, but I had never had the pleasure of seeing inside. The door had always been half-open, and when I entered, I had no idea how many others would be inside.

The room was empty. Spacious and empty. There were a lot of comfortable-looking chairs positioned around the perimeter, pointed towards a television at the end of the room, but none of them were occupied. The television wasn't on. The atmosphere was dead quiet, and it made me feel like an intruder. If I'd felt more at home I might've taken a seat, put on the TV, and flicked through the channels until I found some football or Judge Judy. I decided quickly to just take a walk around the room rather than stay.

There was a coffee table to the left that was home to several tatty magazines and a couple of novels. The paperbacks were titles I didn't recognise, and both had suffered from broken spines in the hands of some overly aggressive readers. It was a pure reconnaissance mission, so I had no intention to make a pit stop. I might have changed my plans, and sat down and read something, had the material been intriguing. I checked out the walls and was encouraged that there were plenty of paintings and pieces of art to mask the duck egg-coloured walls. I stopped and read through one display that held dozens of cards from previous customers. The cards were open behind the glass to show a multitude of Thank Yous to the nurses and staff. It was nice to see that so many people had taken time out to show some heartfelt appreciation. Each letter or card represented a scary, life-changing story that was possibly similar to mine. It was overwhelming to try and comprehend how much pain and suffering had gone on inside that building.

The messages uplifted me, and I felt humbled by them.

'Well done, you lot,' I said to the framed display, as if all the senders and recipients were in front of me.

With my mission complete, I sloped back to my bay, before someone caught me in there, talking to the rest of the pictures.

Back in bed, I held a little video call with Ali, and it was lovely to talk about normal everyday stuff. She showed me the flowers and presents she'd got from her friends at work and asked me if I had any ideas how to fix the water dispenser from the fridge. The weather had taken a big turn for the worse, and the rain hammered down at both ends of the call, and we had to talk about how awful it was because Jayden was at QPR with some bin liners in the absence of a waterproof jacket. They were two-nil up against Birmingham, and I guessed he wouldn't mind too much about the weather if the result stayed like that. We ended the call celebrating that we'd got through another 24-hour step towards being at home together.

Another Day in Paradise

Tuesday night was a good one. Obviously, I'd had thousands of better nights, but it was the best one of that particular week. Since the epidural had been removed, I'd chomped up the pills I'd been given at regular intervals, and I remained fairly comfortable. I had been able to get used to sleeping on my back, and I felt happy that I was headed in the right direction. My mind was in a pretty good place. The fire alarm only went off once at 3am and Lukas had only disturbed me two or three times for my usual drips and pills. In the early hours I had drenched myself with an almighty night-sweat and I had to traipse off to the bathroom twice more to relieve my bladder. At least the fluid was trying to exit my body. Who was I kidding? It was a shit night's sleep.

I attempted to doze for as long as I could get away with, but the 8am staff change-overs started well before that, and the extra bodies and conversations were hard to ignore. The rain kept up its relentless attack on the big window to my left. If that wasn't noisy enough, because one of the panes was ajar, the wind crept in at the side and caused the half-drawn roller blind to move and bang against the wall. It was a dull thud, a dong, which sounded off once or twice a minute. After twenty minutes, the thud seemed to have doubled in volume. It was a noise that I'd found to get more and more irritating as each minute passed. I tried to block out the sound, but it was just too persistent and too bloody infuriating.

My wife had suffered from hyper-sensitive hearing all her life. Misophonia was the scientific name for sound-rage. I thought of her as I lay on my back and listened to the bong of the blind. I guessed that she would have been even more agitated than me, and I found it impossible to concentrate on anything else as the pauses between the thuds were just not long enough.

I hoped that I hadn't caught misophonia, I was certain it wasn't infectious.

Bong.

I couldn't count on the wind to ease.

The sound had got right under my skin.

The dividing curtains between us all meant I could only see Roy, but he didn't seem bothered by the roller blind at all.

Yet that blind continued to clonk against the wall.

I watched it. I saw the blind lift away from the wall, hang there for a moment, and then fall back so that the weighted end struck the side of the wall where it protruded out just enough to make contact. Dong.

And again. Bloody clonk.

Jeez, Louise! What had happened to me? That shitty annoying noise had driven me up the bloody wall. I couldn't take it any longer.

I had come up with a great plan. I moved the sheets out of the way. I pulled myself upright. I moved my legs to the left. I got out of bed. I went to a notice on the wall next to me and removed the Blu-Tack that held the bottom right hand corner in place. It wasn't a lot, but it would be enough. I marched (as much as I could march) to the blind and used the Blu-Tack to stick the banging corner to the wall at the point of contact.

Had I done it?

The wind whistled around the side of the window. It wasn't powerful enough to break the stickiness of the gum. The end held fast. Yes. I had cracked it. The noise had stopped, and I could get on with the rest of my life.

I got back into bed, delighted with myself. Maybe I should've just closed the window.

26 – ANOTHER DAY IN PARADISE

Breakfast was served on time. I'd taken my special pill to settle my stomach and enjoyed two biscuits of Weetabix, nicely softened with some milk (no sugar). It went down fine. The tea wasn't great, but it was good enough to set me up nicely for the day ahead. My plan was a day of uneventful recovery.

When I returned from my morning wash, I saw that the doctors were in town. Dr Haji and Dr Woo were with Roy. The curtains were open, and I tried not to be too nosey, but I couldn't help but listen in.

From what I could gather, it was great news. They were letting him go home.

As soon as the doctors left him, I had to confirm what I'd heard. 'Roy? Are they letting you go home?'

'Yes, they are,' Roy said, as calm as you like. It was as if it was never in doubt.

'Today?'

'Yes, today. Once they've sorted all the paperwork out.'

'That is brilliant news. Well done, you.'

'Thank you. Although I'm not going to get over-excited, we have been here before.'

That explained his calm demeanour. I for one would never forget his previous release date. He seemed to have proved his recovery to the team. They weren't doing much more for him that he couldn't do from the comfort of his home, so it made perfect sense to get the man home.

I smiled at my newfound friend. 'You'll be fine. Just don't do anything sudden, OK?'

'Don't worry, I won't.'

Roy excused himself from our chat. He said that he wanted to let his wife know that he was being discharged. I apologised for holding up that call and felt a pang of guilt that I'd found out such big news before Mrs Sanderson. Roy made his call, and I didn't even attempt to overhear, but I was sure it was lovely one to make.

I wanted to make my version of that call. It was the only call I wanted to make.

Possibly tomorrow, but definitely by Friday. That had been sealed with a high-five, so that was as good as a guarantee.

I'd felt an undeniable urge. It was a familiar urge, but it was one I hadn't sensed all week. My bowels were on the move. I'd squeaked out some farts and relieved a little built-up pressure, but I sensed something a little more substantial was on the way.

As scary as it was, I couldn't put it off any longer.

Every trip to the toilet since my surgery had drawn a blank when it came to the hard stuff. I had finally reached a point where my intestines had stirred themselves back to life. It must have been the same start-up sensations I experienced when I was first born. There weren't pains as such, but it wasn't just wind. I could just tell. Proper movement was afoot.

I had prepared for a long stay in the toilet. I'd even taken my phone in with me.

I sat down to implement Plan A – which was to take things exceptionally easy and to use very little force from my guts.

I was pleased to text Ali that Plan A had worked out like a dream.

Phil: Currently on the toilet giving birth to triplets!

Ali: Oh shit. Literally. Enjoy. Don't strain.

Phil: Didn't need to strain too much - played it perfectly.

Ali: So glad you've been, this is important xx
You must feel better for that x

Phil: I sure do.

Before my industrial scale clean up, Ali reminded me that because my operation had been brought forward a week, my ordeal was nearly over.

> Ali: Just think you were supposed to be going in today and now you're almost home.

> Phil: Oh yeah!

It was true. I was almost home. Almost.

27
When Wishes and Prayers Come True

'Yes. Good. We shall be discharging you later today.'

I could hardly believe what Dr Haji had just said to me.

I wanted to believe it, but anything that sounded too good to be true, normally wasn't. 'Really?'

'Yes. We have some blood tests to confirm this afternoon, but if they are still clear then we can let you go home later.'

'Wow. Thank you, so much.'

I was so taken aback; my reaction must have seemed like 6 out of 10 on the excitement scale. I was way too scared to get carried away. Surely there'd be a spanner chucked into the works somewhere along the line. It couldn't just suddenly happen so quickly. Could it?

I took several minutes to digest everything that had just happened. Mr Chai wasn't in attendance, but Dr Haji and Dr Woo were. They had told me that the results of the bloods they'd taken from me were all positive and the CT scan I'd had the day before had given me the all-clear. The team were satisfied with my progress. Before I could go, the team would need to brief me about all the medication I would be taking home, and about all the vaccinations and jabs I'd need in the absence of a spleen, and other practical things about my wound dressing and getting the staples removed. I asked them about the final drain that was clipped to my joggers and Dr Haji said that part of the deal was that I would have to return to the clinic part of the hospital the following week. It wasn't a problem. Christ, it was true; they were releasing me back into the wild.

27 – WHEN WISHES AND PRAYERS COME TRUE | 241

However, the caveat was that Mr Chai had to pass my afternoon blood test.

Shit, even if I failed that test in the afternoon, I'd pass it soon after. I would have banked a Thursday release date there and then, but Wednesday? That seemed ridiculous!

I immediately let Ali know the incredible news.

> Phil: If my afternoon blood tests are ok - they'll let me home later today. I'm not getting over-excited as I know there's some medication they'll need to get sorted...but it's gotta be soon. Fingers crossed that the blood tests are kind. X

Ali must have been busy at the school because it took her nearly half an hour to even look at her phone. Then, a nano-second later, she sent a reply.

> Ali: What???!!!

Then, after her shock had settled down, she became worried. As delighted as Ali was to get me home, she was equally as desperate to make sure I was being looked after as expertly as possible. So, I forgave her when she sent her second message nine minutes later.

> Ali: I'd feel a lot happier it being tomorrow x
> Please don't rush it x

Normally Ali didn't like personal calls at work, but the one that followed that exchange of messages was a brilliant exception.

I couldn't contain my excitement and Ali couldn't contain her apprehension. She wanted them to continue monitoring me every two hours. I told her we had a temperature gun at home, and a portable blood pressure machine, so I could self-monitor. If I was to get sick, I was under strict instructions to not piss about and get myself straight back to Hammersmith Hospital.

The delicious thought of lying in my own bed, with my own sheets and pillows filled my mind. I could take a hot shower in absolute comfort. I dreamt of trimming my beard back to a respectable length. There was nothing better than being able to sit on my own toilet for as long as I bloody-well wanted to. My daydream extended to every conceivable creature comfort – a proper cup of tea, biscuits, my reclining sofa, my TV. Oh yeah, seeing the kids would be nice as well.

'Look. If everything goes well today and they go through all the medication and nutrition business with me - I'm coming home – whether you like it or not.'

'Oh, Phil. As much as I'd love you to be home, I can't help but feel this is being rushed through.'

The rest of the call was filled with my statements of how the food was killing me and how pleased they were with my recovery. I was never going to convince Ali completely, because if I was honest to myself, I had my own reservations about the sudden, early exit. I had considered that maybe the NHS needed my bed. The difference was, I was prepared to take the gamble, leave the building (and the exceptional people inside), and see how it went from there. Ali questioned me about going to the American Football game. I said, barring a disastrous set-back, I was going to make it. Even if it meant strapping a bag of pancreatic juice to my side. She said that I was crazy, and I said that I agreed.

I wanted to share my update with as many people as I could, as quickly as I could. My phone struggled to keep any battery power it had as I pinged messages out to everyone I could. My mum, my brother, my dad, GaryMan, Tony from work, and every WhatsApp group that knew about my predicament. They had all known how much I'd suffered, and so they all came back with joyous messages in their own different words. I bathed in all the individual expressions of relief and love.

> Sean: I doubt you will get home as there is no fucking petrol anywhere...

> GaryMan: Great news mate. Although, how are you going to cope without your opiates. You smack-head.

It was a massive challenge to not chuckle or laugh because I was in such good spirits. I had been incredibly lucky not to have experienced any of those involuntary muscle spasms that used to grab me from time to time. No sneezes, laughs, or hiccups. There had been some coughs, but I had managed to keep a lid on them, so they were no more damaging than a gentle throat clearance.

The Race For Home

I went over to see Roy.

It wasn't even eleven in the morning, and he had his bags packed and was ready to go.

'I think we have a race on,' I said to him.

'Do we?'

'It certainly looks like it,' I confirmed. 'They've said there's a good chance I'll be chucked out later today.'

'That's fantastic news,' Roy said as his smile grew and the eyes behind his spectacles widened. He knew how much it meant to me because going home meant everything to him as well.

'It sure is. They've got all that paperwork to sort out, so it might not be until the end of the day, but yeah, great news. And you? Have they given you a time?'

'They told me that they are completing the discharge papers right now, then I just have to wait for the medication and then I'm a free man. Hopefully, I've only got an hour or two to go.'

I was so pleased for Roy. He'd been through more than me and there he was, hours away from leaving the hospital. We continued our chat and Roy told me that Grace would pick him up. Because we only lived ten minutes from each other, we discussed the option of a shared lift, but then dismissed it, as the timings would be way off. As much as I'd joked about a race, Roy was hours in front of me. When the conversation ended it wasn't punctuated with a goodbye and good

28 – THE RACE FOR HOME

luck (we were saving that for later), but we did know it was destined to be one of our last chats.

The waiting game was always the most boring. There was only so much time I could soak up with my mobile. I opened up the chess app, and after an hour of intense concentration (on top of the previous hour I'd spent that morning) I made moves in five separate games. With 24 hours to make each move, I knew my opponents wouldn't respond until later that day. I had never got sucked into the world of Facebook, Instagram, Twitter and all that unsocial media business, so I had to rely on amusing myself. I resigned to the idea that the day was going to drag.

One saving grace was that Anika had been tasked with facilitating my release, so at least I knew that there was some oomph behind the practicalities of my release. We had struck up a nice little friendship and she was happy to keep the pressure up when it came to chasing discharge papers and tests. After she'd extracted what I'd hoped would be the last of my blood tests from my arm, she escorted me down the corridor to get me weighed.

As we approached the same scales that I'd stood on when I had first arrived, I wondered how much weight I had lost. I had barely eaten all week. In fact, if I added up everything that I'd eaten since my operation, it still wouldn't come close to what I'd usually have as a Sunday roast. Not to mention the weight of a spleen, a tumour, and half a pancreas. Those chunks of flesh must have equated to a decent sized baby of several pounds. At least I hadn't felt weak from lack of food, and my intention was to keep building myself back up to fighting weight when I got home.

I stood on the scales and with Anika by my side we watched the arrow within the big dial spin clockwise into action. I remembered that before the operation I was 87kgs and thought it was possible that I'd probably gone under 13 stone if the scales showed 83kgs. I hadn't been anywhere near that weight since I'd left school.

The result shocked me.

'You've put on fifteen kilos,' Anika announced before she wrote the result down.

That sounded outrageous to me. There must have been a mistake because Anika wasn't a jokey sort of person.

'What? That can't be right?'

'Yes. Look. The scales show 102 kilos,' she said as she pointed at the number on the dial.

I had been looking at the right place, but I didn't quite believe what I saw. The movable stainless-steel arrow had indeed rested on 102.

'Is that in pounds?' I quizzed, still not understanding how the weigh-in had gone.

Anika laughed. 'No! Of course not!'

'What? How the hell could I have put on fifteen kilos? That's like two buckets of water?' I hoped that I didn't sound rude, but I couldn't contain my surprise. How the hell could I have gained the weight of a medium sized suitcase when all I'd eaten was a few bowls of Weetabix and an egg sandwich?

'It's OK. It does happen.'

As reassuring as Anika tried to be, I had to question her.

'But I've barely eaten; I thought I would've lost two and half stone. Not put it on!'

'It probably is because your body has retained so much of the fluid that has been given to you.'

I paused to take in that information. It was true that from the waist down I'd inherited the bottom half of the Michelin Man. I looked down at my swollen legs and once again registered how tight the red socks had become around my lower calves. I had never felt frail or weak, so I guessed it was possible. I remembered what Mr Chai had told me about how the body could react to the trauma of surgery. My body reacted by soaking up every last drop of liquid that had entered my blood stream via the IV drip.

It seemed bizarre. Yet, the professionals didn't seem to be concerned that their patient had turned into a sponge.

The explanation seemed plausible.

'Oh, OK,' I said.

28 – THE RACE FOR HOME

Anika helped me down from the scales and walked me back. I let her reassure me further as she explained that gradually my body would return to normal. I wondered how many wees I would need to get rid of fifteen litres of water. Or possibly, the equivalent of a hundred night-sweats.

After the shock of my weigh-in and having accepted that I was still officially classed as a heavyweight, I found the wait continued to make me restless and antsy. I got up and went for a walk. There was only one place to go, the day room.

I decided that I would watch some television. Because it was the middle of the day, and a Wednesday at that, I wasn't expecting much to be on. I doubted there would be much channel selection beyond the terrestrial workings of Channel 5. I hoped that Homes Under The Hammer or Bargain Hunt could wash over me for an hour, or until I jumped out of the second-floor window in exasperation.

Surprisingly, there were some signs of life inside the room. The TV was on; it looked like This Morning or possibly Loose Women (technically the same thing) flickered away at the far end of the room. Fortunately, the sound had been muted. More noticeably there was a woman in one of the armchairs on the left, next to the coffee table. I noticed that she furiously texted on her phone. In the space of two seconds, I'd assessed her as being the same age as me, possibly a few years younger, with sandy coloured hair that would have lain just below her shoulders if she hadn't tied it back in a ponytail. With olive skin and dark features, I guessed she had Mediterranean roots. She was clad in a hospital gown and was attached to a machine that held up a foil-covered bag. I noticed that a thin tube came from the bag and wormed its way down and inside the woman's gown. It then came up through the neck and entered a nostril. It wasn't clear like a saline solution, but it was a solid white. It looked like milk.

She sensed me in the room and looked up from her phone.

We patients didn't have to wear face masks, so we politely exchanged smiles.

After the smiles, we both said, 'Hello.'

I would've been happy to leave it at that and to take a seat on the other side of the room, to give her some space and privacy, but I soon discovered she was a bit of a chatterbox.

'Sorry, I'm trying to get hold of my daughter's school. What a nightmare.'

I wasn't sure if she expected me to offer advice, sympathy, or a solution. 'I bet. Nothing's easy when you're stuck in this place.'

'Damn right', she said with authority and gave me a nod that compounded our agreement. 'How long have you been here? I haven't seen you before.'

I then had to become the chatterbox and gave her a short and not-very-sweet account of my stay at Hotel Hammersmith. I did my best to not sound too delighted about it being my last day as she looked like she still had some work to do.

'What are you in here for?' I asked in my most friendly way.

We spoke for twenty minutes or so, but I never found out her name. Her story was not an easy one to forget. It made me realise that I had been extremely fortunate because my illness had been contained and, unless the biopsy came back with something awful, I believed I was on the mend. It was true that there was always someone far worse off than yourself.

Her horror show had kicked off eight weeks before, when she had started vomiting out of the blue, and from then on she simply hadn't stopped. It wasn't a case of food poisoning, or pregnancy that she (and her GP) had assumed. After three weeks of hell, she ended up in A&E. She couldn't keep anything down, hence the white tube that provided some manufactured nutrition. She had scared the life out of her thirteen-year-old daughter and had fainted numerous times in front of her partner, mother, friends, and work colleagues. Despite many tests, the experts were still trying to work out exactly what they should do to fix her. They had told her that she had a rare stomach cancer, but she was currently undergoing more tests to see what else because she had become a complicated case for them. Every result they got back spiralled into a world where they needed further tests. Her time in hospital had been relentless.

28 – THE RACE FOR HOME

I was impressed with her positive attitude. Considering I was a stranger, she was candid and open. I saw a lot of how I had handled my illness mirrored in her demeanour. Maybe she was still in shock and denial like I had been, although it was more likely that she was just incredibly strong. A series of beeps from the computer that controlled her medication interrupted her story of how she was trying to hold down a full time job in the city and being a parent whilst being bed-ridden.

'Ah, sorry about this. I've got to change this over,' she said, referring to the foil covered bag.

'No problem. You go for it.'

As she left the day room, I wished her luck and hoped that she would be back to normal life quickly. She thanked me and said that she hoped I was in the clear and wouldn't be back.

There was always someone worse off. I felt a pang of guilt that I was due to leave that day, whilst she would be stuck in the middle of a medical maelstrom without a positive exit plan.

I couldn't find the remote for the TV, so it stayed muted. I stared at Schofield and Willoughby as they silently stood next to a big prize wheel. They seemed to be highly amused with whatever was being said in the studio. I wasn't certain, but it looked like Kim from Lincoln had won £1,000. The presenters continued to laugh inanely like a couple of teenagers sharing a spliff. I was glad that I couldn't find the remote. Having completed a 30 minute chunk of the day, I got up and left the day room. I'd only visited it twice, and I hoped that everything would go well enough that I wouldn't have to visit again.

Roy waited patiently. His bag hadn't moved. He was as calm as I was restless.

'Have you got a time yet, Roy?'

'Not yet. The paperwork is done, I'm just waiting for my medication.'

'OK, that's good. So, nearly there.'

'Yes. Nearly.'

I started to pack. That would burn up some time.

I took my time because I was naturally slower and also, I deliberately wanted to drag it out. The holdall had a few pairs of discarded pants inside, but otherwise it was empty and light. I wasn't quite ready to powerlift heavy bags about. I carefully packed my washbag, my phone charger, towel, and some clothes. Sixty seconds later I was done. So much for killing time. I hadn't packed my book because, like Roy, I intended to keep reading right up to the time of my release. It was the only thing that would keep me sane.

My day dragged on into mid-afternoon. Waiting for blood test results was boring. As I lay, propped up on my bed, my hero turned up. I put my book down to my right. I knew Mr Chai was an exceptionally busy man; every day was non-stop, packed with one life-threatening emergency trumped by the next. It must have been a bizarre environment to work in. He could easily have sent one of his team, yet he made the time and came to see me. It was a classic fifty-fifty situation and he'd arrived personally to announce his ultimate decision. As The Clash once sang, '*Should I stay, or should I go?*'

He had his mask under his chin so I could hear him clearly. 'Hello, Philip. How are you?'

Please don't break my heart. Don't break my spirit by snatching away this opportunity to get home.

'Hi. I'm doing OK thanks. You?'

'Yes, I'm fine thank you.'

I felt a bit sick. The anticipation was horrible. I teetered on the brink of losing my manners and almost barked out – *Am I leaving today, or were the blood tests no good?* Like an innocent man in the dock, praying for a non-guilty verdict, I waited for the main man to deliver my fate.

'Well look, the blood tests have confirmed that you have been fighting an infection, and we've spoken before about your temperature.'

The Clash sang on, '*It's always tease, tease, tease.*'

Come on. Just say it.

'What we are going to do is to let you do the rest of your recovery from home.'

Home. He'd just said the magic word.

28 – THE RACE FOR HOME

A powerful cocktail of relief and excitement whooshed through me. I didn't question it; there was no way I was going to say anything that might make him reconsider. 'That is such brilliant news. Thank you so much. Thank you. Genuinely, thank you.'

I held eye contact with him. Those brown eyes were windows to the man's intelligence and, more than that, his kindness. I couldn't summon up any profound words to express the emotions and gratitude that I felt. The man had saved my life. We shared a moment, a smile, and I'd like to think, some mutual respect.

'You are very welcome,' he said.

Obviously, he had held similar conversations with countless patients over his distinguished career. For me, it was the first time.

'Thank you for saving my life. And, my wife says, "Thank you" as well.'

His smile was sincere. 'The team and I are just doing our job, but thank you, it is appreciated. I also have to say that you're not quite out of the woods yet.'

Our glorious moment was tinged with some unpleasant realities. Every silver lining had a cloud. My surgeon went on to remind me about making sure I kept my wound clean and insisted that I gave my body time to heal. I was not to exert myself. No driving for six weeks, the same advice as though I'd had a C-section. He said that the team would be by to talk me through all the medication that I would be on, and to help arrange all the vaccinations I'd need over the following weeks. No spleen meant nasties like meningitis and hepatitis were a greater danger to people without a complete immune system.

He said they'd booked me in to attend his clinic session the following week to make sure I was on track. Hopefully, my final drain and bag could be removed at that point because until then, it was going to be a constant companion and it was coming home with me.

The main point Mr Chai wanted to make was that I was still on their radar. They were still a week away from understanding the results from the biopsy of the tumour, and they would need to scan me in three-month intervals. The support team would arrange everything, and all I had to do was turn up.

I acknowledged all the information. I felt reassured and safe that they would continue to look out for me. The service was exceptional. They could not have done anything better to fix me. Apart from the food – the food was shocking.

He wrapped things up. 'If that is all OK, I'll see you next Monday.'

'Yes, that all sounds perfect to me.'

He held out his right hand. 'Excellent. Well goodbye for now.'

I grabbed it between both my hands. It was a handshake that deserved to be doubled-up to demonstrate as much gratitude as I could muster. 'Goodbye. And thanks again.' I let go of his skilful hand; a more passionate person may have squeezed hard enough to break it. He gave me a final nod of acknowledgment and left me to complete my departure plans.

I didn't have an exact time, but I needed to ensure my lift home knew that we had a bright green light and to get ready for the trip. I was on a massive high. I'd forgotten all about the dull ache of my abdomen, but my chest seemed fine, and my sore throat was long gone. Good times all the way.

> Phil: They are deffo chucking me out today!
> Might be 6/7pm or whatever but it's happening. All results and opinions are in. They've got stuff to do before I leave - new dressing/medication/paperwork etc all I have to do is come in on Monday for the clinic people to remove my last tube. Get in.

> Ali: Oh my...OK. I think...
> You need to check all aftercare instructions also things like driving etc and make sure you understand it all x

> Phil: Yeah yeah yeah. Call me when you can ...
> could be 6/7pm... obviously don't leave until we know x

It felt so good to confirm my release in writing. It made it seem even more believable. Nothing would stop me; I was out of there, no matter what.

As promised, Anika came to me armed with all her paraphernalia to change my dressing. It had been two days, so a change was due, but it was satisfying to be sent home all clean and packaged up, and as up to date as I could possibly be.

I knew the drill with Anika. Once the new dressings had been cut up and ready to be fixed in place, she put herself into a low gear and her speed became completely unhurried, as if she had all the time in the world. As gently as she could, she removed the old bandages.

I had a brief spell of bravery.

As Anika moved all the used dressings to the medical waste bin, I looked down at my exposed tummy.

I was shocked by what I saw. The sight made me draw in a sharp breath.

The damage looked far worse than what I'd hoped or expected. The whole area was numb, probably because of the cut nerves and all the painkillers so the appearance was miles away from the nothingness that it had felt like.

I saw a long series of brutal-looking metal staples that stretched from my solar plexus down to just above my naval. Then the mini-train tracks took a ninety-degree left turn and travelled all the way to my left flank. The staples were industrial versions of the ones I'd used at work to hold multiple-paged contracts together. How the hell had they physically achieved this? The staple machine must have looked like something out of a Saw movie. I had expected dozens of stitches, and I was aware of the term staples, but what I saw was a massive zip. I looked like I wore a skin-coloured onesie.

It wasn't neat. The clips weren't exactly evenly spaced, and the patched-up line was higgledy-piggledy. There was a noticeable puffy bulge where the lines had crossed. The shaved skin around each entry point looked bruised and tender. There were areas along the length that held patches of congealed blood and I could see immature scabs had tried to take shape.

It was one ugly motherfucker of a scar.

Anika returned before I morbidly started counting the staples. The way she cleansed my wound was just as measured and tender as before. I watched her with fascination. I barely felt anything; it was as if she was touching someone else.

I knew that the scar had become a part of me. It represented the darkest time of my life and yet it also acted as a symbol of how strong I could be when faced with genuine terror. Not many people would ever see it, but I wondered how others would perceive the physical reminder of my operation. As grotesque as it was, I guessed it would settle down and Ali would, in time, get used to it. The scar was a reminder for every step she had been through with me. The kids would get to see it from time to time, assuming I would be allowed to go swimming on holiday or whenever, and I hoped it wouldn't make them too queasy. As for anyone else? Well, I figured I could impress them with tales of a shark attack that I'd heroically escaped from.

Anika completed my new dressing and it all looked neat and tidy. The bandages were pure white and hid the fucked-up mess below as perfectly as they could. She told me that I needed to book an appointment with my local GP surgery to get the dressings changed in a few days. The random box of plasters I had at home were simply not up for such a massive job, so I was more than happy to book an expert. As if on cue, Anika handed me a big selection of wipes and sterile bandages that were large enough to cover my whole tummy. I couldn't get those mega-sized plasters at Boots, so I thanked Anika and hid them in my A4 folder that contained all my case notes.

Before I could lay back and admire my neat tummy, Anika had changed gears again. She sped off with her trolley only to reappear sixty seconds later. The trolley had gone, and instead she had a clear plastic bag with her.

She had brought me a shitload of drugs.

Anika sat down at the end of my bed with a bag full of little boxes. It seemed strange that she'd chosen to sit. I guessed that the instructions were going to take some time because it was the first time I'd ever seen her take the weight off her feet.

28 – THE RACE FOR HOME

She emptied the bag on the bed, and the many boxes made a monster game of medical Jenga. She sorted through the boxes and found the first two she wanted. She took me through the course of antibiotics that I was on. Like a good boy I was expected to finish the current course and it meant taking one pill three times a day for seven more days. Then, after I'd finished that little lot, there was a different box for me to consider – prophylactic antibiotics. Anika explained they were to prevent infection before it started. I needed two a day, one in the morning and one in the evening. When I asked for how long I was supposed to take the prophylactics, she looked at me and said that I would be on them indefinitely. Forever. For the rest of my days.

From what I could gather, those pills were intended to help replace my spleen.

What I needed was a pill box because I knew that I was bound to forget to take a pill at some point. And then I'd be in intensive care the following day.

Once home (I'd soon be home) I'd get straight on to Amazon and get myself a nice colourful daily dispensing pill box. And I'd set reminder alarms on my phone. All of that could help keep me alive.

That wasn't the end of the antibiotics. Anika showed me a third batch that consisted of two boxes that had red flashes on them. 'These are emergency rescue antibiotics.'

I was a little puzzled. 'Er...OK.'

'Yes. If you feel unwell then you are to stop the prophylactics and start these.' She took a pen from the chest pocket of her uniform and wrote RESCUE PACK in black on both boxes. 'And then you must check yourself into the hospital straight away.'

She was deadly serious.

I wanted to get a better definition of what unwell meant. Were we talking a bout of diarrhoea, cardiac arrest, or everything in between?

'How do you mean unwell?' I asked, hoping it wasn't going to mean just a simple headache.

'If you have a fever, or a temperature. You know, if you're sick or if you think your body is not winning against an infection.'

Her clarification made things a little less woolly for me. 'Oh, OK.'

I took the boxes from her. Red for danger I thought. I accepted that I would need to take them at some point. I knew I wasn't going to stay well forever.

'These do have an expiry date on them, so make sure you get them replaced before they run out of date.'

I checked one of the boxes. August 2023. I had a two-year window. I wondered how long I could last until I needed to be rescued by the emergency pills.

Anika dug out the box of Omeprazole. I already knew what it was for, but I let Anika explain it to me. I had to take one a day, in the morning, thirty minutes before I ate anything. My new life would have to adjust to that restriction. My morning routine for as long as I could remember had been to wake up, toilet, shower, get dressed, eat breakfast, leave for work. I worked out that I would need to add in a new stage of take Omeprazole straight after wake-up otherwise I'd be sitting around for the best part of half an hour until it was deemed safe to have a bowl of cereal.

Next up, Anika went through a wonderful cocktail of painkillers.

For starters, they'd given me a bumper box of paracetamol. I knew I had some at home, but it was nice to have extra supplies for free. They weren't extra special ones; I was allowed to take two of them every four hours. If they didn't hit the spot, I was allowed to dip into the Dihydrocodeine tablets. The label on the codeine box told me I was not allowed more than four 30mg pills in a day. If that combo didn't help, then I had a third line of defence within a box of Pregabalin capsules. I was only allowed two of them over a 24-hour period. Unlike the codeine, they weren't opioid based, but were prescribed for neuropathic pain. My father-in-law had taken Pregabalin recently and he'd had a rough time on it, so I made a decision to take them only if I truly needed the extra boost.

Anika said that was it for medication and handed me the A4 sheet of paper that listed all the drugs she'd spoken about. What I needed was a schedule, or a timetable, which gave me each weekday and the times I needed to take each pill. I calculated that I would have to set an alarm on my phone to go off every thirty minutes to keep on top of my new drug-taking life.

There had been a lot to absorb. What I wanted to ask was: *If I missed any of these pills, how long would I live for?*

Then there was another bit of paper for Anika to go through. No wonder she'd chosen to sit down. It was a comprehensive list of all the vaccinations that I would need to book in with my GP once I was safely home.

Within the first two weeks post-op, I needed to have had jabs to cover two different types of meningitis strains. There would be initial injections and then a further series the following month. Then there was a Pneumococcal polysaccharide vaccine to arrange. That one was to help me fight off pneumonia in case that extremely common bugger wanted to seek me out when I could be at my lowest. Those nasty ones would last a few years at least. Added to that I was down for seasonal flu vaccines and covid boosters. There was no getting away from it; I had been promoted to the local GP's number-one customer.

Anika told me that if I had any intention of going on holiday to exotic countries, I needed to make sure I understood what other vaccinations I would need. She made it clear to me that there would be some places that were out of bounds. Even if I went to the most developed countries, I would always have to take my rescue pack with me.

Just to make sure I understood my spleen had gone, I was handed a card. It was business-card sized to fit snuggly in my wallet. White with bold red lettering to express the importance of the message. I read the words – *I have no functioning spleen.* I turned it over and saw that Anika had filled in some blanks, my name, date of birth, and the medication I was dependant on. I was supposed to carry the card with me at all times in case I fell so unwell I couldn't explain my organ loss to any potential lifesaver. That was fantastic, with the assumption they checked through my wallet. I considered the possibility of having the words tattooed on my chest, inspired by soldiers that have their blood types tattooed on their bodies. I looked at the card again, the words were factually correct, but they seemed so harsh and matter of fact. I hid it in the folder.

Anika then pulled out some industrial looking hardware.

I knew that it was coming because I'd seen it fall into the mountain of pill boxes when she'd tipped the bag out. Still sealed in their sterile bag, Anika placed the bolt-cutters in front of me.

'You will need to take these with you to the district nurse in two weeks. They'll need them to remove your clips. Don't take them out as they need to remain sterile.'

I picked up the bag. They were hand-held bolt-cutters, but they were sturdy ones. I gave them a squeeze and saw the pincers bite together through the bag.

'Err...OK,' I said with some trepidation.

They were a modern stainless-steel version of a medical instrument from medieval times. Brutal and frightening. I tried not to picture how a nurse would use them in a fortnight to free me from the dozens of staples that were tightly fastened against my torn skin. I left that mental bridge uncrossed and did my best to move on.

Finally, Anika handed me her last two sheets of paper that confirmed my consented discharge. I saw the words DISCHARGE SUMMARY at the top, but I didn't bother reading further because I'd catch up on all the technical blurb when I was at home. At home! Thank you, you merciful God.

'I just need to remove your cannula, and then you really are free to go.'

Rejoining my Favourite Timeline

The cannula came out and was replaced with a cotton swab whilst I was still on my high. I barely noticed Anika's swift work, although I did thank her and told her I would say goodbye before I left. I had reached the point where I had been given everything I needed and all of the restrictions that had kept me in hospital had been cut. I called Ali and told her that I was all packed and ready to be picked up.

It was a quick call, and Ali ended it when she said, 'I'm on my way. I love you.'

The stars were almost complete in their alignment. Ali was on her way. If the traffic on the A40 was kind, she was less than an hour away.

It was almost 7:00pm. I'd completed a final double-check of my bedside unit to make sure that I hadn't left anything behind. My holdall was zipped up and it wasn't too heavy. If I took my time, I was confident that I could walk out of the hospital with the bag over my shoulder, exactly the way I'd walked in with it.

Roy was still in his chair. Just like me he, was packed up and ready to leave.

'I'm embarrassed to say that I'm going to beat you out of here,' I said to him.

He was as calm and unflustered as ever. 'I've got all the paperwork; I'm just waiting for my medication.'

Anika was busy attending to Stefano, but she must have heard us speak. She came straight over.

'Have you checked in your locker?'

Roy looked as confused as me. 'What? No. What locker?'

She pointed above his head. 'The box behind you, on the wall. I think they locked it in there.'

Roy and I looked at each other. Surely not. He'd had his discharge letter since just after lunch. He put his book down and got up to check. He turned his back to me, turned the key that was still in the lock, and opened the door of the small box.

'Aah,' he said without any emotion. He turned back to face us, and he held the packet of drugs out in front of him, to show us what he'd found.

I would have been furious if that had happened to me. Every minute in that hospital was a torturous one. I was incredulous. 'They'd been in there all the time?'

Anika didn't answer. She seemed somewhat embarrassed.

'Hmm, so it would seem,' Roy said, as if he didn't have a care in the world.

Maybe he was just pleased that he had his medication. If he wasn't that bothered, then I wasn't going to make a huge fuss about it. I wondered how long he might have waited if Anika hadn't overheard us. Nobody seemed to have been aware of Roy's situation. I was pissed off for him, yet he was so cool. I think he just wated to phone his Grace and say he was ready to be picked up.

It wasn't a time to be angry. I kept it light because it was a time to celebrate. 'I just want to say that it wasn't me that hid them in there just to win our little race.'

He gave me a side-eye look. 'I wouldn't put it past you...'

'Well, I'm going to make a move out of here, before you find out the truth.'

'You're leaving now?'

'I sure am.'

'Good for you,' Roy said, and he shot out his right hand. 'Thanks, Phil. And good luck with everything.'

I shook his hand. It was a proper old-fashioned, mutually respectful handshake. Our goodbye was honest and heart-warming. We'd been thrust together for the most intense and distressing week of my life, but we had survived. It would be true to say that we had helped each other through a terrible storm, and without each other, it would have been lonely and even more traumatic.

'No. Thank you, Roy. You've really helped me through all of this.'

'Likewise.'

'Cheers, Roy. And good luck to you too.'

Our handshake ended. I returned to my bed, carefully loaded the holdall on to my shoulder and left. I paused to exchange goodbyes with Stefano. He was his usual dramatic self and made out that I had been his favourite and he would never forget me. He always made me laugh.

Incredibly, Boring Dean was still mumbling into his phone. He probably wasn't even aware that I was walking out of the bay for the last time. I offered a sheepish wave in his direction. He looked away. I couldn't help but think *fuck you*.

I ambled past the long reception desk. Anika had returned to her base after telling Roy where his medicine was. I noticed her in a state of concentration whilst she typed up some notes. She was on the last hour of yet another ridiculously long, exhausting shift.

'See ya,' I called out as I sneaked by.

Anika had already given me a goodbye, but she looked up and shrieked out a final farewell. 'Goodbye, Philip! Good luck with everything.'

'Thanks. You and the team have been incredible. Thank you for looking after me so well.'

'Aww. You're welcome. It has been a pleasure.'

A pleasure? That was something that I seriously doubted.

'Well, keep up the good work, you've been brilliant.'

I hadn't stopped, and I kept up my steady pace and made my way through to the lift lobby. Anika watched me leave and then returned to her computer. Life for everyone on the ward continued. Life in the hospital was relentless.

The lift took me down to the ground floor and then opened its automatic doors to present me to whoever was there to greet me. Bizarrely, there was an audience of one; someone I knew. Stood in front of me was Lukas. He, too, had a sports bag on his shoulder. He wore a jacket and jeans which looked odd as I'd only ever seen him in scrubs. I assumed he was on his way to change shifts with Anika.

He appeared surprised to see me. 'Oh vow. You are go-ink home?'

I smiled. The big man had generated moments of sheer terror for me. Those moments were well and truly behind me, though. Weren't they?

'Yes, I am officially a free man.'

'Ah. Goot fur you. Are you feelink OK?'

'Thanks, and yes, I'm good thank you. Thanks to you and the team.'

We swapped places. Lukas stepped aside to let me move away from the lift, and he walked inside the metal box to replace the space I'd left. There was no handshake and that was fine with me.

'Sank you,' he said as the doors began to close. 'Guttbye!'

'See ya,' I said as the doors closed and, just like that, I was safe from any last second psychopathic behaviour. I was glad I got to say a goodbye to him. I never did work out quite what made the male nurse tick, but I couldn't deny that he had played a significant part in getting me through those awful nights when I was at my most vulnerable.

I had plenty of time, so I took deliberately short steps along the first long corridor to protect my energy levels. The bag felt a bit heavier. I was determined not to stop. I remembered the route out and there were signs fixed up high to confirm that I was going in the right direction.

Midway along there was a left turn, which led to another lengthy corridor. I kept left, near to the wall, just in case I needed some support. I trudged on and each small step took me further away from my personal hell and a step nearer to the love of home, so although my steps were short, they were doubled because of their meaning.

Maybe I should have accepted the offer to get a porter to wheel me out? No. It had turned into a walk of glory to prove to myself that I had conquered the entire ordeal. Phil the Warrior.

29 – REJOINING MY FAVOURITE TIMELINE

At the end of yet another long corridor, I found myself in the opened-up reception area. Because the normal working day was done it was quiet. Only a few people were about. There was no guard of honour to mark my departure, not that I expected one.

At the end of the reception lobby, I saw the doors.

They looked beautiful.

My body had become tired. It simply wanted me to stop, to put the sodding bag down and to take a rest. No chance. Those double doors were just yards away, no way would I stop. I'd rest the other side of those doors.

Body, if you want us to stop, you're going to have to do better than to ache and creak.

As I approached the doors, the magic of the automation worked. The sensor had seen me come near and it activated the glazed doors. They parted and glided in opposite directions to present a huge opening.

I crossed the threshold.

The bright lights of the lobby behind me lit the paving ahead of me as I strode into the autumnal evening. The sun had just set. The air felt cool, and it made me realise that I'd grown acclimatised to the stuffiness of the hospital without thinking about it. Similarly, the sounds and acoustics were obviously unlike everything I'd got accustomed to. Being outside felt wonderfully familiar and strangely different. The outside world had carried on, whilst I'd been suffering in the parallel universe of Hammersmith hospital.

I spotted a bench that was located perfectly to where I expected Ali to park. The bench faced the low boundary wall, and I would be able to look over it to see the cars go past on the main road. I kept up my steady pace and promised my body that it could rest once it got me to that ideal seat.

My legs kept moving and didn't let me down. They got me to my target.

I slowly placed my bag on the bench, and then turned and sat next to it.

My breathing had become laboured, and I hadn't noticed I'd

sweated until my T-shirt had touched the skin of my back as I sat down. I'd ignored all of those signs of fatigue as I was so fixated on making it to the outside and to that bench. I let myself recover from the exertion. I sat up as straight as I could and concentrated on my breaths. It only took a couple of minutes to get myself comfortable with regulated breathing.

I checked the time on my phone. Ali was probably ten minutes away. That wasn't too bad.

It gave me time to reflect on what had happened to me. I thought of Roy puking up blood in front of me on day one; coming out of the blackness of my operation; I thought of my crazy Saturday when I was convinced I'd witnessed all sorts of debauchery and illegal drug-dealing – everything seemed outrageous and unbelievable. It made me question my own sanity.

Ten minutes had turned into fifteen and I had started to feel the chill of the late September air. I shivered and it made my core ache. I didn't want to go back into that bloody building just to use its heat. Come on, Ali.

Then, I witnessed the most glorious vision...I saw our car.

Over the wall, I spotted Ali's handsome blue SUV drive by from right to left and slow down as it approached the main entrance. Seconds away, my rescue was seconds away.

I got up. My body sent a jolt of pain through me that should have manifested itself as a wince written on my face. I converted it into a smile. I left the bag on the bench, as the extra weight might have stolen my smile away. No way was I going to show any weakness. I stood up strong, and proud that I'd made it out. Well, 98.5% of me had made it out.

The car slowed and came to a stop right next to me and my bench.

I saw Ali. She had wound down her window and I could see her beautiful smile.

'Alright?' I said.

'Alright, Mr Gorgeous?' she replied.

'Yeah, not bad.'

29 – REJOINING MY FAVOURITE TIMELINE

'My God! How long have you been outside? It's freezing. You'll catch a death of cold!'

Harrison wasn't there because he was stuck at work, but Jayden and Lydia were in the back of the car and Ali's strangely worded statement had cracked them up.

'A death of cold?' Jay mocked as Lydia giggled away. I'd missed their laughter.

Ali looked at me for support. 'That's what you say, isn't it?

I offered no support at all. 'I have no idea. It's almost right.'

Ali jumped out of the car. She ran over and our hug was perfect. Not too passionate to cause pain, but loving enough to tell each other that everything was going to be alright. If we were together, everything would be OK. It was wonderful to feel the warmth of her cheek next to mine. She smelt so lovely, and it made me smile some more. I don't think I'd overflowed with the emotions from a happiness/relief combination before.

Ali let go of me and took my bag from the bench. She loaded it in the boot and got in the driver's seat whilst I tentatively got myself into the passenger side. The blue scissor-clip held the bag and tube to my side, but I still took care, so I didn't knock or catch it on anything. Once inside, I immediately felt the electric excitement from everyone in the car. The chat and banter started up between us as a group. We'd all been through the experience; it hadn't been just me. We were all overjoyed that it was all over. I was back in the right universe; I could restart my life and I might even be able to finish that bloody painting of Pelé.

Ali drove us home.

Epilogue

It took several weeks, but life for me, Ali and the family managed to return to normal. In that time, I was told that the biopsy results were good and was given an all clear. I had suffered a significant pancreatic tumour, and not the almost always deadly pancreatic cancer. The regular check-ups and CT scans have continued to give us good news. I've looked back at everything that happened and can consider myself lucky; lucky that they caught that monster before it enveloped even more vessels and took more organs and tissue with it. Compared with many others that have had their own journeys with their health, I am extremely lucky. Not that my tumour had been a walk in the park, because it had taken me to gates of hell, and it had changed me in a lot of ways.

My sons helped get me safely to the Jets game and I managed to keep my bag of pancreatic juice strapped to my side and out of harm's way. It was a big achievement, and the ninety thousand people around me had no idea what struggle I'd been through to get there. We lost the game, but the result was secondary; I had a soppy grin on my face throughout because I was simply delighted to be alive and mobile.

I chose not to extend the writing of my experiences beyond hospital, simply because I had to draw the line somewhere. My physical rehabilitation and working hard to stand up straight were tough but unremarkable. After three weeks I had the pleasure of handing over the sterile bolt cutters to a nurse and she unzipped me from my metal staples. Four weeks back and I finally had the last drain and bag removed (I'd lost count how many times that bloody tube snagged itself on the kitchen unit handles). All was good, no more drama. It took dozens of slowly eaten meals before my digestive system got back to anything normal and eventually the doctors decided to put me back on Metformin because my damaged pancreas didn't quite squeeze out enough insulin. My recovery was a steady and calm one.

I also discovered, several months after my return, that I had contracted sepsis whilst in Hammersmith hospital. My surgeon had explained about the dangers of infection after an operation, but when it bit, I had been kept in the dark. Or at least, I couldn't remember being told, and I hadn't realised or worked it out either.

Sepsis got a foothold and almost took full control, and it could have beaten me.

It certainly made a massive impression. It attacked me by making my body attack itself. With my spleen missing, my immune system didn't know what to do, so it just went into overdrive and started a massive fight with everything. It caused havoc with my body temperature as my defences continued with its angry, heated war. It explained why my breathing had become so erratic and painful, and the compromised oxygen levels further hampered any recovery. Ali noticed how ill I had looked; she had been alarmed by my pasty, white-grey colour. I had been unaware that they had put me on powerful antibiotics; I simply accepted one IV bag after another.

Fortunately, the drugs had done the trick. Surviving sepsis was a huge triumph.

For me, the most troubling effect of sepsis was what it did to my brain. I had assumed that the bizarre thoughts, emotions, and convincing hallucinations I experienced on that insane Saturday had been caused by half a ton of opiate-based morphine.

I was wrong.

I have checked it out since and many people with sepsis suffer hallucinations, delirium, confusion, nightmares, and panic attacks. As it turns out, going crazy is common.

Writing about my hospital adventures has helped me unpick most of the insanity. And whilst I can accept that my orgy of brain-fucks was a result of raging sepsis, I do wish I could see the video footage of my time in the grips of it, just so I could put all those ridiculous, unexplained events to bed.

Acknowledgements

The majority of my thanks for the successful publication of both of these books should really go to the many insanely good people within the NHS. I changed all the names to protect the innocent and, because of the way of the world, to protect myself against any lawsuits for defamation of character. When the shit really hit the fan, I found the staff to be incredible. It is scandalous how they are expected to share each twenty-four-hour day between just two people and to still be flawless in the most responsible of jobs. They saved my life, no doubt about it. For the time being.

My close family, extended family, my many friends, colleagues and ex-colleagues all deserve some gratitude from me here. For all the messages, love, prayers, thoughts, advice, and help I can hardly begin to tell you all how much it has been appreciated. The support you all gave to me and Ali has been nothing short of phenomenal.

All technical thanks go to AJ Humpage, my wonderful editor. From what I gave her to deal with, she has pulled off a miracle. After she'd stopped laughing at the first draft I sent her (because it was so amateur rather than funny), she kindly set me on the right path and dragged out some emotions and creativity that I struggled to put down on paper. I have learned a lot - although the true professionals still reading this may well disagree. Passive sentences, mixing up my tenses over and over, and lacking detail. I don't mind admitting that I never even knew what a gerund was or why they are frowned upon. The adventure has been educational in the extreme.

Beyond the technical help, AJ has been the most superb support I could have wished for. I will be eternally grateful to her for sticking with me, believing in me, and for the endless encouragement. I have thanked her many times within our correspondence over the past couple of years and it is wonderful that I can memorialise my gratitude here. AJ, you have been the bolt of lightning to fire up this personal monster of mine. Thank you so very much for every single comment or message, you have made a massive difference to the telling of my story.

Stepping into the world of books has been a truly enlightening experience. Therefore, massive thanks must also go to Alexa Whitten for her expertise and magic as she has managed to turn some basic Word documents into physical books. If any aspiring writers are looking for some help to get their work published, I can only say good things about Alexa. You can find her at www.thebookrefinery.com and her Pen to Published podcast covers the many, many vital elements needed that I didn't even know existed beyond simply writing a story. Thank you Alexa for giving my monster project eyes and legs to explore the big bad world.

Finally, I can thank Ali.

All those dozens of weekends when she'd wake up alone, then come downstairs and see me scrunched up in the corner of the same sofa. Tapping away on my laptop. Thank you, Ali, for not giving me a hard time as I selfishly sacrificed our time together as second best to getting this beast-of-a-project done and dusted. Unwavering support, love, understanding, compassion, I couldn't have asked for more from my little Wifey. The whole hospital experience taught us to cherish every moment that we have been given (in the words of Kool and the Gang) and now that both of these books are complete, we can do exactly that.

About the Author

Pelé Can Wait... Some More is PS Honey's follow on book from *Pelé can Wait*, which he split into two heart-warming, painfully true stories.

Not only has he amassed over thirty years of experience as a quantity surveyor in the construction industry, he is also a commissioned artist, has played poker on the World Poker Tour, and was part of Team England's World Chess League online win in 2022. He has been married to Ali for over 25 years and they live in South Buckinghamshire with their three children.